DATE DUE

Demco, Inc. 38-293

D0161009

INDEPENDENT STUDIES IN POLITICAL ECONOMY:

THE ACADEMY IN CRISIS
The Political Economy of Higher Education
Edited by John W. Sommer
Foreword by Nathan Glazer

AGRICULTURE AND THE STATE
Market Processes and Bureaucracy
E. C. Pasour, Jr.
Foreword by Bruce L. Gardner

ALIENATION AND THE SOVIET ECONOMY
The Collapse of the Socialist Era
Paul Craig Roberts
Foreword by Aaron Wildavsky

ANTITRUST AND MONOPOLY
Anatomy of a Policy Failure
D. T. Armentano
Foreword by Yale Brozen

ARMS, POLITICS AND THE ECONOMY
Historical and Contemporary Perspectives
Edited by Robert Higgs
Foreword by William A. Niskanen

FREEDOM, FEMINISM AND THE STATE
Edited by Wendy McElroy
Foreword by Lewis Perry

OUT OF WORK
Unemployment and Government in Twentieth-Century America
Richard K. Vedder and Lowell E. Gallaway
Foreword by Martin Bronfenbrenner

PRIVATE RIGHTS, PUBLIC ILLUSIONS
Tibor R. Machan
Foreword by Nicholas Rescher

REGULATION AND THE REAGAN ERA
Politics, Bureaucracy and the Public Interest
Edited by Roger E. Meiners and Bruce Yandle, Jr.
Foreword by Robert W. Crandall

TAXING ENERGY
Oil Severance Taxation and the Economy
Robert Deacon, Stephen DeCanio, H. E. Frech, III, and M. Bruce Johnson
Foreword by Joseph P. Kalt

THAT EVERY MAN BE ARMED
The Evolution of a Constitutional Right
Stephen P. Halbrook

For further information and a catalog of publications, please contact:
THE INDEPENDENT INSTITUTE
134 Ninety-Eighth Avenue, Oakland, CA 94603
(510) 632-1366 FAX: (510) 568-6040

The INDEPENDENT INSTITUTE

THE INDEPENDENT INSTITUTE is a tax-exempt, scholarly research and educational organization which sponsors comprehensive studies on the political economy of critical social and economic problems.

The politicization of decision-making in society has largely confined debate to the narrow reconsideration of existing policies, the prevailing influence of partisan interests, and a stagnation of social innovation. In order to understand both the nature of and possible solutions to major public issues, the Independent Institute's studies adhere to the highest standards of independent inquiry and are pursued regardless of prevailing political or social biases and conventions. The resulting studies are widely distributed as books and other publications, and are publicly debated through numerous conference and media programs.

Through this uncommon independence, depth, and clarity, the Independent Institute pushes at the frontiers of our knowledge, redefines the debate over public issues, and fosters new and effective directions for government reform.

Beyond Politics

Markets, Welfare, and the Failure of Bureaucracy

William C. Mitchell and
Randy T. Simmons

WESTVIEW PRESS
Boulder • San Francisco • Oxford

Copyright © 1994 by The Independent Institute

Published in 1994 in the United States of America by Westview Press, Inc., 5500 Central Avenue, Boulder, Colorado 80301-2877, and in the United Kingdom by Westview Press, 36 Lonsdale Road, Summertown, Oxford OX2 7EW

Library of Congress Cataloging-in-Publication Data
Mitchell, William C.
   Beyond politics : markets, welfare, and the failure of bureaucracy /
William C. Mitchell and Randy T. Simmons.
      p.   cm.
   Includes bibliographical references and index.
   ISBN 0-8133-2207-3 — ISBN 0-8133-2208-1 (pbk.)
   1. Social choice.   2. Bureaucracy.   I. Simmons, Randy T.
II. Title.
HB846.8.M57   1994
350—dc20   94-12008
                                                                                  CIP

Printed and bound in the United States of America

The paper used in this publication meets the requirements
of the American National Standard for Permanence of Paper
for Printed Library Materials Z39.48-1984.

10   9   8   7   6   5   4   3   2   1

Contents

List of Tables and Figures   xi
Foreword, *Gordon Tullock*   xiii
Preface   xvii

PART 1
Market Failures and Political Solutions:
Orthodoxy   1

1   Market Failure and Government Intervention:
    The View from Welfare Economics   3

    The Market Process, 4
    Market Failure as Justification for Restraining the
       Invisible Hand, 6
    Conclusions, 19
    Bibliographical Notes, 20
    References, 21

2   Political Presuppositions of the Idealized State   22

    Human Nature in Politics, 23
    Participation as Salvation, 24
    Visions of the Polity, 25
    Omnicompetent Scientific Managers, 30
    The Idealized State, 32
    Conclusions, 34
    Bibliographical Notes, 35
    References, 36

PART 2
In Dispraise of Politics:
Some Public Choice   39

3   Unromantic Side of Democracy   41

    The Polity as an Economy (of Sorts), 41
    The Fundamental Nature of Collective Choice, 44

Contents

Confused Voters and Ballot Box Logic, 46
Politicians and the Universal Political Touch, 49
Hard-Working Bureaucrats and Nonworking Bureaucracy, 58
The Impassioned Organized Interests, 62
Conclusions, 63
Bibliographical Notes, 64
References, 65

4   Pathological Politics: The Anatomy of Government Failure   66

Citizen Sovereignty and Efficiency, 66
Perverted Incentives, 67
Separation of Costs and Benefits, 68
Political Signaling: Votes and Rhetoric, 70
Institutional Myopia, 73
Dynamics: Uncertainty, Innovation, and Welfare, 75
Electoral Rules: Paradoxes and Impossibilities, 77
Justice and Redistribution, 80
Conclusions, 82
Bibliographical Notes, 82
References, 83

PART 3
Case Studies in the Anatomy of Public Failure   85

5   Politics of Free and Forced Rides:
    Providing Public Goods   87

How Much to Supply, 88
Free Riders and Forced Riders, 89
Technological Gains and Public Pricing, 94
Sharing the Burden of Public Goods, 95
Publicness and Free-Rider Arguments Questioned, 96
Public Goods and Decentralization, 98
Conclusions, 100
Bibliographical Notes, 100
References, 101

6   Political Pursuit of Private Gain:
    Producer-Rigged Markets   102

Welfare Losses from Rent Seeking, 104
Rent Seeking: A Precarious Future? 107
Conclusions, 108

Bibliographical Notes, 109
References, 110

7   Political Pursuit of Private Gain:
    Government Exploitation   111

    Exploitation Defined, 111
    Official Exploitation of Citizens: Taxation, 112
    Bureaucratic Exploitation of Citizens, 114
    Manipulating Median Voters: Agenda Control, 116
    Profscam and Price Fixing at State Universities, 118
    Limits on Exploitation, 123
    Bibliographical Notes, 125
    References, 126

8   Political Pursuit of Private Gain:
    Consumer Protection   127

    Agoraphobia, 127
    The Market as a Positive Game, 128
    Monopoly: Sources, Power, and Welfare Losses, 129
    Consumer Protection: How Much Is Enough? 133
    Protecting Citizen-Consumers: The Case of Government
        Goods, 139
    Bibliographical Notes, 144
    References, 145

9   Political Pursuit of Private Gain:
    Environmental Goods   146

    A Primer, 147
    Choosing Inefficient Policies, 149
    Pollution by Government Agencies, 153
    Trading Dirty Air: Markets for Optimal Pollution, 155
    Market Limitations, 157
    Other Environmental Markets, 158
    Conclusions, 160
    Bibliographical Notes, 160
    References, 162

10 Political Pursuit of Private Gain:
    Coercive Redistribution   163

    The Quest for Equality: Some Inconvenient Facts, 166
    Redistribution in the Real World of Democracy, 169

Distributive Justice in a Transfer Society, 172
Bibliographical Notes, 174
References, 175

11   Micro-Politics of Macro-Instability   176

Uninformed Governments,   176
Self-Interest in Instability, 178
Politically Manipulated Business Cycles, 179
A Note on Supply-Side Economics, 183
Micro-Basis of Macro-Policies, 185
An Economic Bill of Rights, 189
Bibliographical Notes, 193
References, 194

PART 4
In Praise of Private Property, Profits, and Markets   195

12   Rediscovery of Markets, Competition, and the Firm   197

New Views of Market Processes, 198
The Business Firm: New Understandings, 201
Virtues Reclaimed, 205
Bibliographical Notes, 207
References, 208

13   Privatization, Deregulation, and Constitutionalism   210

Privatization, 214
Economic Efficiency, 215
Regulatory Reform, 216
Constitutional Reform, 217
Not Perfection, but Improvement, 219
Bibliographical Notes, 220
References, 221

About the Book and Authors   223
Index   225

Tables and Figures

TABLES

4.1	Inefficiency of log rolling	71
10.1	Percentage income shares for families, 1952–1979	168

FIGURES

3.1	The political system	42
5.1	Preferences for government spending	89
5.2	Preferred amounts of welfare	90
5.3	School district realignment	99
6.1	The costs of cartels	103
7.1	Laffer curves	113
7.2	Exploitation by a Niskanen bureau	115
7.3	Romer-Rosenthal exploiters	117
7.4	Profscam at state universities	120
7.5	Price discrimination at the university	124
8.1	Welfare losses from monopoly	131
8.2	Supply and demand for safety	134
9.1	Controlling pollution	147
10.1	Taxes and transfers as a percent of family income	169
11.1	The political business cycle	180
11.2	The yearly growth in the money supply	182
11.3	Tax revenue	184
11.4	Ratio of deficit to GNP	191

Foreword

THE STUDY OF POLITICS has initiated a revolution in recent years. That this revolution has hardly begun is attributable not to any caution or incompleteness but to the fact that most people are ignorant of it.

The new approach begins by assuming that voters are much like customers and that politicians are much like businesspeople. Bureaucrats in the federal government are much like bureaucrats in many large corporations. These statements seem simple and straightforward. One would think few would disagree.

Nevertheless, this approach is, rather mysteriously, very controversial. I have been denounced with great vigor for saying simply that the customer in the supermarket and the voter in the voting booth are the same person.

On the basis of these assumptions, it is possible to develop a new theory. Although the theory, called public choice, is based on economics and uses many of its tools, it is a genuinely original creation of political science rather than simply a transfer. (It should be noted that awareness of the new theory is fairly common in economics departments, though the subject is regarded as a little odd because economists are, after all, not students of politics.) The economic conceptions and tools, although helpful, were inexact for use in political theory, and hence it was necessary to develop new ones.

For this approach, the government is not a romanticized generator of public goods or a protector of virtue but simply a rather prosaic set of instruments for providing certain types of goods and services that may be hard to provide. Instead of thinking of the government as something that stands above the market, public choice theorists regard the government and the market as parallel organizations sharing a basic objective: filling the demands of the citizens.

Some of these demands, that for food for example, are no doubt best served by the market. Nonetheless, governments around the world are involved in the food production business. They make bread more expensive and transfer funds from the rather poor consumer of bread to the much-better-off farmer in Western countries. Interestingly, in Africa, where the farmers are poorer than the consumers, the system is used to transfer money from the farmers to the consumers.

In contrast, such problems as air pollution are widely viewed as properly handled by government even though they are resistant to both market and government solutions. People do not hold this view because air pollution is a more important matter than bread—on the contrary, food is fundamentally more vital to our lives than cleaner air—but because they see government rightly or wrongly as a better instrument for coping with it. Once again, society maintains two parallel organizational structures in the hope that they will provide for citizens' wants better than either one could by itself.

Most public choice theorists do not think the government provides very high-quality service. Nor do they think that the market is perfect. In economics, the theory of perfect competition is considered by many to be a mathematical convenience that permits analysis of some economic problems with greater speed than is permitted by the classical economics of Smith and Ricardo; the theory does not fit the world perfectly.

Similarly, the new theory of how politics works does not yet fit the world perfectly. We hope for its improvement. One of the advantages of being in a new field is that we can legitimately blame gaps and holes on the newness of the work. Economics has been around for a long time, and expectations of further revolutionary change are not so easy to come by.

There is a subdivision of public choice with a good deal of elaborate mathematical work. It is normally called "social choice." The bulk of the authors in public choice are not particularly mathematical and resemble Ricardo more than they do Hurwiez. Whether the mathematical complications in either public choice or economics are pioneering in important new areas or practicing mere escapism is an open question.

However, this book is about a new approach, one just making its imprint. There are now public choice societies in the United States—where the field has reached its highest development—as well as in Europe and Japan.

The originator of the subject was an Englishman, Duncan Black, but its first major development occurred in the United States. The American journal *Public Choice* is now twenty-five years old and the American Public Choice Society has almost 1,000 members. The European Public Choice Society is smaller, but nevertheless flourishing, and has its own journal, *Scelte Pubbliche*. The Japanese have also vigorously entered into this field, although they have not yet established structures as formal as those provided by either the American or the European societies. The Japanese journal is *Public Choice Studies*. In January 1994, public choice scholars from Japan, Taiwan, and Korea met in Hong Kong, where they were attending the Pacific Rim Conference of the Western Economic Association. They decided to establish an Asian Public Choice meeting and were hopeful that it would draw participation from more than just those three countries.

The flourishing state of the field in the past few years has been evident especially in the United States, where four additional journals have been started: *The Journal of Constitutional Political Economics, Rationality and Society, Journal of Theoretical Politics,* and *Economics and Politics.* Thus, the academic side of public choice is now well established at the higher levels. There are many scholars actively writing, publishing, and doing research in the field.

Some gaps exist, however. It is possible to teach excellent graduate courses in political science using a number of specialized books. However, we badly need more college courses in public choice at both the graduate and the undergraduate levels. It is therefore fitting that the authors of *Beyond Politics: Markets, Welfare, and the Failure of Bureaucracy* are both political scientists. This book will go a long way toward improving on the thinly scattered material found in political science courses.

If the new approach is to have impact on our political system—it does, after all, give a more accurate and useful picture of government than the old approaches did—then people without graduate degrees need access to it. We need a book for the general reader, the kind one might find in the popular bookstore chains.

Mitchell and Simmons again come to our rescue. This book clearly is excellent for the ordinary informed citizen. I cannot truthfully say that it is an easy book, because the ideas included will be new to a great many of its readers. It is, however, not written as a book to be studied instead of read. Ordinary readers who are willing to temporarily leave aside the conventional wisdom about our politics will find that they can go through this book quickly and productively.

The book is a major contribution to informed public comment. There are many very difficult problems in connection with government, and we should try to solve them on the basis of the best learning available. This book will make that learning available to almost anyone who has a normal education and who is willing to devote a little effort to the task.

In fact, the book is so well written and the subject so important and exciting that a great many people will find it very entertaining even if they do learn while reading it. We can welcome this work as a major step forward in understanding the dynamics of government and markets and how both affect us all.

Gordon Tullock
University of Arizona

Preface

UNTIL A CENTURY AGO, students of economics, politics, and policy studied "political economy." Today, some study politics while others study economics. Although the change allowed for greater specialization in each field, it masked the fact that politics and economics cannot be separated. Economies do not exist in a vacuum and neither do politics. Political systems shape, sometimes control, and often misdirect economic systems. Likewise, economic interests shape, sometimes control, and often pervert politics.

No one argues with these simple assertions, but they have not motivated mainstream economic or political analysis for most of this century. One of the most glaring examples has been welfare economics, a branch of economics that studies imperfections in markets or "market failures." Because no human institution is perfect, it is easy to find imperfections or "failures." It is even easier if, like the welfare economists, you only concentrate on the economy and do not recognize the effects of the political system on the shape, direction, and rules of the economy. It is also easy to call for government intervention if you have no corresponding theory of how government functions.

One of the most influential works in welfare economics was William Baumol's *Welfare Economics and the Theory of the State*—a study in market failures that contained no theory of the state, no theory of whether government could respond rationally to calls to intervene in markets. It simply identified market failures that "ought" to be corrected. Baumol's book was followed by Paul Samuelson's 1954 article, "The Pure Theory of Public Expenditure," and Francis M. Bator's 1958 article, "The Anatomy of Market Failure." Baumol's book and these two landmark articles clearly established the fundamentals of the market failure argument—the most important economic argument for government intervention.

While welfare economists justified government, political scientists developed theories that presented government as generally benevolent and at worst benign. These modern students of politics argued that government could serve the public interest through competition among the multiplicity of interests in a society. To most political scientists and policy analysts, politics is where conflicts of values are resolved, inequalities narrowed, and, according to some, people reach their potential. Their faith in government

xvii

is often matched by their skepticism of markets, a skepticism fueled by the market failure literature.

Countering these visions of the economy and the polity is a discipline that recombines the study of economics and politics. This modern political economy, known as "public choice," questions the purported causes of market failure and the competence of government to cope with alleged difficulties. James M. Buchanan, Anthony Downs, Mancur Olson, Gordon Tullock, and William Niskanen are especially prominent in this revolutionary discipline. They and others have identified perversities of majority rule and have shown that the polity has a powerful propensity to adopt less efficient policies and to restrict personal liberty—all in the interest of special groups or equalization of wealth and income. They have developed a theory of government failure.

A much different picture of our modern political economy emerges than that accepted by mainstream political scientists and welfare economists when the insights of public choice are combined with other, modern studies of the value of property rights, markets, and the firm. Our purpose is to provide students of economics, politics, and policy with a concise explanation of public choice within the context of modern economics and political science. Students of all these disciplines will benefit from our challenge of cherished assumptions and conclusions about market failures and government successes. They will acquire positive and normative measures for evaluating claims about government and markets and, regardless of their ideological leanings, gain a foundation upon which rational policy may be built.

Part One, "Market Failures and Political Solutions: Orthodoxy," begins with a chapter on market failures in which the standard welfare arguments are set forth and duly cited. We identify and explain fundamental principles and review orthodox policy solutions to market failures. In Chapter 2, we examine the political theory employed by proponents of government action. The task is not simple or easy because few proponents of the polity have set forth a positive explanation of how the polity functions, what incentives face government officials, or whether the tasks assigned government are even possible. Accordingly, much of our discussion is necessarily inferential and apt to assign more systematic qualities to the argument than are in fact present.

In Part Two, "In Dispraise of Politics: Some Public Choice," we offer a public choice perspective on politics—a view that embraces both description and diagnosis and shows the optimism inherent in the orthodox positions to be untenable. In Part Three, "Case Studies in the Anatomy of Public Failure," we present a public choice analysis of a series of case studies to demonstrate how and why government cannot deliver on the promises of its champions. We deliberately chose a broad range of issues—

public goods, interest-group politics, consumer protection, the environment, redistribution, and economy-wide stability—to illustrate the breadth and power of public choice analysis.

In Part Four, "In Praise of Private Property, Profits, and Markets," we summarize and integrate recent, more realistic understandings of the market process, property rights, and contracts as well as proper roles for government, given these understandings. In the final chapter we offer a few thoughts on a more humane, responsible political economy.

Although there is no large-scale, easily mobilized constituency for expanding personal liberty, reducing government's arbitrary power, and promoting market efficiency, some recent events suggest that responsible politics are not as infeasible as once thought. More remarkable still is the fact that fiscal improvements at the constitutional level are not only thinkable but even fashionable and, perhaps, politically expedient. Our analysis does not lead us to expect wholesale, positive changes, but a cautious optimism might be in order. This book is our effort to promote the kinds of changes that will improve our political economy.

This book has taken some time to come to fruition. Along the way we received assistance from the Political Economy Research Center, Utah State University's Institute of Political Economy, and the Earhart Foundation. Kathy Streckfus did a superior job of copy editing. Bruce Johnson, research director for The Independent Institute, appreciated our efforts long before anyone else, and David Theroux, president of The Independent Institute, persisted in making the book a reality. We are grateful.

William C. Mitchell
University of Oregon

Randy T. Simmons
Utah State University

PART ONE

Market Failures and Political Solutions: Orthodoxy

"MARKET FAILURE" is the modern justification for government action. And that justification has been used by consumers, activists, politicians, special interests, and bureaucrats to produce broad-ranging programs, rules, and agencies to control and influence economic choices. Political control over private economic action has become a fact of life during the past century. Rent control, pollution regulation, safety rules, import restrictions, fuel economy standards, and thousands of other controls have been enacted to overcome perceived imperfections in markets.

The vision underlying this expansion is that government succeeds where markets fail. It is a vision we do not share. We have more faith in markets than in governments. There is a story, probably apocryphal, about a Polish economic adviser who sought direction from U.S. policymakers about moving from a socialist to a market economy. They reminded him that markets are chaotic and difficult to control and predict and that they produce inequitable distributional outcomes. They cautioned him to maintain strong government control over the economy, keep certain sectors under direct government control, and regulate economic activities. The Polish adviser listened politely and finally said, "Oh we know all about regulation and control, we call it socialism. We want to try capitalism." We sympathize with the Polish economic adviser. Like him, we prefer capitalism, but to understand why, it is necessary to understand the justifications and assumptions of the progovernment position. Let's begin.

1

❧ 1 ❧

Market Failure and Government Intervention: The View from Welfare Economics

WHEN WELFARE ECONOMISTS dethroned markets they also administered the coronation of government. Even the most elementary of modern economics texts routinely inform the reader that markets—free and unfree alike—suffer from serious and inherent imperfections. We are told of undersupplied public goods, exorbitant and ubiquitous social costs of private actions, inevitable business cycles, unprotected consumers, and unfairly distributed wealth and income.

Such discussions have a powerful impact because they are intuitively appealing and understandable to the general public and especially to idealistic students. Moreover, the causes of failure are seemingly clear and the solution readily at hand. When markets fail, this argument goes, we must resort to and can rely on politics and governmental administration. Resources will be allocated efficiently, and wealth and income will be fairly distributed, that is, more equally divided. Furthermore, political activity will ennoble individual citizens while the unseemly, raucous, and self-interested competition in the market will debase them.

Although most economists reject the more extreme indictments portrayed here, the thrust of economists' arguments in recent years has been in this direction. Moreover, social scientists untutored in the formalities of economics and the general public are even more inclined to take a jaundiced view of the workings of a market economy. For them, any activity motivated by self-interest is at best suspect and at worst contaminated. Adam Smith's notion of an "invisible hand" at work in market forces is widely regarded as a contradiction in terms; public benefits cannot emerge from competition and self-interest. In contrast, since political actors are considered selfless and well informed, the public interest can be readily and accurately divined; since the political process is considered costless, the public interest is easily achieved. And political conflict debases no one.

We reject this simplistic political view and contend that market failure is

3

seriously misunderstood. Further, we maintain that normal political responses to alleged market failures usually make things worse. In fact, we think our nation's chief problems stem not from market difficulties but from political intervention in otherwise robust markets.

To set the stage for our arguments, we begin by explaining how markets work and discussing how mid-twentieth-century critics—led by welfare economists—criticized them and justified the government intervention so prominent today.

The Market Process

"The market" is an abstract concept referring to the arrangements people have for exchanging goods and services with one another in all aspects of economic life. Thus, it is a process rather than a clearly defined place or a thing that we can observe easily, although some markets are located in particular places. Markets can be as formal and well organized as the stock market and as informal and unorganized as Saturday garage sales or, as one popular introductory textbook suggests, a singles bar (Heyne 1994, 177).

Markets coordinate human activity by taking advantage of self-interest, as Adam Smith ([1776] 1981) first pointed out. In the trucking and bartering of the market, a person is "led by an invisible hand to promote an end which has no part of his intention" (p. 456). In one of Smith's most famous passages, he asserted, "It is not from the benevolence of the butcher, the brewer, or the baker that we expect our dinner, but from their regard to their own interest. We address ourselves not to their humanity, but to their self-love, and never talk to them of our own necessities but of their advantages" (pp. 26–27). Notice that Adam Smith's example shows how markets use self-interest to cause people to act *as if* they care about others. Consumers get what they want from butchers, brewers, and bakers by making them better off. Conversely, butchers, brewers, and bakers improve their own wealth by making consumers better off and they seek to do so not because they necessarily like consumers (although brotherly love is not precluded) but because they do "well" in markets by doing "good" for others.

No one is in direct charge of markets—no one declares how much of a product will be produced, by whom, in what quantities, and at what prices. Products are produced and prices set spontaneously, without central direction or central planning, although individual companies and entrepreneurs do a great deal of planning and coordinate their activities across time and space with little or no knowledge of each other.

Markets develop and expand by relying on voluntary exchange as a way for people to obtain what they want. Markets promote exchange by providing information about the qualities of a particular product, especially compared with the qualities and costs of competing products, and the cost of negotiating and monitoring agreements. When the costs of making decisions and trades are reduced, new opportunities can be exploited, and as the new opportunities are exploited, wealth increases and economic growth occurs. More opportunities mean more wealth.

Markets provide information, in part, by generating prices. Each price is a piece of potentially valuable information about available opportunities. The more prices there are and the more widely they are known, the wider the range of opportunities available and the more wealth that is generated. The prices consumers are willing to pay at a particular time and place indicate the relative value the consumers place on goods and services. As prices become known, individual suppliers send goods and furnish services where they are wanted most; that is, where they bring the highest price.

Because prices indicate the relative values other people place on goods, prices discourage wasteful use of scarce resources. The fact that something is expensive is an indication that others value it highly and that it is costly to replace. In contrast, if something is free for the taking—if it has a zero price—that fact indicates that it has little value to others and can be replaced easily. Low prices encourage consumption. High prices discourage it.

Markets, then, are decentralized processes for directing human activity. No central committee or decisionmaker determines how or when resources will be used. Instead, values are expressed by monetary bids and self-interest is usually the dominant motive for participation. When such a process produces outcomes that seem unacceptable or less beneficial than what is believed possible, many people—economists and noneconomists—tend to support attempts to impose the visible hand of government on the invisible hand of the market.

Markets function best within a stable legal structure containing a set of well-defined rights. These rights include the freedom to contract with one another, the right to property, and the right to have contracts enforced. Policing of rights and contracts against fraud, deceit, destruction, and theft is a necessary part of such a legal structure. Without these minimal activities by government, markets could exist only with great difficulty. Thomas Hobbes, for example, argued that a power had to be erected to enforce contracts because "covenants without the sword are but words, and of no strength to secure a man at all . . . if there be no power erected, or not great enough for our security; every man will, and may lawfully rely on his own strength and art, for caution against all other men" (Hobbes [1650] 1977, 129).

More recently, Paul Samuelson (1967) suggested that the legal system is a public good and that providing it is an indispensable activity of government:

Government provides certain indispensable *public* services without which community life would be unthinkable and which by their nature cannot appropriately be left to private enterprises. Government came into existence once people realized "Everybody's business is nobody's business." Obvious examples are the maintenance of national defense, of internal law and order, and the administration of justice and of contract. (p. 47)

Providing a legal system establishes the framework for exchange—it sets the rules of the game. Establishing this framework does not require that there be any direct intervention into the voluntary exchanges of people by government officials or agencies. It means there is a power to whom people may appeal if contracts are broken, if fraud occurs, or if private property is taken.

Providing a legal system is only one of the many activities that enable modern governments to affect market processes. Most of the others are based on arguments that markets, although useful for directing some human choices and behavior, are ill suited for directing others. Put bluntly, markets fail, and that failure justifies government action.

Market Failure as Justification for Restraining the Invisible Hand

Economists tend to begin their investigations of markets and market activity by postulating a perfect market; that is, one in which all opportunities for mutually advantageous exchange are being exploited. Under a set of rigorous assumptions about preferences, motivations, and technology, they show that markets will reach a point at which no one can be made better off without making anyone else worse off. Market failure simply means the failure of real world markets to achieve the standards of the imaginary market.

Those economists most active in developing theories of market failure are welfare economists. One early welfare economist was A. C. Pigou. In 1920 he showed that the performance of markets in supplying social amenities is likely to be unsatisfactory. By 1952, the arguments were well enough developed for William Baumol to bring them together in his book *Welfare Economics and the Theory of the State*. Baumol's work became the economic profession's standard for the study of market failures and provided an intellectual foundation on which to base proposals for government programs designed to improve on markets.

Baumol's work on the theory of market failures was taken up by many of the other leading economists of his time. One notable contribution was made by Francis Bator ([1958] 1988), whose essay on "The Anatomy of Market Failure" summarized what was developing into a large body of literature as well as analytical consensus.

Bator and others identified a set of market failures that eventually became central to modern economic analysis. Specifically, they clarified the characteristics of "public goods" and the reasons why markets are expected to under-produce them. They explained the nature and reasons for overproduction of negative externalities. They identified market power, lack of information, and market instabilities as having ruinous effects on the efficient operation of the private economy.

In the following pages, we discuss the most commonly accepted forms of market failure developed in the welfare economics literature. We also identify the orthodox policy solutions.

Ubiquitous Externalities

One pervasive market failure results from "spillover" or "external" costs of a private action. That is, one or more person's activities create costs for a second person without the second person's permission, and sometimes without his or her knowledge.

Private costs are those paid by the individual taking action. The spillover costs of an action are those that are passed on to others. For example, if you neglected to change the oil in your automobile and the engine was damaged, you would have to get it repaired. Your negligence would have produced private costs. If, however, your negligence caused the engine to emit noxious fumes, some of the costs of your failure to keep your car in good repair would spill over to all breathers of the air contaminated by the fumes.

People generally undertake only those activities for which the additional personal costs are expected to be less than the additional personal benefits. When there are no costs created for others, an individual comparing costs and benefits in this way avoids waste and searches for efficiency. But if some of the costs of the action spill over to others while the individual captures the benefits, then comparing private costs and benefits will lead to actions that are costly to society.

Let's return to the example of your automobile. If all of your auto's exhaust fumes were pumped into the interior of your car so that you were the only one to breathe them, you would not be likely to drive very much or you would find a means of making the emissions breathable. But if you were able to vent your exhaust fumes into the atmosphere where others would breathe them, you would not be likely to reduce your emissions voluntarily. Your personal cost of reducing emissions would outweigh the benefits, because you would be suffering little. Other people, plants, and animals who used the air would share the cost, and you would get a net benefit from polluting. Furthermore, your emissions by themselves would have a negligible effect on air quality regardless of whether others used the air as a waste repository.

Spillover costs are also known as negative externalities. When costs can be socialized—externalized, as in the automobile example—the individual weighs the total benefits against only a portion of the costs (the ones he or she bears) and improves his or her own position at the expense of others. Socialized costs and privatized benefits mean that people get a "free ride" at others' expense.

Where such spillovers do occur, most economists assume the market will respond imperfectly, *if at all*, to the desires of the public. The belief in the pervasiveness of negative externalities and the dangers they pose, as well as the implied need for government action, is demonstrated by the following quotation from a book on environmental quality by William Baumol and Wallace Oates (1979):

> Externalities pervade virtually every sector of our economy; they are the un-avoidable element of the productive process; and their consequences tend to grow disproportionately with increasing population and expansion of the economy's activities. . . .
>
> *Our central point is that externalities are not exceptional phenomena; they are everywhere about us, embedded in the workings of our economy.* (pp. 77, 79; emphasis in original)

For government to reduce spillover costs, four broad categories of policy instruments are commonly advocated. The first three aim at influencing the behavior of the externality producer: They are persuasion, regulation through direct controls, and regulation that relies on market incentives. The fourth instrument, direct government expenditure, is generally used for large construction projects such as sewage treatment plants.

Appeals to conscience—campaigns to encourage individuals to stop littering, to recycle trash, or to join carpools and calls to industry to recognize its social responsibility—are crusades to persuade people to internalize the costs of their actions. The hope is that people who produce externalities will subject their immediate self-interest to a general group interest. Such appeals rely on a moral resurgence and usually fail in the long run, although there are occasional short-term successes.

Most economists are highly skeptical of appeals to conscience. Economic analysis instead emphasizes the importance of making individual self-interest coincide with the group interest. In his book *The Public Use of Private Interest*, Charles L. Schultze (1977) reflected this view nicely:

> If I want industry to cut down on pollution, indignant tirades about social responsibility cannot hold a candle to schemes which reduce the profits of firms who pollute. . . . In most cases the prerequisite for social gains is the identification, not of villains and heroes, but of the defects in the incentive system that drive ordinary decent citizens into doing things contrary to the common good. (p. 18)

Although many economists also reject regulation of externalities through direct controls—commonly known as "command and control"—such direct regulation is central to current U.S. public policy to control externalities such as pollution. A government agency prescribes certain procedures and places limitations on the kinds of activities that may be undertaken. A petroleum refinery, for example, may have a combination of potential pollution sources that include 8,000 valves (500 for gas, 6,000 for heavy liquids, 1,500 for light liquids); 24,000 flanges; 450 pumps (50 for light liquids, 400 for heavy liquids); 50 process drains; and 3 flares. Each valve, flange, pump, drain, and flare might be subject to individual point source limitations established by the government. The command and control approach also often requires a specific technology or a specific treatment procedure. Thus, government decides on the kind of control, the appropriate standard measurement, and the level of control.

A central argument against command and control regulation is that it takes little advantage of the skill and enterprise of company managers. Once a specific technology is mandated, little incentive exists to search for more effective or less costly technologies. There is also the often overwhelming administrative problem of prescribing procedures and issuing permits individually tailored to thousands of different companies or individuals.

Some economists have proposed that externalities can best be corrected by having government mimic the market through a system of pricing measures—user fees, taxes, and penalties. The government should allow the creation of tradeable pollution rights, for example, or place a charge (price) on pollution that equals the value people give to environmental quality. Firms could then respond to that price and achieve levels of environmental quality selected by a market rather than by political fiat. These policies would create incentives for firms to seek more efficient ways of reducing pollution, encourage innovation, and cause the people creating the spillover costs to recognize those costs. Polluters would then be less likely to produce beyond the point where the costs of production begin to exceed the benefits. Some examples of environmental policies proposed include sewer charges, emissions trading, "bubble" and "offset" policies, which allow firms to build new pollution-creating facilities in exchange for equivalent reductions at other sources, and "banking," which allows discharge reductions to be stored for future use. Economists, paradoxically, created the justification for government intervention but have had little success in getting their preferred solutions enacted.

Public Goods

Welfare economists argue that private goods (consumer products such as pencils and automobiles, for example) are efficiently produced and allocated by markets—as long as externalities are controlled. Because a private good is exclusive—that is, nonowners can be kept from using it unless they pay for it, and suppliers can obtain the full value of the good from those who want it—it is distributed to the people who want it the most. Another characteristic of a private good is that one person's consumption prevents or reduces another's consumption of that good. If a person wants to consume a private good, he or she usually has to pay for it. (Note that many government-supplied goods, such as food stamps and sawtimber from the national forests, are also private goods.)

Public goods differ greatly from private goods in ways that make their provision through markets problematic. In Paul Samuelson's (1954) original formulation, public goods have two distinctive characteristics. First, a public good is nonexclusive; it cannot be withheld from any member of a group once it is supplied to the group. One commonly used example of a public good is national defense—once a protective missile is supplied, all the people in the nation benefit, whether they pay for it or not. If it is available to one, it is available to all. Second, one person's consumption of a public good does not affect another's consumption. That is, the enjoyment or benefit of a public good is shared by all members of the group receiving the good regardless of whether the individual members have chosen to pay for it. Because one person's consumption of a public good does not preclude anyone else's consumption, the cost of providing the public good to an additional consumer is zero. If it is provided for one it is provided for all, and all can benefit without reducing its value to others. Police protection, parks, roads, and aids to navigation are commonly cited examples, as are flood control and sanitation.

Since people obtain the benefits of a public good regardless of whether they pay for it, there is a powerful incentive to offer nothing or little in exchange for the good. Richard McKenzie and Gordon Tullock (1978) identify how difficult it is to collect payment after a public good has been supplied: "The public good producer can be expected to have the same luck in collecting from beneficiaries as a baker would if he flew over a city, tossing out loaves of bread, and then went from door to door to ask for payment from all those who picked up the loaves he dropped" (p. 342).

McKenzie and Tullock's baker may get some payment for his bread, but it is in the interest of each person from whom payment is requested to understate the amount he or she received or is willing to pay. This lack of incentive to participate in providing public goods is another manifestation of the free-rider problem. Because the benefits of a public good are received upon production, not upon payment, people can benefit without paying. They get a free ride because benefits are socialized while costs are privatized.

Public goods pose several serious problems for markets. First, how can one charge for a product when many "free riders" can refuse to pay? And even if it is possible to charge for the good, how can the appropriate price be established? Finally, without the guidance of prices, how can one decide how much of the good to produce? Although a bridge is an imperfect example of a public good because of crowding and because it is possible to exclude people from using it, bridges do illustrate the pricing problem. If a bridge has excess capacity, the cost to users of allowing an additional person to cross the bridge is zero. The additional person's use of the bridge does not decrease anyone else's use. But charging a toll in this situation would discourage some people from using the bridge who would otherwise use it. The result is that total social welfare is less than optimal. The difficulty lies in determining how to pay for the public good without reducing the potential social welfare.

Increasing total social welfare is a justification many welfare economists use for government provision of goods that have a public nature. Jules Dupuit, the originator of the bridge example, claimed that the pricing problem is so difficult that "as long as activities have even a trace of publicness, price calculations are inefficient [see Bator 1958]." In a footnote to this conclusion, Bator noted: "This is not to say that there exist other feasible modes of social calculation and organization which are more efficient" (p. 64). Regardless of such caveats, there is a strong presumption that the government must intervene to provide public goods and to price them appropriately.

The argument that government should produce public goods did not originate with welfare economists. David Hume ([1740] 1975), for example, provided part of the foundation upon which modern scholars justify government activities. Hume maintained that individuals, left to themselves, "wou'd lay the whole burden on others." The solution was obvious to Hume because "political society easily remedies ... these inconveniences. ... Thus bridges are built; harbours open'd; ramparts rais'd; canals form'd; fleets equip'd; and armies disciplin'd; everywhere by the care of government" (pp. 538–539).

In order for "political society" to remedy the inconvenience of free riding, it must find a means of paying for the public goods. Government's answer is to turn free riders into forced payers through taxation. The presumption is that forced taxation is often the only way to pay for the public goods that members of society desire.

No one claims there are many *pure* public goods. National defense is one of the few possible ones. However, less rigorous or partial definitions are frequently used to justify government supply of goods and services. For example, Paul Samuelson (1967) argues that the public should finance any good whose (marginal) cost of supply is zero. Remember Dupuit's bridge example: Once the bridge is constructed and until capacity is reached, the cost of providing the bridge to an additional user is zero. This approach suggests that bridges, roads, harbors, and a host of other similar goods should be sufficiently "public" to require provision through taxation.

As academics we have frequently heard colleagues complain that the small university towns in which they live do not provide them with all the amenities of civilized life that they experienced while graduate students in Cambridge or Berkeley. One such complaint is that cultural facilities and events are lacking; another is that there is little or no public transportation.

Smaller cities lack such facilities and services because no entrepreneur can make a profit from the limited demand for them. Our colleagues, however, want the facilities even though they do not make extensive use of them. The option for which there is a demand is of value, but there is no way to collect sufficient fees to pay for it. Suppose that our professors live several miles from campus and own private cars, but that the cars now and then fail to function. If a bus costs fifty cents one way and the only alternative is a cab at $10, a professor with a car that malfunctions, say, five times a year would pay $100 for five round-trips by cab. But if a bus were available, the annual cost would be just $5 for the five emergency trips. The annual savings would amount to $95. A professor should then be willing to pay up to $95 annually to ride the bus. But how is the public bus company going to collect that $95? The value of the option is not the $5 for five fares, but $95.

Option demands and public goods present similar problems. If they are to be provided, some way must be found to collect the fees to pay for them. For most welfare economists, the obvious answer is to tax the public to subsidize the agencies or companies that will provide the service. The result is half-full municipal buses and seldom-used city-owned concert halls.

The bus and concert hall examples preview our arguments in Chapter 6 about the difficulties governments face in providing public goods. If nonexcludability means free riders exist when markets supply a public good, it also means free riders will persist if government supplies the good. Government can coerce payment from taxpayers whether they consume the good or not, but there is still no guidance as to the optimal amount to produce or the appropriate price to charge. Given the other limitations faced by government, the arguments for public provision of public goods are not as compelling as they may seem at face value.

Imperfect Competition

One of the most widely accepted and feared forms of market failure is imperfect competition, especially when it is perceived to lead to monopoly power. Economists' concerns differ somewhat from those of the general public: Economists recognize that monopoly power can lead to prices higher than those that would exist under perfect competition, while the voters and politicians worry about the effects of concentrated market power on the "little guy"—small businesses and average working people. The U.S. Supreme Court reflected this general sentiment in the following famous passage from an 1897 decision:

> [Large business combinations] may even temporarily or perhaps permanently, reduce the price of the article traded in or manufactured, by reducing the expense inseparable from the running of many different companies for the same purpose. Trade or commerce under these circumstances may nevertheless be badly and unfortunately restrained by driving out of business the small dealers and worthy men whose lives have been spent therein and who might be unable to readjust themselves to their altered surroundings. Mere reduction in the price of the commodity dealt in might be dearly paid for by the ruin of such a class. (United States v. Trans-Missouri Freight Ass'n, 166 U.S. 323 [1897])

Economists, as opposed to judges, are concerned over the fact that monopolists can make consumers worse off. If a competitive industry is monopolized, prices increase, availability decreases, or both. These losses in consumer welfare can be avoided if regulatory agencies prevent monopolies from forming in the first place.

There is another and possibly more compelling argument against monopoly than the one asserting misallocation of resources. Competition is the force that compels people in business to seek new and more efficient production techniques, to produce new products, and to take risks. Given the relative security of monopoly power, the monopolist lacks incentive and drifts into managerial and technical stagnation. The creativity that could be channeled into producing new goods and services in the presence of competition does not exist. Thus, according to this argument, the major cost of monopoly is not necessarily reduced output and higher prices than would be obtained under competitive conditions; rather, it is the lost wealth that would otherwise occur because of competition spurring the creation of new ideas.

The traditional political response to monopoly power has been to institute antitrust laws. There is, however, not a close connection between the economists' concerns and the solutions attempted through antitrust laws because the laws were established during the nineteenth century before the economic theories of imperfect markets were developed. Besides, the size of corporations has been largely unaffected by the existence of antitrust laws. Perhaps antitrust laws are used as a policy tool because they are politically popular, not because they have economic benefits. As we will learn in Chapters 7 and 8, antitrust may be redundant since the economy is far more competitive than the supporters of antitrust recognize and consumers benefit far more from these contestable markets than many welfare economists and consumers themselves recognize.

Inadequate Information

Models of market competition typically rest upon the assumption of perfect information. They assume that consumers know everything they need to know about a product's quality, about the quality and price of competing products, and so on. Such an assumption is unrealistic, partly because the costs of obtaining such information outweigh the expected benefits. Consumers prefer to make purchases with imperfect information because the cost of obtaining full information would be too great.

One consequence of this choice is that prices of certain commodities are not uniform across the market. Some sellers are able to charge higher prices than others. But as long as prices are not outrageously out of line, consumers will pay them rather than pay the price of reducing their ignorance.

Why does inadequate information or uncertainty exist in the first place? There are many reasons. Products may be too complex for nonspecialists to understand or their effects may be felt only in the longer run when it is too late to change one's decisions. Products may also have serious unknown side effects (as in the case of some prescription drugs). Of course, it is not unknown for sellers to exaggerate claims for their products and services. Buyers who do not make repeat purchases from the same seller may be at the mercy of unscrupulous persons.

For such reasons, information problems do arise. And while consumers devise handy rules of thumb and other protections to prevent fraud or reduce the costs of information, welfare economists and politicians have been all too willing to offer consumers the services of government. The question remains: Are consumers better protected by reducing their information costs or by prohibiting producers and sellers from marketing inferior goods? We attempt an answer in Chapter 8.

Ensuring Economy-wide Stability

The overall business climate experiences fluctuations known as business cycles. A business cycle is defined as a recurrent (but not periodic) fluctuation in general business activity over a period of years, usually measured in terms of unemployment levels, inflation, and income. The existence of a business cycle is often taken as evidence of a market failure requiring government attention.

Governments claimed no particular advantage at combating business cycles until John Maynard Keynes published his *General Theory of Employment, Interest, and Money* in 1936. He argued that markets are not self-correcting—that some swings in the business cycle will not be corrected unless governments take action. To bring the economy out of depression, the government must find some way to stimulate consumption, investment, and capital expansion. He proposed that a combination of fiscal policies—deficit spending and regulation of tax rates and money supply—would allow governments to fine tune economies so that full employment and stable prices could be achieved. Keynesian policies have been adopted widely since *General Theory* was published.

Keynes blamed unemployment on inadequate demand for labor. This view reflected his interpretation of the cause of the economic depression of the 1930s, during which the unemployment rate in Britain rose to more than 30 percent and many of the unemployed remained so for more than a year. He claimed the unemployment of the depression was caused by a lack of spending—too much saving. Keynes's reputation and the power of his theory combined to convert a new generation of economists to the view that markets could fail to correct economic fluctuations. The prolonged depression provided evidence for this view, and traditional theories were insufficient to explain economic fluctuations or to provide the guidance necessary for designing political responses.

The prevailing view of how the government should respond to business cycles is still based on Keynesian economics. A simple explanation of the Keynesian view of the business cycle is that both economic expansion and contraction will be magnified if a market economy is left to its own direction. Erratic fluctuations in aggregate demand will lead the economy to waver between inflationary overexpansion and recessionary unemployment. A deficient level of demand results in abnormally high unemployment; excess demand produces inflation.

The Keynesian cure for such fluctuations is to adopt flexible fiscal policies. The government budget becomes the primary instrument for fine tuning the economy to achieve full employment, economic growth, and price-level predictability. During a downswing, government needs to increase demand by reducing taxes and increasing government spending. The government should *not* run balanced budgets, but should run a deficit to stimulate the economy and move it toward full employment.

To deal with inflation, government must do the exact opposite of what is required to increase employment. Once full employment is reached, taxes should be increased, the money supply tightened, and the government should run a budget *surplus,* not deficit. Such policies will counteract the wave of business optimism and consumer spending that is pushing aggregate demand beyond a level consistent with stable prices. Restrictive fiscal policies will reduce disposable income, causing consumption to decline, and will dampen investment. In addition, reduced government spending will diminish aggregate demand directly. The combined result should maintain both full employment and price stability.

Attempts to manipulate the economy in this manner are relatively recent phenomena that required a revolution in thinking about government budgets. Widespread popular and political support for the view that the budget could be used to dampen fluctuations in the economy occurred only after the balanced-budget norm was destroyed or at least undermined. The extent to which Keynesian manipulations replaced other views about government's proper role is suggested by President Richard Nixon's statement as he announced the imposition of wage and price controls, "We're all Keynesians now."

In later chapters we will respond in detail to Keynesian arguments. For now, let us suggest that, even if the Keynesian analysis of the causes of inflation and recession is correct—an assumption we dispute—governments will be unable to implement the policies necessary for Keynesian economics to work. Moreover, we conclude that Keynesian policies exacerbate some of the problems they are intended to cure.

Distributive Inequities

The distribution of income in the United States depends largely on the operation of market forces. Markets reward people in accordance with their contribution to the production of goods and services that consumers wish to purchase. Thus, a person whose productivity is low will earn little, regardless of whether the low productivity is attributable to lack of effort, lack of skill, or low demand for the skill.

Just as a university professor grades an exam according to the quality of the answers, not according to the effort that went into studying for the exam, markets reward output, not effort. People who lack skills, people with poor intellectual ability or poor health, and those who produce goods and services for which there is little demand or for which there is a large supply and low prices are likely to earn less than the more fortunate and the better educated.

There are two main arguments against relying solely on markets to allocate wealth and income: market failures and injustice. These two arguments are summarized in Arthur Okun's (1975) book *Equality and Efficiency: The Big Tradeoff.* He began by describing the outcomes of a perfectly competitive market that pays "workers and investors the value of their contributions to output." But, he argued, real markets are not perfectly competitive. Imperfections such as inadequate information, discrimination, inequality of opportunity, and monopoly power prevent the distribution that would be reached in the perfect market. He concluded from this argument that rewards based on productivity are just but markets are imperfect. Therefore, ways must be found to make markets more competitive, to provide adequate information, and to prohibit discrimination.

Okun's second argument addressed the notion that rewards based on productivity are unfair. Since people's natural abilities are genetically based, they have in no sense "earned" them; those with a superior genetic heritage enjoy an undeserved and unfair advantage over their less fortunate fellows. Thus, Okun claimed, "Society should aim to ameliorate and certainly not to compound, the flaws of the universe. It cannot stop rain, but it does manufacture umbrellas. Similarly, it can decide to restrict prizes that bestow vastly higher standards of living on people with greater innate abilities" (p. 44). Thus, the arbitrary distribution of natural abilities calls not for rewarding those endowed with superior ability but for rewarding those endowed with lesser ability.

This redistributionist view suggests that markets do not distribute income and wealth as they ought to—even if we accept the premise that the allocations by a perfect market are justified. What is more, even perfect markets will fail to "justly" allocate the rewards of labor.

By the mid-1970s, one of the greatest single forces changing the role of the federal government in the United States was the push for equality. The federal government expanded its role through a series of income redistribution programs that had the explicit goal of reducing inequality by aiding the poor.

Retired and unemployed persons benefit from social insurance programs providing income payments in prescribed situations. The best known of these is Social Security, which is essentially a program of forced saving financed by compulsory payroll taxes levied on employees and employers. Although Social Security was originally envisioned as a social insurance program that workers would pay for in exchange for later benefits that would vary according to the level of contribution, it evolved into a system for transferring wealth from those who work to older, retired persons, regardless of the personal wealth or income of the retired person or of the younger, working person.

Poor people who do not qualify for Social Security benefits are provided for through other programs. These include the federally financed and administered Supplemental Security Income program and the state administered but partially federally funded Aid to Families with Dependent Children (AFDC) program. These programs attempt to provide a minimum income for the aged, the blind, the disabled, and dependent children who do not have the financial support of a father because of desertion, disability, or death.

In 1964, just after the Johnson administration's "War on Poverty" got under way, there were 367,000 Americans receiving food stamps. This program expanded to the point that by 1990 there were 20 million recipients; the annual cost had increased from $860,000 to more than $14 billion. Along the way, more than 1 in every 12 persons had become regular users of food stamps. Eligible recipients now include striking workers and college students as well as those normally considered poor.

In order for government to redistribute incomes, it must tax. Taxes are a necessary means to the end of redistribution. A variety of tax tools are available, including taxes on income, sales, property, and corporations as well as Social Security taxes. The favorite of these taxes for redistribution purposes is the income tax because it can be used to take more from those who have a greater ability to pay. The principle of ability to pay has been used to justify progressive tax rates, that is, rates that require high-income groups to pay proportionately more than low-income groups.

The redistribution of wealth and income has become the major activity of government, supplanting the traditional functions of supplying public goods and controlling externalities. It is our view that this development has been spurred by the reasoning of welfare economists. For many, the chief failure of the market economy is its maldistribution of income and the most effective instrument for correcting this lamentable situation is use of the political process. Those who do not do well in the economy, welfare economists contend, can exert influence through sympathetic political representatives in the political process and thereby increase their share. Unfortunately, experience shows that the political process rarely works this way; politicizing redistribution does not prevent those who do well in the economy from doing even better through the political process. Chapter 3 documents this conclusion.

Transaction Costs

Some potentially formidable barriers to well-functioning markets are transaction costs—the costs of negotiating and monitoring agreements to exchange. Transaction costs are part of every sale or contract: Buyers and sellers must search each other out, agree on what it is they are exchanging, and gain some assurance they are getting what they bargain for. If sellers are to get the whole value of their product, they must incur the transaction costs of excluding nonpayers. In turn, buyers must have a way of measuring or evaluating the product to be sure they get full value for their money.

Transaction costs are used to justify a substantial amount of government regulation. If for every purchase of gasoline consumers had to bring a set of containers and devices to measure gallons and determine octane ratings, for instance, they would be wasting time and money and face additional dangers from exposure to gasoline and its fumes. The average person can take a tape measure to the lumberyard to measure the length of a two-by-four, but it is more difficult to measure the load that can be supported by a prebuilt truss or a glue-laminated floor joist. But with government regulation of weights and measures, people buy gasoline without worrying about whether the amount on the pump is what really goes into the gasoline tank and whether the posted octane rating is accurate. Government inspections allow consumers to purchase pressure-treated or kiln-dried lumber without having to certify for themselves that the advertised treatment processes actually happened. Building regulations allow people to build roofs with prebuilt trusses without having to hire engineers to check the structural capacities of the trusses or joists. This justification for using government coercion is that it dramatically reduces the costs to the consumer of acquiring information. It also assumes that markets will fail to provide information of similar quality.

This defense of regulation must be modified, however. If sellers are intent on taking advantage of buyers because of the sellers' superior information, we must account for the enthusiasm with which sellers seek to be regulated. The demand for government regulation most often arises from sellers. As we learn in upcoming chapters, regulation is a way for sellers already in the market to use government coercion to restrict competition, choice, and opportunities. In addition, private entrepreneurs have become quite inventive at devising new ways to provide information and reduce transaction costs. There are superior alternatives to government regulation, and we provide several examples in Part Three.

Conclusions

When welfare economists consider the market economy they usually do so by examining the market environment within which economic agents—consumers and producers—make decisions. They ask whether any improvements can be made. Are there artificial barriers to entry that reduce competition? What are the relevant externalities? Are there inequities? Is the market responding to demand? These are legitimate questions.

The analysis of markets usually encourages the welfare economist to recommend government policies to change the offensive or inefficient situation. All too often they find "solutions" that require government intervention: more and/or different taxes; price controls; subsidies and tariffs; penalties for collusion through antitrust laws; more controls over private property; and, of course, more government-directed planning.

During this century, government responses to perceived market failures have produced steady increases in the sizes of government budgets, regulatory agencies, and legislative staffs. This growth resulted from a faith in government activism: the belief that the government could correct market failures by appropriate regulations, discretionary fiscal policies, and redistribution. The role of government is no longer limited to providing necessary public services like a legal system and national defense. Instead, government is expected to use its power to cure social ills that are not adequately addressed by private markets.

This view of government contains implicit assumptions about the motives and abilities of people who hold positions of power in government and who carry out government policies. It is based on faith that government can and will carry out the strategies necessary to correct market failures. Chapter 2 describes and analyzes these assumptions as a prelude to discussing, in subsequent chapters, the actual effects of political responses to market imperfections.

Bibliographical Notes

Despite the joke that if we laid all the economists in the world end-to-end we would not reach a conclusion, economists are remarkably consistent when it comes to the basics of their paradigm. They make the same assumptions about human nature, how markets function, the role of prices, and the effects of changes in supply and demand. In fact, it has been said that a demand curve is the closest the social sciences come to an analog to the law of gravity. Except in extremely rare circumstances, demand curves are downward sloping to the right, meaning that quantity demanded increases as price falls.

We suggest one classic article, an introductory text, and a book chapter for those wishing to better understand the basics. The article is Frederich A. von Hayek's definitive, "The Use of Knowledge in Society," *American Economic Review* 35 (September 1945), 519–530. It is the best description we know about how prices coordinate human activity and, incidentally, why markets coordinate better than politics. The introductory chapter of *The Best of the New World of Economics* (Homewood: Richard D. Irwin, Inc., 1989), by Gordon Tullock and Richard B. McKenzie, is a wonderfully concise and complete introduction to the basic assumptions of economics and how to use them. The authors pose clever and sometimes disconcerting questions at the end of each chapter to encourage the reader's understanding. Although there are now several good introductory textbooks, the one we find most pleasurable is Paul Heyne's *The Economic Way of Thinking* (New York: Macmillan, 1994), now in its seventh edition. His writing style is conversational and his examples are easily understood and compelling.

Anyone beginning to read about free riders and collective action should begin with economist Mancur Olson's book *The Logic of Collective Action* (Cambridge: Harvard University Press, 1965). Olson describes the incentives to free riding and explains how successful groups provide "selective incentives" to overcome it.

The classic work on externalities and the environment is Garrett Hardin's "The Tragedy of the Commons," first published in *Science* 162 (December 1968), 1243–1248. Hardin's article, one of the most reprinted articles on the environment, describes how rational, individual action destroys commonly owned property. H. Scott Gordon's earlier article, "The Economic Theory of a Common Property Resource: The Fishery," in *Journal of Political Economy* 62 (April 1954), 124–142, provides a more mathematical and scholarly treatment of the same subject. Of course, instituting defined, enforceable property and use rights solves the problem of the commons. We suggest a recent collection edited by Bonnie J. McKay and James M. Acheson for examples from several different cultures. This book, *The Question of the Commons: The Culture and Ecology of Communal Resources* (Tucson: University of Arizona Press, 1987), contains eighteen chapters describing management of common property resources.

For a thought-provoking treatise on distributional questions, we refer readers to Charles Murray's *In Pursuit of Happiness and Good Government* (New York: Simon and Schuster, 1988). Murray uses thought experiments and case studies to reconsider basic assumptions about income distribution, government, and happiness.

An extensive discussion of public goods can be found in John G. Head, *Public Goods and Public Welfare* (Durham: Duke University Press, 1974). Head discusses questions of demand and supply of public goods by markets and government.

Finally, we suggest a book by Charles E. Lindblom that captures the conventional wisdom about politics and markets as well as any we know. The title is, appropriately enough, *Politics and Markets* (New York: Basic Books, 1977). Lindblom writes of the limited competence of governments, but especially of markets, and discusses the virtues of policymaking and planning. We believe the book to be badly flawed and refer the reader to James M. Buchanan's critical review in *Journal of Economic Issues* 13 (March 1979), 215–217, but recommend the book for readers wanting to understand the vision of politics and markets popular among many academics, especially political scientists.

References

Bator, Francis. "The Anatomy of Market Failure," reprinted in Tyler Cowen, ed., *The Theory of Market Failure* (Fairfax, Va.: George Mason University Press, 1988), 35–66; originally published in *Quarterly Journal of Economics* 72 (August 1958), 351–379.

Baumol, William J. *Welfare Economics and the Theory of the State*, rev. 2nd ed. (Cambridge: Harvard University Press, 1965; 1st ed., 1952).

Baumol, William J., and Wallace E. Oates. *Economics, Environmental Policy, and the Quality of Life* (Englewood Cliffs: Prentice-Hall, 1979).

Heyne, Paul. *The Economic Way of Thinking*, 7th ed. (New York: Macmillan, 1994).

Hobbes, Thomas. *Leviathan, or the Matter, Forme, and Power of a Commonwealth Ecclesiastical and Civil* (New York: Macmillan Publishing Co., 1977; originally published in 1650).

Hume, David. *A Treatise on Human Nature,* edited by L. A. Selby Bigge (Oxford: Clarendon Press, 1975; originally published in 1740).

Keynes, John Maynard. *The General Theory of Employment, Interest, and Money* (New York: Harcourt, Brace, & World, 1936).

McKenzie, Richard, and Gordon Tullock. *Modern Political Economy: An Introduction to Economics* (New York: McGraw-Hill, 1978).

Okun, Arthur. *Equality and Efficiency: The Big Tradeoff* (Washington, D.C.: Brookings Institution, 1975).

Pigou, A. C. *The Economics of Welfare* (London: Macmillan, 1920).

Samuelson, Paul A. "The Pure Theory of Public Expenditure," *Review of Economics and Statistics* 36 (November 1954), 387–389.

———. *Economics,* 7th ed. (New York: McGraw-Hill, 1967).

Schultze, Charles. *The Public Use of Private Interest* (Washington, D.C.: Brookings Institution, 1977).

Smith, Adam. *An Inquiry into the Nature and Causes of the Wealth of Nations,* edited by R. H. Campbell and A. S. Skinner (Indianapolis: Liberty Fund, 1981; originally published in 1776).

Political Presuppositions
of the Idealized State

WELFARE ECONOMISTS proposing government action to remedy market failure have found ready allies in the political science profession. The prevailing view among political scientists is that democratic governance is essentially benign and, although perhaps not efficient by economists' standards, fundamentally fair. Although political scientists lament problems such as special interests' excessive power, an "imperial presidency," and voter apathy, by and large they tend to think that representative democracy results in overall justice and equity—or that it would if certain reforms were implemented.

A minority view among political scientists is that elites rule by directly initiating or vetoing political and economic decisions. Although elite theorists worry about the abuse of power, many argue that elites actually protect democratic values in order to preserve their own positions in the system. Elites are concerned about a well-functioning government and economy and have the connections, expertise, and experience to manipulate either in order to overcome failures.

Both positions provide intellectual support for the welfare economists' article of faith that the government can remedy market failures and imperfections. And the economists need that support, for, as George Stigler (1975) put it:

> Economists have long had a deeply schizophrenic view of the state. They study an elaborate and remarkably complex private economy, and find that by precise and elegant criteria of optimal behavior a private enterprise system has certain classes of failures. These failures, of which some are highly complex in nature and all are uncertain in magnitude, are proposed for remedial or surrogate performance by the state.
>
> Simultaneously, the economists—along with the rest of the population—view the democratic state as a well-meaning, clumsy institution all too frequently diverted by emotion and administered by venality. The state is often viewed as the bulwark of "vested interests"—and in fact where else can an interest vest? The state is thus at one and the same time the corrector of

subtle disharmonies between the marginal social and the marginal private products of resources and the obstinately unlearning patron of indefensible protective import quotas and usury laws. (p. 103)

We believe economists take such a schizophrenic view because they have not applied their own powerful tools of analysis to the state. When they do, they are less likely to assume the state can easily improve on markets. We present such an analysis in Part Two. But before undertaking that analysis, we provide an overview and discussion of the presuppositions that underlie welfare economists' and political scientists' faith in political processes.

Although proponents of government action seldom make explicit statements about the motivations of people in government or about how government will actually carry out the functions assigned to it, they do have assumptions about these things—political behavior, the expected effects of political participation, political processes, and the expected outputs of those processes. To describe these, we have relied heavily on classics of political science because they articulate what the economists usually leave unsaid and seem to us to summarize the conventional view shared by welfare economists. In later chapters we contrast these conventional views with a model of *government* failure.

Human Nature in Politics

Although interaction through politics may produce outcomes greater than the sum of the parts, the fact remains that policies, choices, and decisions are made by individual people. When the media report that "the government attempted to counter a cyclical downturn with a countercyclical policy," readers and viewers should recognize what is really meant—some individual person or members of a group of persons made a particular decision. A set of beliefs about how government works makes little sense without some assumptions about what motivates those individuals making up government.

Conventional wisdom among political scientists and economists promoting government intervention appears to be that humans shift mental and moral gears (or at least they should shift gears) when moving from the economic sphere to the political one. Some argue that while market choices are based on simple preferences, political choices require complex judgments, sometimes based on moral or ethical rules. Thus, to most political scientists, bureaucrats are well-meaning civil servants who apply their professional training and expertise in the public interest. Politicians balance the claims of competing interests and trade votes to produce socially beneficial outcomes. Bargaining among interest groups is guided by a beneficent invisible hand. Voters seek to enhance the general welfare by choosing carefully among competing politicians and ballot proposals. The result of all this is a process that enables the participants to become part of a cause greater than themselves.

Government, therefore, is basically passive, waiting to be acted upon by voters and interest groups, and politicians and bureaucrats are middlemen who arrange exchanges and deals for others and protect the public interest. In this view, politics is a benign, competitive process having close parallels with competitive markets; in politics, however, people participate primarily to serve interests other than their own, although serving their own interests is not precluded from the analysis.

Participation as Salvation

One theme underlying many modern discussions about politics and markets is the capacity for political participation to inspire individual fulfillment and improvement. Participating in the political process is seen as a way of lifting oneself above the crass self-interest many believe characterize market transactions. In this essentially Aristotelian vision, people are not able to reach their highest potential *unless* they participate in the political process. In fact, such participation is deemed necessary for human moral development. Only by connecting oneself with others through participation in political processes does one become whole. A central purpose of political participation is, therefore, to cause people to change

> from seeing themselves and acting as essentially consumers to seeing themselves and acting as exerters and enjoyers of the exertion and development of their own capacities. . . . For the latter self image brings with it a sense of community which the former does not. One can acquire and consume by oneself, for one's own satisfaction or to show one's superiority to others; this does not require or foster a sense of community; whereas the enjoyment and development of one's capacities is to be done for the most part in conjunction with others, in some relation of community. (Macpherson 1977, 99)

Participating in the political system, even if it is simply to exercise one's right to vote, takes on a religious quality. It suggests a willingness to fulfill one's life within the bounds established by the community and to bear witness of the value of the community. As one author suggests,

> To join is not simply to buy shares in a Lockean joint stock company but to give oneself up to an experience with others, to enter a relationship not as in the market but as in a marriage. . . . The language echoes the Bible (as well as the rhetoric of the New Left). It appeals to human feelings, to their spiritual and mystical dimension, in its call for a spontaneous, emotional sharing of experiences apart from any calculation of advantage. (Spitz 1984, 7–8, 33)

Visions about the value of political participation may be just that— visions. People may join civic organizations, churches, youth sports programs, or even run for local elected office out of a sense of community, but there is little evidence that a sense of community is what drives political participation outside the local community. There is, however, strong evidence that much political participation is based on a calculation of personal advantage. As we suggest in the next chapters, even voting and nonvoting may well be based on such calculations.

Visions of the Polity

Few political scientists accept the notion that America or any other democracy is a populist democracy governed by the common man. The accepted position is that policy decisions are made by a small group of people—elites who are better educated and more wealthy than average. Political scientists differ, however, over whether and how interest groups and elections affect the decisions of the elite and whether elites compete with each other or maintain a well-functioning oligopoly.

Pluralism

The most widely accepted model of the governmental process comes from the pluralist tradition begun by David Truman (1951), Robert Dahl (1956), and Charles E. Lindblom (1977). Although Truman's pluralist democracy differed from Dahl's and Lindblom's polyarchy, each built on the view of government developed by James Madison in *Federalist 10*. Madison argued that it is impossible to stop factions—or, in today's terminology, "interest groups"—from organizing and attempting to use the political system to their own ends. The effects of one faction can, however, be controlled by vigorous competition from other factions. An existing multiplicity of interests competing with one another in the political arena produces a market-type competition that becomes the collective choice version of Adam Smith's "invisible hand." It produces socially beneficial policies—policies that no one necessarily intended but that are in the public interest. Although this political marketplace is seen as suffering from some inherent limitations, the process is judged to be essentially healthy. Consider Robert Dahl's (1967) arguments:

> Because one center of power is set against another, power itself will be tamed, civilized, controlled and limited to decent human purposes, while coercion, the most evil form of power, will be reduced to a minimum.
>
> Because even minorities are provided with opportunities to veto solutions they strongly object to, the consent of all will be won in the long run.
>
> Because constant negotiations among different centers of power are necessary in order to make decisions, citizens and leaders will perfect the precious art of dealing peacefully with their conflicts, and not merely to the benefit of one partisan but to the mutual benefit of all the parties to a conflict. (p. 24)

Possibly the most succinct summary of this vision of government as an agent for creating positive changes in society was developed by Theodore Lowi (1969). He called this model of government "interest-group liberalism" and summarized it as follows:

> It may be called liberalism because it expects to use government in a positive and expansive role, it is motivated by the highest sentiments, and it possesses strong faith that what is good for government is good for society. It is "interest-group liberalism" because it sees as both necessary and good that the policy agenda and the public interest be defined in terms of the organized interests of society. (p. 71)

In language more familiar to economists, liberal welfare analysts assume that the political process is an efficient one in which all actors possess more or less complete information, transactions are almost costless, and there is an absence of externalities. Such a view of the polity is strikingly similar to the notion of a perfectly competitive market. In a perfect market there are no unexploited opportunities for gain; Pareto optimality has been achieved. All plans of the participants have been realized through the perfect coordination of activities. Under this scenario, the political process, like the perfect market, is assumed to be efficient. Lowi, in fact, wrote that the assumptions underlying interest-group liberalism "constitute the Adam Smith 'hidden hand' model applied to groups."

The pluralist position is supported, surprisingly enough, by two prominent members of the Chicago school of political economy. Gary Becker (1983) and George Stigler (1975) have each argued at length and in detail that present policies are politically efficient, that is, nothing better can be done under existing rules. Protectionist policies are the rational outcomes of the current political process. Politicians and voters adopt the more efficient or less inefficient policies—a rather startling claim in view of all the rent-seeking evidence. In any event, although the pluralists surely would not employ the same reasoning process as the Chicago analysts, it is clear that these groups share an essentially benign view of politics.

Anyone can see that these assumptions, like assumptions about perfect market conditions, are unrealistic. Balancing all these interests is cumbersome, tedious, and costly, especially since the medium of exchange is composed of votes, support, status, and time rather than something as simple as money. Another complication is the sheer number of participants in the process. As numbers increase, the costs of achieving agreement also increase and the ability to make efficient decisions declines.

Such considerations are irrelevant in the pluralist tradition. Truman argued, for example, that efficiency is not an appropriate tool of analysis or an appropriate criterion for evaluating the governmental process. Instead, stability of the political system, equality, and control by "the people" are the valued criteria. These concepts become both positive statements describing the governmental process and normative statements describing how it ought to function.

Elitism

Elite theorists are in a minority but their arguments are well regarded. They claim that societies are ruled by a single, relatively closed, upper-class elite that responds to public pressures only when the elite's position is threatened. The elite's power comes from controlling the essential resources of society, including wealth, education, legal and executive experience, and connections to government, military, business, and education leaders. Socioeconomic status determines membership in the elite, not elections or expertise.

Elite theory claims that in Western democracies, the elite ironically protects such basic tenets as individual liberty, due process, limited government, and capitalism. Members of the elite protect these values in order to preserve the existing system and their position in it. Elite theorists refer to *Who's Who in America* to show that a relatively small group of people dominate executive positions in government, finance, and industry. They claim that government regulatory agencies often become covert lobbies for the interests they are supposed to regulate. Since political appointees at the heads of the agencies expect to return to the business or industry they are supposed to be regulating, they make decisions to promote their own future job prospects. Besides, agency heads and industry lobbyists are in frequent contact socially, recreationally, and professionally. They belong to the same clubs, civic groups, and churches. That familiarity at all levels of their lives is believed to promote similar views.

Politicians serve, in large part, at the pleasure of the elite. Candidates find it difficult to get elected without the elite's money, connections, and endorsement. Corporations influence elected officials with contributions, personal favors, and promises to locate or threats to close plants in the officials' districts. Elections are symbolic exercises that reinforce the masses' perception that they are real participants in democracy. But elections do not bind politicians to particular courses of action. Those courses are chosen or at least influenced by the elite.

Interest groups themselves are elitist. Because the only politically successful groups are the organized ones, they must have hierarchy and leadership. Elites gravitate into that leadership and, like government and business leaders, gain a vested interest in maintaining the status quo and their position in it. Thus, interest groups become co-opted by and a tool of the elite.

Is a government of elites likely to use the power of government to overcome market failure? The answer would seem to be that it depends. It depends on whether remedying the failure would preserve the system, benefit some elites without harming others, or disturb the existing power structure. Some argue that, since the New Deal, elites have had an increasing sense of *noblesse oblige* and that increased public-mindedness has led them to use government to address a broad range of societal ills that cannot be addressed directly by markets.

Polyarchy

To accommodate the insights of the elitist view, pluralist scholars have developed a synthesis model, called polyarchy, that depicts society as collections of organized units, each headed by an elite. These "plural elites" interact, compete, strike bargains, and manage conflict within their own units. This model recognizes the existence, influence, and power of elites but retains the invisible hand component of pluralism. The public good comes from the competition between elites as well as their cooperation and public-mindedness.

According to Charles Lindblom (1977), "Constant and varied interaction between leadership and citizenry ... enables citizens to form volitions and guides leadership's response to them" (p. 137). He further claims the key process is formed by leaders persuading masses of voters. The process of persuasion is not simply the leader communicating with a homogeneous citizenry. Instead, leaders communicate with intermediate leaders who in turn attempt to persuade lesser leaders. These leaders include other local politicians, writers and broadcasters, religious leaders, union officials, and active, informed citizens who are opinion leaders in their neighborhoods.

Polyarchy is clearly not a system of majority rule, nor is it a system of elite rule. A political party is a coalition of political leaders who cooperate to win elections. The parties agree on those issues for which there is massive, clear support. They divide on issues that have not been clearly decided by public opinion. The outcome is that majority positions prevail when they are clear and unmistakable. Where they are not clear, elected and appointed officials are able to pursue their own agendas, which may or may not be in the public interest.

Although political scientists criticize polyarchies as systems in which the organized can benefit at the expense of the unorganized, in which leaders are able to use rather than serve the membership of their groups, and in which majority rule is not always followed, they generally see them as effective tools for addressing problems, at least those problems identified by organized groups. Competition among leaders and groups causes pertinent information to reach decisionmakers. The abuse of power is controlled through several mechanisms: the election of officials by ordinary citizens, the sharing of authority between bureaucrats and elected officials, and the formation of alliances between interest-group, legislative, bureaucratic, and executive leaders. Lindblom described the polyarchy as "a vast process of mutual accommodation to win votes, to assemble the votes of smaller groups in ever larger blocs and, for some leaders, to achieve influence by delivering votes to others" (p. 140).

Countervailing Power

An idiosyncratic twist on the elite model was offered by economist John Kenneth Galbraith. His arguments are worth summarizing because they are influential among political leaders and political scientists—probably more so than among economists. An overriding theme of his writings has been that the economy has broken up into two sectors, a competitive one and a relatively monopolistic one. He claimed that giant corporations dominate large segments of the economy and channel consumer wants to meet corporate interests through manipulative advertising. In *The Affluent Society* (1958) he put his argument this way:

> Consumer wants can have bizarre, frivolous, or even immoral origins, and an admirable case can still be made for a society which seeks to satisfy them. But the case cannot stand if it is the process of satisfying wants that creates the wants. For then the individual who urges the importance of production to satisfy those wants is precisely in the position of the onlooker who applauds the efforts of the squirrel to keep abreast of the wheel that is propelled by his own effort. (p. 125)

Galbraith maintained that consumers' wants ought to be sovereign but that advertising and any other means of manipulating wants *violate* consumer sovereignty. Thus, consumer sovereignty is only a useful concept after consumers have been liberated from wants induced by large corporations.

Galbraith also argued that the American economy suffers from a lack of "social balance"; that is, a "satisfactory relationship between privately produced goods and services and those of the state" (p. 201). He proposed remedying this imbalance through "a system of taxation which automatically makes a pro rata share of increasing income available to the public authority for public purposes. The task of public authority, like that of private individuals, will be to distribute this increase in accordance with relative need" (p. 242).

As government distributes public goods and services in order to achieve social balance, no real test of how to distribute this increase in accordance with relative need is possible, according to Galbraith, but he dismisses the problem by saying that the "mark of an affluent society is the opportunity for the existence of a considerable error on such matters." Private goods are so clearly overprovided relative to public goods in his view that the approaching balance will be evident as society moves toward it: "When we arrive, the opulence of our private consumption will no longer be in contrast with the poverty of our schools, the unloveliness and congestion of our cities, or inability to get work without struggle, and the social disorder that is associated with imbalance" (p. 249).

Galbraith's vision of the future society may differ from that of the mainstream, but his assumptions about government illustrate widespread current thinking: Change is only likely to occur through *political* battles among competing interest groups, and once change is mandated the government's army of scientific managers will carry it out. The major concern is not how bureaucrats and politicians will spend tax revenues but how society can get the money into their hands in the first place. Instead of being concerned with the ability of government officials to manage effectively, policymakers should worry about monopoly power and consider strict regulation of industries, even nationalization if necessary, so the industrial sector will serve the public interest. Protective, concerned government substitutes for failing markets.

Omnicompetent Scientific Managers

In order for a government, whether elitist, pluralist, or polyarchal, to carry out its ends, it must rely on managers. Information must be gathered, policies reviewed, and programs implemented and administered. The managers who undertake these tasks are known as civil servants, public administrators, or bureaucrats. They are an essential part of any attempt to manipulate markets, and an understanding of the conventional view of their capabilities and expected tasks is important to analyzing their ability to correct market failure.

For the past one hundred years the basic vision of bureaucracy has been that efficiency is promoted by professional, nonpartisan administration directed and coordinated by a strong executive. The beginning of this theme came from an 1887 article published by a young political scientist who later became president of the United States—Woodrow Wilson. To Wilson ([1887] 1992):

> The field of administration is a field of business. It is removed from the hurry and strife of politics; it at most points stands apart even from the debatable ground of constitutional study. It is a part of political life only as the methods of the counting-house are a part of the society; only as machinery is part of the manufacturing product. (p. 18)

Wilson laid out what came to be known as the politics-administration dichotomy, the distinction between the proper sphere for partisan politics and the proper sphere for nonpartisan administration. He asserted, "More important to be observed is the truth already so much and so fortunately insisted upon by our civil service reformers; namely that administration lies outside the proper sphere of politics." And he believed that "this discrimination between administration and politics is now, happily, too obvious to need further discussion" (p. 13).

Wilson's dichotomy became the base for other academic studies but also fit well with the arguments of muckrakers like Lincoln Steffens, Ida Tarbell, and Upton Sinclair. In addition, Frederick Taylor and others were developing techniques for factories based on the ideas of "scientific management," and these ideas were adopted by promoters of a scientific, nonpartisan, public administration.

Scientific management of public agencies became an ideal of both the Left and the Right. It is based on the belief that "right-minded" managers, who are not motivated by profit or other selfish goals, will protect the public interest while managing government agencies, programs, and properties. In order to accomplish this purpose, however, managers need to be insulated from politics. Once the political system has produced policy direction, scientific managers need to be left alone to manage according to their professional training.

Scientific management, as viewed by its proponents, allows a well-trained, competent bureaucracy to apply technology and expertise to the tasks of eliminating the waste commonly found in market transactions, protecting the people from the excesses of business, and distributing society's wealth fairly. In fact, Wilson argued that such a manager "ought not to be a mere passive instrument" and that "large powers and unhampered discretion" were the cornerstones of a good bureaucratic system. Bureaucratic misconduct would be controlled by granting more, rather than less, power. He argued, "The greater [the manager's] power the less likely is he to abuse it, the more he is nerved and sobered and elevated by it. The less his power, the more safely obscure and unnoticed does he feel his position to be, and the more readily does he lapse into remissness." In addition, a strong professional ethic, inculcated in schools of public administration and reinforced by the virtues of public service, was to guide public managers to employ their science in the public interest.

One of the purported virtues of scientific management is its ability to divine not only what people want but also what is good for them. Consumer sovereignty, or the preference of citizens, is not valued as highly as the truths of science wielded by powerful, nonpartisan administrators. Keynesian fiscal policies are examples. Few citizens will want their taxes increased, but scientific management dictates that they be increased during times of prosperity in order to forestall a future, greater evil. Scientific management of the economy is thus supposed to protect people from their shortsighted, selfish vision by substituting the foresight and wisdom of the Keynesian planner.

Other examples include regulation of individuals and business by government agencies. Ordinary citizens must be protected from themselves in a host of activities: New automobiles must have bumpers that pass government-imposed crash tests, seat belts that activate buzzers when not hooked up, and fuel-efficient motors; new homes and additions to existing homes must be built according to standard building codes; lawnmowers must have devices to automatically stop the blade when the operator lets go of the handle. Citizens must be protected from business as well: Meat cannot be purchased without a government inspection; medical services cannot be bought from someone who has not graduated from an accredited medical school; businesses must pay their employees a wage at least equal to the minimum set by the government; advertising messages must conform to the guidelines established by the Federal Communications Commission; new drugs must meet tough standards and undergo extensive testing and review by the Food and Drug Administration. Science establishes the standards for protecting individuals from themselves and from others, and the standards are then enforced by the government.

Modern students of public administration have modified many of the assumptions and claims of scientific management, but the examples in the previous paragraph indicate that those assumptions still drive the structure and content of modern policy. Current analysts emphasize that bureaucracy has to be much more politicized than proponents of scientific management had thought. Agencies have to build and curry the favor of a clientele in order to survive, for example. In addition, administrators do not have perfect information or certainty. Rather than choosing the best course of action from among a complete and certain list of alternatives, administrators must seek improvement by making what Herbert Simon ([1947] 1976) called "satisficing" choices among a limited number of alternatives.

Whether the description of bureaucracy is made by an old scientific manager or a new systems theorist, however, the same model of political behavior underlies the argument. Managers may maximize or suffice with perfect or imperfect information, but they act in the public interest.

The Idealized State

Using the state to remedy market failures requires planning—not necessarily the central planning of production as has been attempted in Communist countries, but the substitution of human intelligence for the perceived crudities of politics. Less crassly put, such planning requires the depoliticizing of decisions at intermediate and low levels.

Although all governments have implemented this type of planning, it became conscious government policy with the advent of the Progressives and the "good government" movement. Planning was justified as a search for a more or less objective public interest undertaken by technical experts and statesmen. It has been aided by the proliferation of systems-analysis mathematical modeling and input-output analyses.

By now, almost everyone approves of some form of government planning—fiscal, plant closings, accident prevention, income security, population, investment, development, transportation, housing, employment, and on and on. Notice that these types of planning are far more extensive than the "good government" planning advocated by the Progressives because they address market interventions that attempt to create "good markets." They are attempts at resolving perceived market failures.

Although welfare economists are generally reticent about expanding government planning to include planning and coordination of economic activities, this concept has broad support across the political spectrum. In the 1992 presidential election, for example, President Clinton campaigned on a planning and coordination platform and Ross Perot claimed there were several plans already in existence that would get the economy rolling—they just needed to be implemented.

Given the belief in pervasive market failures, national planning is advanced as a means of ending "mindless growth" and "excessive development" arising from uncontrolled market activity and replacing them with quality growth and controlled location and timing of economic development. One official governmental statement of this sort was contained in the *Global 2000 Report to the President* (1980), a widely circulated report issued at the end of Jimmy Carter's presidency. The report began by claiming:

> If present trends continue, the world in 2000 will be more crowded, more polluted, less stable ecologically, and more vulnerable to disruption than the world we live in now. Serious stresses involving population, resources, and environment are clearly visible ahead. Despite greater material output, the world's people will be poorer in many ways than they are today.
>
> For hundreds of millions of the desperately poor, the outlook for food and other necessities of life will be no better. For many it will be worse. Barring revolutionary advances in technology, life for most people on earth will be more precarious in 2000 than it is now—unless the nations of the world act decisively to alter current trends.
>
> This, in essence, is the picture emerging from the U.S. Government's projections of probable changes in world population, resources, and environment by the end of the century, as presented in the Global 2000 study. They do not predict what will occur. Rather, they depict conditions that are likely to develop if there are no changes in public policies, institutions, or rates of technological advance, and if there are no wars or other major disruptions. A keener awareness of the nature of the current trends, however, may induce changes that will alter these trends and the projected outcome. (p. 1)

The proposed way out of these impending calamities was centralization of planning and greater control of economic activity. According to the report, the economy is characterized by unplanned and uncontrolled economic growth. People are constantly obtaining more, newer, and better products they do not need; because the world is running out of resources, an era of scarcity is replacing a world of growing affluence.

There are strong calls for action to avert this impending scarcity. As part of his narration of a three-part series for NBC's "Today" show (January 9–11, 1990), ecologist Paul Erlich asserted that humans are "destroying the entire ecological system." He claimed, "The most explosive social reality of the next century is that the world's ecosystem cannot support the spread of the American lifestyle to the underdeveloped nations of the world." Vice President Gore's book *Earth in the Balance* identifies impending ecological crises and calls for federal action. The November 2, 1993, *Wall Street Journal* reported on Representative Gerry Studds's bill to establish a National Biological Survey. Studds is quoted as saying the survey would have "a simple, yet awesome mission—catalog everything that walks, crawls, swims, or flies around this country." The article then reported that the science adviser to the secretary of the interior, Dr. Thomas Lovejoy, claims the survey's findings would "determine development for the whole country and regulate it all" (p. A20).

Efforts to establish such political action generally focus on the need for central information-gathering. Several bills introduced in Congress during the 1980s sought to create a new agency or office responsible for identifying key economic and environmental indicators, generating data about them, plugging that data into computer models to analyze trends and interactions, and then using the results to make policy. Several assumptions underlie this view of scientific management of information by government. First, it is assumed that the information is available and can be collected. Then, it is assumed that the information is time and place specific; that is, that it can be applied to particular products in particular situations. It is also assumed that the information will be used in the policy and regulation process. Finally, it is assumed that information unavailable in the market—or too costly to gather—will be available to government at reasonable cost.

Conclusions

We included the discussion of national planning to illustrate the assumptions behind the idealized state and the direction such a state might take. Advocates of using the state to respond to market failures believe in government planning. Others believe markets are fine as long as they are directed by government. A currently popular phrase asserts, "Markets can row but government must steer."

Many advocates of greater government planning and direction see exchange as a competitive activity producing winners and losers. The "little guy" is at the mercy of the "big guys"; consumers are manipulated by advertisers into buying products they don't need or even really want; buyers are at the mercy of sellers; and labor loses to management. Although mutually advantageous gain is considered a possibility, the usual expectation is that someone's gain is often someone else's loss.

Politics are assumed to makes things better. Political processes distribute wealth more equally with the result that the political and economic power of those who operate the economy is reduced. Political interference in the workplace protects labor from being victimized by management, and political actions afford consumers greater protection. This idealized democratic state is guided by an invisible hand that improves on the chaos of the market. It lifts people from the morally degenerating or at best amoral self-interest of the market into more responsible and more socially beneficial activities. Government allows for the expression of competing values and becomes the tool for resolving conflicts between them. Competent, scientific managers protect citizens from themselves, from organized interests, and from big business.

Although it is doubtful that many economists who advocate government intervention to reverse market failure are as optimistic or as naive as the preceding summary suggests, the summary does reflect the view animating discussions promoting government to resolve market failures. The problem is that few economists have applied their powerful tools for analyzing market processes to an analysis of government processes. Those who argue that market failure justifies government action don't stop to ask certain questions: What incentives exist in government? Who wins and loses? Are the actual outcomes different from those we hope for? Do good intentions in government produce good results?

The following chapters provide such an analysis. They show the idealized democratic state to be just that—idealized but not realized and with no potential for realization. They also show the earlier claims of market failure to be far weaker than supposed even just a few years ago; as a result, the initial justifications for relying on the state, ideal or not, are seldom justifications at all.

Bibliographical Notes

In this chapter we identified some of the most important works for understanding the pluralist vision of the state. They are worth identifying again: Robert Dahl's *A Preface to Democratic Theory* (Chicago: University of Chicago Press, 1956), David B. Truman's *The Governmental Process* (New York: Alfred A. Knopf, 1951), and Charles E. Lindblom's *Politics and Markets* (New York: Basic Books, 1977). We also recommend a slim volume on interest groups by Alfred O. Hirschman entitled *The Passions and the Interests* (Princeton: Princeton University Press, 1977).

The basic books on elite theory are those of the Italian sociologists Gaetano

Mosca and Vilfredo Pareto. In *The Mind and Society* (New York: Harcourt Brace, 1916), Pareto argued that elites hold power because of psychological advantages over the masses such as strength, decisiveness, cunning, and deceit. Mosca's 1896 book, *The Ruling Class* (New York: McGraw-Hill, 1939; translated and edited by A. Livingston), stressed the value of organization. Another classic work in elite theory is *Political Parties: A Sociological Study of the Oligarchic Tendency of Modern Democracy* (Glencoe, Ill.: Free Press, 1958), written by Robert Michels in 1911. Michels believed the ideal of democratic rule was futile, given the power resources of ruling elites, and that despair led him to support fascism. More modern works of importance include C. Wright Mills, *The Power Elite* (New York: Oxford University Press, 1956), and the popular classroom text by Thomas R. Dye, *Who's Running America: Institutional Leadership in the United States*. The text is published by Prentice-Hall and the most recent edition was released in 1990. It contains fascinating case studies of elites and how they make choices.

Public administration is its own academic field complete with academic journals and professional conferences. Thus, the literature on the subject is voluminous. We suggest a few we find interesting and useful. First, we suggest Herbert Simon's *Administrative Behavior: A Study of Decision-Making Process in Administrative Organization* (New York: The Free Press, 1976), first published in 1947. Simon, who later won the Nobel Prize in Economics for his work on decisionmaking theory, provides the basis for much of the modern study of bureaucracy.

Another book we recommend as "must reading" about how bureaucracy functions is Aaron Wildavsky's *New Politics of the Budgetary Process* (Glenview, Ill.: Scott, Foresman, 1988). Wildavsky argues that the budget lies at the heart of the political process and provides clear, insightful descriptions of how bureaucrats, politicians, and interest groups interact to produce the budget. The analysis is much like that upcoming in the next two chapters and is basic to understanding political processes.

Finally, we suggest *Inside Bureaucracy* (Boston: Little, Brown, 1967) by Anthony Downs. He uses economic analysis to develop a theory of bureaucratic decisionmaking that produces hypotheses about life cycles of bureaus, different types of bureaucrats, ideology, and budgeting, to mention just a few. The examples he uses are a bit dated now, but the theory remains basic to understanding bureaucracy.

References

Becker, Gary S. "A Theory of Competition Among Pressure Groups for Political Influence," *Quarterly Journal of Economics* 98 (1983), 371–399.

Dahl, Robert. *A Preface to Democratic Theory* (Chicago: University of Chicago Press, 1956).

———. *Pluralist Democracy in the United States: Conflict and Consent* (Chicago: Rand McNally, 1967).

Galbraith, John Kenneth. *The Affluent Society* (New York: Mentor Books, 1958).

Global 2000 Report to the President (Washington, D.C.: U.S. Government Printing Office, 1980).

Gore, Al. *Earth in the Balance: Ecology and the Human Spirit* (Boston: Houghton Mifflin, 1992).

Lindblom, Charles E. *Politics and Markets* (New York: Basic Books, 1977).

Lowi, Theodore. *The End of Liberalism: Ideology, Policy, and the Crisis of Public Authority* (New York: W. W. Norton, 1969).

Macpherson, C. B. *The Life and Times of Liberal Democracy* (Oxford: Oxford University Press, 1977).

Simon, Herbert. *Administrative Behavior: A Study of Decision-Making Process in Administrative Organization* (New York: The Free Press, 1976; originally published in 1947).

Spitz, Elaine. *Majority Rule* (Chatham, N.J.: Chatham House, 1984).

Stigler, George. *The Citizen and the State: Essays on Regulation* (Chicago: University of Chicago Press, 1975).

Truman, David B. *The Governmental Process: Political Interests and Public Opinion* (New York: Alfred A. Knopf, 1951).

Wilson, Woodrow. "The Study of Administration," reprinted in Jay M. Shafritz and Albert C. Hyde, eds., *Classics of Public Administration,* 3rd ed. (Pacific Grove, Calif.: Brooks/Cole, 1992); originally published in *Political Science Quarterly* 2 (June 1887), 197–222.

PART TWO

In Dispraise of Politics: Some Public Choice

GOVERNMENT FAILURE is the topic of Part Two and is a central research topic of a relatively new academic discipline known as public choice. Public choice scholars apply economic reasoning and analysis to the study of both individual and collective political choices. Their conclusions quickly disabuse one of the notions of the idealized state explained in Part One.

Public choice scholars have shown that governments do not easily fix market failures; they usually make things worse. The fundamental reason is that the information and incentives that allow markets to coordinate human activities and wants are not available to government. Thus, voters, politicians, bureaucrats, and activists who believe themselves to be promoting the public interest are led by an invisible hand to promote other kinds of interests.

Our analysis is confined to democracies, not authoritarian regimes, and our criticisms of democracy should not be taken as support for those regimes. We believe strongly in self-government. Democracy can be structured to provide appropriate protections for individual rights and opportunities for voluntary, collective action. But modern democratic politics is often exploitative, wasteful, and destructive of individual rights. The analysis presented here prepares the reader to understand the case studies of Part Three and anticipates the reforms we propose in the final chapter.

❦ 3 ❧

Unromantic Side of Democracy

THE EVOLUTION OF public choice theory over the past thirty years has certainly demystified and deromanticized political processes. Perhaps the field's major discovery has been the welfare-diminishing propensities of real world politics. These propensities, known as government failures, are as ubiquitous as market failures and apparently more difficult to cure.

The conclusions drawn from public choice are in many ways a restatement of the warnings given 200 years ago by the authors of *The Federalist Papers*. The Federalists were concerned about the abuse of power, the ability of organized groups to exploit unorganized groups, and other forms of the political pursuit of private gain. Public choice uses economic reasoning and analysis to show why the Federalists' fears were well founded and to uncover the institutions and processes that lead to government failure. In this and the following chapter we explore in some detail how democratic politics really operate and with what results.

The Polity as an Economy (of Sorts)

The public choice model of politics and democracy is actually quite simple. Politics is assumed to be a system consisting of four groups of decision-makers—voters, elected officials or politicians, bureaucrats, and interest groups. Individuals are assumed to be rational utility-maximizers who seek benefits from the political system. Politicians are assumed to seek votes, and bureaucrats seek job security and budgets. Interest groups and voters seek more wealth and income. Although there are serious limitations in the political institutions of exchange, each actor is assumed to want something possessed and/or controlled by others; for example, voters and interest groups want services from politicians and bureaucrats, and bureaucrats want greater revenues or budgets from politicians and taxpayers. And, of course, politicians want votes and other forms of support from citizens and interest-group members. For convenience the system is depicted in Figure 3.1.

41

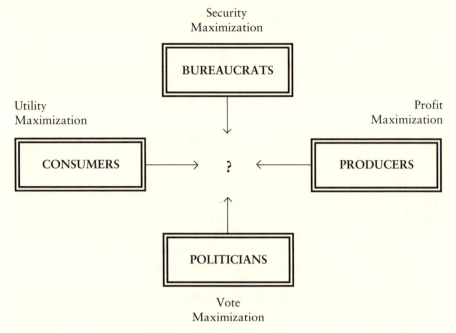

FIGURE 3.1   The Political System

Like markets, politics operate in an environment of scarce resources and uncertainty. The polity offers a means of allocating these scarcities, distributing income and wealth, and providing for the common welfare. In one sense, the polity is a substitute for the market; in another sense, it is a complement designed to fulfill certain tasks markets find difficult to perform.

In our model, each individual is assumed to control certain assets. Each is self-interested and purposively oriented, and each engages in rational decisionmaking. Unfortunately, and precisely contrary to markets with well-defined and defendable property rights, political processes have certain properties that lessen efficiency and discourage harmony among the self-interested.

In assuming self-interested political agents, we are simply asserting that most people identify more easily with their own concerns than those of other people; we are not saying individuals are without interests in others (e.g., their family) and their welfare. Still, most of us get up in the morning asking what we must do for ourselves, not what we can do in the public interest or for the GNP. So long as we operate within well-designed economic and political institutions such self-interest is not bad; in fact, such institutions will, like Smith's "unseen hand," serve to convert selfishness into the general good. Most people most of the time find it impossible to argue for any sustained period against their own manifest best interests. Few people possess the wisdom and information to divine the best interests of others, and still fewer offer to continuously sacrifice themselves to improve the well-being of others. People find the most time to do the things they value most and find the least time for the onerous or for that which shows little promise of significant payoff for themselves. We do not claim that every normal individual always knows his or her own best interests but that no one else is likely to know them better. That is what Aristotle meant when he wrote that the wearer of shoes knows better than the cobbler whether a shoe pinches.

As maximizers who follow their own strongest impulses, without necessarily having the most noble ends in mind, citizens in the polity act much like economic agents in the economy. Whether consumers or citizens, they seem capable of organizing their objectives in some order of relative importance. Like consumers, citizens prefer more to less, other things remaining constant or equal.

Although their wants, in general, are insatiable, specific wants are quite satiable or limited. Their consumption of any one good, in particular, seems governed by the "law of diminishing marginal utility," that is, as an individual consumes more of some good the value of successive units decreases and eventually levels off so that no additional value is obtained by further consumption of that good. This fortunate fact not only limits consumers' particular demands but provides them with the opportunity and incentive to transfer the less wanted items to another person who places more value on them in exchange for other goods.

Individual preferences in the polity and economy alike are also characterized by a strong concern for time of consumption; in other words, in seeking gratification people usually prefer now to later. In order to overcome short-term preferences, rewards must be offered, as in the payment of interest for borrowed funds. Preferring now to later is, however, reversed in the matter of payment of costs; the utility-maximizer prefers to pay later or, better, to avoid payment altogether.

Both rational economic and political agents make their choices at or on the margin, that is, they ask how much additional benefit is to be expected from spending additional sums of money or employing additional resources. Such decisionmakers observe the rule of equating marginal benefits and marginal costs (MB = MC). Should marginal benefits exceed marginal costs (MB > MC), the rational person opts to continue the activity until the two terms are equalized. If the marginal costs exceed the marginal benefits (MC > MB), the decisionmaker does not continue the activity or cuts back until the two values are equal.

This discussion of decisionmakers leads us inevitably into considering the environment of choice and how that environment affects both individual and collective choices. Again, we stress the fact that resources are, at any given time, scarce relative to demands for their use. Such scarcity forces people to allocate resources so as to make the best or most efficient use of them; otherwise they pay the higher costs of inefficiency and become less well-off. In short, scarcity poses opportunity costs, and unlike benefits, such costs increase, usually at an increasing rate. If the law of diminishing marginal productivity did not operate, the world could be fed from someone's backyard garden; adding unlimited labor, water, and fertilizer would cause unlimited production. In reality, benefits increase at a decreasing rate while costs increase at an increasing rate! Additionally, the decision environment is best characterized by varying degrees of uncertainty; that is, we only rarely know with confidence what will happen. We always choose in varying states of ignorance with respect to what other rational, self-interested people and Mother Nature are contemplating. Thus we cannot accurately predict and control the future or undo the past. Try as we might through science and hedging our bets (insurance), we cannot know all there is to know. Fortunately, we need not be omniscient or omnicompetent.

Imposing various forms of order through political institutions is one way people seek to reduce uncertainty and advance their self-interests. Such institutions structure the behavior in the political game. Among those rules are constitutions, which prescribe how subsequent policy choices and rule changes are to be made. For example, constitutional rules governing civic and property rights, contracts, and so on serve to better define who commands which resources and how they may be employed and transferred. The important point is that collective institutions are highly important matters with good and bad consequences for individual and joint welfare.

The Fundamental Nature of
Collective Choice

On the basis of these elementary but fundamental considerations about decisionmakers we are ready to explore the nature of politics. In the first place, to have a government and a system of democratic processes is to decide that henceforth certain choices will be made not by individuals in the isolation of markets but *jointly with others*. In order to decide with others, rules must be adopted enabling authoritative joint choices to be made in spite of differences among those choosing. Plurality is one such rule; simple majority and supra-majorities are others. Such rules necessarily imply that when choices are made there will be relative losers and winners. To put it another way, a voter on the losing side is required to comply with the winning decision because government has coercive power to impose its will on the dissidents; majorities may use the power of government to tyrannize and exploit minorities. The coercive power of political systems provides evidence that government is a monopoly—control over which is desired by many and protected by a relative few. Social scientists have long noted the jealousy of rulers in harboring their authority. Rulers do not cheerfully tolerate competitors, and they guard their treasuries with special zeal since the revenues collected are their means for doing what they will.

Although governments are best thought of as monopolies, it is important to remember that they are rather peculiar monopolies. They are *not* profit oriented in the same sense as the market monopolist. They conduct their fiscal operations in ways radically different from the private firm and even the private monopolist. Governments rarely seek profits for their "owners" by selling goods and services at prices that enable costs to be met and profits earned. As we discuss later, these differences make governments act in ways that are very different from the ways private monopolies act.

In Chapter 2 we identified the production of public goods as a justification for governmental action. Since public goods are really gratuitous or indiscriminate goods once they are produced, nonpaying citizen-consumers cannot be easily prevented from making use of or enjoying the benefits. This situation creates special problems of pricing and supply that cannot easily be resolved by government. How much is enough? Who shall pay how much? How should payments be made? Since price tags are not found on individual units of public goods, tax systems are devised to meet the costs of offering them. But when everyone has equal access to the same quantities of the same goods, how is the government to determine tax rates? In the market, consumers or buyers confront price tags to which they can relate their own estimates of the value of the good. Not so in the polity, where there is no direct connection between the costs and benefits of a good or service. As a consequence, those who benefit most from a service may not be taxed, and those who are taxed most may not place a high value on the service or even use it.

These several attributes of collective choice at once distinguish the political process from the market, where free, independent, individual choice is the norm. Politics inevitably involves conflicting preferences, majorities versus minorities, coerced participation, enforced sharing, and extraordinary inefficiencies and inequities. That so many citizens wish to extend these attendant controls over their personal lives appears paradoxical, but we will resolve that dilemma shortly. How monopolistic governments can be restrained also becomes an important issue, one we reserve for the last chapter.

Confused Voters and Ballot Box Logic

In Latin, "votum," from which we get our word "vote," means "ardent wish." But obviously many American voters are not terribly ardent and are, in fact, highly frustrated; we know this because the right to vote is not regularly exploited by many citizens. Apparently, voting is viewed as neither a highly rewarding nor an efficacious activity. Without substantial reforms, electoral participation will remain low, and even with reforms voting can never provide a truly effective means of representing citizen preferences. In brief, voters can make electoral choices but they do not have much individual influence over policies.

It is important to view the voter as a citizen who commands a number of civic assets, or rights, enabling participation in civic endeavors. Like all assets, these assets vary in value even though we often speak of the vote as "free," implying, therefore, that it is valueless. But, the expenditure of time, effort, and money by both voter and contending politicians suggests that a vote is worth a good deal to those involved. Most citizens acquire the right to vote as a matter of birthright. The right is distributed universally and equally, and unlike most market assets, votes are nontransferable. This precious right to vote provides the legal basis on which each citizen may express, however inadequately, civic preferences. Undergirding the vote is an entire set of constitutional freedoms—including those of speech, print, religion, and organization—that enable the individual to function as a sovereign member of the polity. Without these freedoms democracy could not exist. Even so, these valued assets do not necessarily promote effective and efficient choices. The high cost of information, for example, encourages people to remain uninformed. The fact that we cannot sell votes prevents resources from being transferred to their highest-valued uses. Furthermore, voters cannot choose among specific policy results but must rely upon political promises—promises that cannot be legally enforced. If politicians could be sued or otherwise penalized for failure to honor commitments, politics would be a great deal different.

As beneficiary and taxpayer, the voter plays dual roles. Although these roles or positions are mutually contradictory in the abstract, no contradiction exists in the concrete world of politics; one role does not discipline the other as in the market. In the market, prudent consumers must consider income and prices before deciding to buy, and this must be done at the margin and with an eye to one's future prospects and obligations. In the polity, in contrast, citizens are not constrained by income or prices. The goods and services of government are provided whether one wants them or not. And frequently people vote for goods to be consumed by others and/or paid by still others. Voting for more spending may seem appealing because of the intended benefits, but such good intentions are not immediately disciplined by the knowledge that someone must pay for these benefits. Under the system of taxation, voters may hope that some other taxpayer, a wealthy one, preferably, can be forced to finance their private desires and altruistic impulses. Voters should not be indicted for profligacy when nothing in the voting decision requires considering income and prices.

The situation is even worse, though. In playing out the taxpayer role, well-meaning, public-spirited voters have every incentive to opt for reductions in their own tax payments and every incentive to pursue private gains at public expense. Ignoring the public cost of one's own demands is highly rational; then, too, a prudent citizen must pay a steep price to even be informed about the costs and benefits of policy options. That most voters choose to remain rationally ignorant is hardly surprising. And only in politics can a person make ethical imperatives of logical contradictions. For example, a citizen might advocate more defense, increased spending on social programs, and consumer protection while also promoting lower taxes, balanced budgets, and reduced government controls. When the price of something in the private market changes, consumers can alter their consumption—that is, buy less of that which increases in price and purchase more when the price decreases. Given fixed quantities of publicly supplied goods and public sharing of the costs, individual citizens cannot follow this eminently sensible course of action. Coerced collective consumption does not permit, let alone encourage, responsible marginal adjustments by the citizen-consumer.

Certain consequences of irresponsibility for the citizen and polity are fairly clear. As a taxpayer, the citizen is interested in the aggregate size of the budget and supports reduced spending, reduced inflation, and increased economic growth. As a beneficiary of governmental spending, the same citizen supports an increase in subsidies or favors for his company or employer and governmental regulation of his profession; he or she has little interest in the total size of the budget. Predictably, these latter interests are generally apt to be more intensely felt than taxpayer commitments.

By this analysis, we should expect the spending incentives to outweigh the revenue considerations not only for the individual but for society as well. The complexity of this situation warrants further explanation. The citizen-beneficiary must appeal primarily to legislative bodies to obtain government services. Legislators usually represent localized interests and have a constitutional mandate to enact appropriations. Thus, citizens and interest groups appeal first to Congress, their state legislatures, and city councils to voice demands for funds, programs, and other privileges. They appeal, too, to the president, governors, and the bureaucracy. Although the president and governors are subject to spending forces and incentives, they are more sensitive than legislators to taxpayer complaints—taxpayers are strongly inclined to blame chief executives before blaming state legislatures and Congress for tax increases. In addition, almost all chief executives are elected every four years, so they are apt to respond to a longer time horizon than are legislators, most of whom are elected every two years.

Our concentration on the fiscal aspects of voting and elections should not overshadow other considerations having important consequences for public life. Although the vote is a visible, central feature of democracy, we should recognize how really insignificant it is in the entire process of collective choice. We sometimes overestimate what can be accomplished by spasmodic attendance at the polls. The limitations are as dismaying as they are pronounced. As voters we are normally confronted not with marginal choices—a little more or a little less—but with either/or decisions, and the either/or's usually consist of "tie-in purchases": In order to obtain one good, we must also accept a variety of other commitments we view as less desirable or even as negative. To get a labor policy I like, I may also have to accept a foreign policy I abominate. To have a president of my choice, I must accept his selection of a vice president. Of course, markets create similar situations for consumers. Complex products and services do pose such dilemmas and we should not minimize them. But these dilemmas are more easily resolved than their electoral counterparts.

Voting is a painfully limited way to express one's values and preferences. It accomplishes its results only indirectly; the vote does not immediately call forth that which is voted for. In fact, if we vote for something but are in the minority we do not get it at all; if we vote against something and are in the minority, we get it and are compelled to pay for the unwanted goods or services. Furthermore, because of secrecy in the casting of the vote, individual voters cannot collect on their votes, and even if they could collect, their votes are practically worthless among the thousands and millions of other votes. Rarely can one vote swing an election. Such is the paradox of participation: The more voters participate, the lower the power or value of the individual vote. This dismal prospect is made even more discouraging by voter free-riding. If everyone believes his candidate will win, few will go to the polls, thereby encouraging the candidate's defeat. Likewise, if everyone thinks her candidate is without a chance of winning, most will fail to vote and thus produce the same result.

Whether voters are sovereign or manipulated, restless or stable, apathetic or interested, ungrateful or appreciative, prospective or retrospective, maximizing or satisfying, they are put into an unpromising choice situation. And, as we have stressed, without a convincing cost-benefit nexus to discipline choices, voters are led necessarily to practice that most ancient art—the art of having it both ways. The ambiguous status of the vote reminds us that Eugene Debs, the nineteenth-century labor organizer and socialist, was perhaps right: "It's better to vote for something you want and not get it than to vote for something you don't want and get it."

Politicians and the
Universal Political Touch

American politicians are elected for set terms of office, provided a fixed salary, and expected to enact public laws and policies binding on all. Their formal roles are defined in constitutions and often surrounded by considerable pageantry, pomp, status, and titles. As long as they are in office, they are important and powerful people.

Fiscal Orientations of Public Office

Like all political agents, the politician spends other people's money and spends it on still others who may not have contributed to the common treasury. Officers of private corporations also spend the money of others (stockholders), but the constraints on their behavior are considerably more direct and powerful than those experienced by politicians. In brief, anyone who spends money not his own on people other than himself will not have as powerful an incentive to get his money's worth as the person who spends his own money on himself.

A businessperson attempts to obtain sales receipts that exceed payments to produce the goods; if successful, a profit is earned that can be retained and used as that businessperson deems wise. The politician is under no similar constraint. The politician who invents a new way of doing something may be rewarded by the voters at the next election but is not allowed to recapture any profits his civic innovation may produce. In fact, saving money for the government and for the taxpayers may defeat the politician's own interests. Those citizens who receive fewer government resources will be more likely to coalesce and vote against reelection than the many taxpayer-gainers—each of whom realizes but a small savings, one not worth the costs of organizing—are to reward the helpful politician.

The difficulties of supporting the general interest are compounded when concentrated interest groups are considered. The politician faces more powerful incentives to spend than to economize. One reason has just been alluded to, namely, that small groups who benefit from government expenditures have more incentives and cheaper means of organizing than do the diffused taxpayers. If a politician has a choice of dividing $1 million equally among 1 million citizens or equally among 1,000 people, he will rationally opt for the latter because he is more likely to win the gratitude of those who gained $1,000 than of those getting but $1 apiece. Conversely, if the same politician has to choose between taxing 1 million taxpayers $1 apiece and taxing 1,000 taxpayers $1,000 each, he will under most circumstances choose the former option. The logic is similarly clear; the electoral implications of concentrated gains and dispersed losses prevail.

In our treatment of the citizen-voter, we emphasized the absence of a constraint to inform and discipline fiscal choices. The same is true for the politician. Spending the public's money to buy votes is considered unethical. But in administering the public's money, the official does not treat spending and revenue decisions as one and the same process as corporate executives do; instead, these crucial decisions are divided into two distinct choices, often made at different times by different people serving on different committees and in separate offices. Wouldn't we all spend more in our private lives if we were not faced with price tags and monthly bills? In some traditional families, that is how fiscal matters are handled: Father worries about the income while mother deals with expenditures, and neither talks to the other. Unhappily, such a family may soon find itself dealing with creditors, financial consultants, lawyers, and bankruptcy court. Governments, in contrast, rarely permit their creditors to sue them, and governmental bankruptcy is unheard of.

We have described in somewhat abstract terms the political setting within which politicians seek office and make policy choices and have examined how this setting contrasts with the marketplace. We have yet to examine the strategies, tactics, and other practices that politicians follow in their everyday political lives. These matters need attention if for no other reason than to sharpen our familiarity with real-life elected officials and policymaking. Then, too, these daily practices and rules of thumb are their adaptations to political settings imposed upon them. We believe these job adaptations are as rational as the decisions of the consumer, producer, and middleman.

Competition, Compromise, and Bargaining

Because votes are so crucial to political success, politicians are required to be competitive, to bargain, and to compromise. Rarely can the individual politician achieve his or her own goals and those of constituencies without allies. Workable public policies for divided constituents and live-and-let-live arrangements with colleagues become all-important goals. Accordingly, politicians are fond of such expressions as "I can buy that" or "I can live with that." Or, "Let's run it up the flagpole and see if anyone salutes." Seeking allies and grounds for compromise are important activities for most politicians and necessarily so, because power is divided and decision-rules require some minimal agreement. In fact, one of the textbook definitions of politics is "the art of compromise."

At the same time, politicians are competitors for office. They compete over final terms of agreement and have diverse interests to protect and advance, including not only their own interests but also those of constituents, party followers, and financial contributors. Like all bargainers, individual politicians are enmeshed within a game of mixed motives, that is, a game characterized by both shared and competing interests. The task then is to advance one's own interests without driving other politicians from the bargaining table. All can be made better off by some agreement, but not all agreements are equally valued. The situation is roughly analogous to that of buyers and sellers haggling over a selling price and other considerations in a market exchange. Unfortunately, the political marketplace does not provide a mechanism for resolving disagreements as facilitative and efficient as market prices. Seemingly, endless compromising is not without its costs. Legislating tax policy is a process of give and take, but taking from some and giving to others. The process also seems to generate some less than admirable personal behavior. Successful politicians become the mirror image of what they do, shifting, smoothing, evading, concealing, lying, and diffusing hostility. Insincerity and flattery are common forms of political behavior; so, too, are paranoia, hatred, envy, and cynicism. Examples abound. President Nixon promised the nation, "I will not take this nation down the road of wage and price controls, however politically expedient they may seem." Two months later he enacted the very controls he said he would not enact. Admittedly, the popular wage and price controls played just a small part in the election, but Nixon was reelected two years later by the largest margin in history! In the campaign of 1988, Vice President Bush promised not to raise taxes; in 1990, he agreed with Congress to do just that.

The courting of voters forces practitioners to adopt tactics rivaling those of Machiavelli's prince. Successful politicians garner credit for popular programs and policies while simultaneously diffusing their responsibility among underlings and opponents for anything that turns bad. They conceal mistakes and embarrassments. They deploy "trial balloons" to reduce the risk of innovation, and they never knowingly allow opponents to define themselves or the issues or to monopolize attention. They usually avoid flat, forthright statements and commitments about uncertain futures and unabashedly steal popular issues and proposals whenever possible. They trust few and pick their enemies with care, for competing politicians are highly valuable targets. And they always honor the self-interests of those to whom they appeal but cloak those same interests in the language of the national interest, social needs, and entitlements.

Successful politicians must be good tacticians. When seeking allies they usually seek only as many as are necessary to win and prefer those who can be dominated. They treat coalitions as temporary, unstable groupings and today's opponent as tomorrow's ally. If losing, they broaden the scope of the conflict in order to enlist supporters. When ahead in a race, they ignore their opponents.

Politicians are never all-powerful; they must contend with demanding and conflicting voters and competitors, real and potential. To some extent they must become responsive to the wishes of the median voter. Still, political institutions are imperfect devices for registering the popular will, and politicians do have some distinct advantages in their relationships with voters. If the politician is engaged on a full-time basis while the citizen is a part-time, inattentive bystander, how could it be otherwise?

Buying Votes with Public Money

Spending money on voters has obvious appeal, but politicians quickly learn that maximizing votes does not result from simply throwing words and funds at citizen demands; something more sophisticated is required. There is a basic calculus enabling the politician to minimize vote losses from enacting or supporting tax legislation while at the same time maximizing favorable votes for money spent. In short, the politician asks two questions: (1) How many additional votes will I receive for each additional dollar spent? (2) How many additional votes will I lose for advancing the welfare of some groups at the expense of others? In choosing among alternative spending projects, politicians attempt to compare the added votes from each added dollar of spending per project and determine the mix that guarantees the maximization of votes. Minimizing votes lost from increasing taxes is assured by the same logic, that is, when choosing among alternative taxes, it is best to match the marginal votes lost from each tax. In Chapter 5 we will show how this impeccable logic for promoting the self-interests of the politician leads to log rolling and a diminishment of the public welfare.

The general rule of marginal calculation must, however, be extended to particular spending programs as well as taxation. The politician deals not in the vast and mystifying aggregates of national income but with particular spending and taxing proposals. Some spending is politically more profitable than others. Perhaps the basic consideration is this: Spend money on private benefits that are not only highly visible but also sufficiently large to make a difference to recipients. Likewise, a payment received now or in the near future is better appreciated than a larger, but uncertain, future installment. Furthermore, to insure lasting gratitude, the flow of income or other benefits ought to be more or less continuous. Spending on public goods may be highly useful in the long run, but individual gains are not easily or readily appreciated by most citizens. Our supply of public goods is assured, however, by the fact that their production confers considerable benefits on the holders of contracts for their provision (for example: highway construction and defense expenditures). Finally, most people receiving monies from the public treasury rarely appreciate having them described as outright pork barrel or subsidies; better that they be considered entitlements or needed investments in the public interest.

Politicians recognize that in evaluating spending they must also take into account the status positions of recipients. Nothing irritates people more than a belief that the undeserving—poor or wealthy—are being made better off. Advantages must not only be cloaked in the public interest but conveyed in less visible but legitimate ways. Rarely are the rich given outright grants; instead their gains are provided indirectly through the tax code and market advantages. Whether beneficiaries get their government income in the form of a check through the mail or through a reduction in their income tax, the same result in net income and wealth is produced. But if the less well-off do not know that is happening, the beneficiary and politician are both better off.

Spending on the less well-off cannot be hidden through tax privileges since they pay little or no taxes. Thus, spending on the poor is more visible, making the task of the politician more difficult and the status of the poor more demeaning. One political way out for the politician has been to provide the poor with more direct aid-in-kind, such as housing, clothing, food, medical services, and education. With certain strings attached, these forms of aid satisfy the need of the politician to show middle-class taxpayers that they are getting their money's worth and that taxpayer support is not being used for immoral, frivolous, or unhealthy endeavors. To gain the support of private producers and government bureaucrats, programs are administered with innumerable controls, checks, and red tape.

Since depressions and recessions temporarily reduce government revenues, budgetary crises challenge the ingenuity of political leaders. If budgets must be reduced, they will be lowered by the smallest amount politics will permit. The programs reduced least will be the big-ticket items that confer well-known, substantial benefits on many people. As reformers of the Social Security program have learned, flows of benefits, once begun, are virtually impossible to terminate or even reduce. Once installed, they become habitual to both recipient and conveyor or bureaucrat. Threats to terminate programs are perceived as imposing greater losses than gains, even if long-term gains would accrue to many more taxpayers. Threat of losses will inspire recipients to organize in defense of their benefit faster and more effectively than any greater but more amorphous gain could inspire diffused taxpayers. It is for this reason that old programs rarely die or fade away; the fact is, they get bigger as officials devise attractive new programs to add to the old. The "Reagan Revolution" is the prime example. Reagan's, and Bush's, policies did not reduce the size of the federal government; they may have only reduced the rate of increase.

But suppose that sacrifices must be made. One strategy is to undertake "meat axe" or across-the-board reductions. This strategy rings the bell for equality and fairness. Although it has the disadvantage of ignoring the size of programs and their differential social value, this approach has undeniable political appeal. The politician will not appear to be picking on some while protecting others. Finally, if cuts must be made on some other basis, the best approach from the politician's perspective is to cut back on those beneficiaries offering the least resistance. For instance, in universities it is the maintenance department and the libraries that are prone to cutbacks and not the professors and chief administrators. Public investments, no matter how sound, are deferred. And, to create the impression of cutting back, the government may publicize how many employees have been removed from the rolls. Of course, most will be retirees, transfers, resignations, and those who die but are not replaced. Salaries are not reduced, but increases are delayed. Some sacrifices are made but mostly by the less powerful.

These propensities of government strongly suggest that the politician's compassion for meeting ever-increasing social wants is being translated into legislation with ever-increasing price tags. Unfortunately, but understandably, public opinion is less preoccupied with checking public expenditures than with redistributing the burden of taxation, perhaps because average people feel they have little influence over expenditures. Accordingly, most citizens voice far more concern over personal taxes than over increased expenditures, most of which go to other citizens. After all, taxes decrease someone's welfare and expenditures make someone better off. In addition, taxes are necessary evils, but something good can always be said about every spending proposal. The fact that expenditures lead to tax increases is usually lost in the discussion of an expenditure's benefits.

The Exchequer Against Taxpayers

Given the obvious fact that a conflict of interest exists between the government and the taxpayer, the government has an incentive to devise tax stratagems that will lessen the conflict. Taxes are resented more than market prices because they are not directly related to one's benefits and because they are imposed from above. Understandably, taxpayers believe a good tax is a small one; if taxes must be enacted, the best one is paid by someone else. Since the politician must take account of these sentiments, we should hardly be surprised to learn that politicians are even more Machiavellian about tax policies than about their spending habits. After all, politicians want people to know about the good they are doing while concealing the costs. So a premium is placed on deception. Still, as George Harrison of the Beatles wrote:

> If you drive a car I'll tax the street
> If you try to sit I'll tax the seat
> If you get too cold I'll tax the heat
> If you take a walk I'll tax your feet.
> (from "Taxman")

Politicians follow a calculus of revenue gathering that in form is identical to the one observed in choosing spending activities. Again, the most power-ful concern for the politician wishing to remain in office is how many votes he or she will lose for each added dollar of taxation. In making choices among revenue instruments the idea is to balance these vote losses among the different taxes so that the total vote loss is minimized. This task is not as difficult to perform as it may seem because economists and politicians have learned much about the real and perceived incidence of different taxes. Worse yet, government is in the unique position of being sufficiently powerful and informed to manipulate citizen perceptions. The fact that in all democracies tax loads have increased enormously over the past eighty years is powerful testimony to the abilities of politicians and the capacities of governments to extract revenues. How is it accomplished?

When legislators assemble to levy taxes, the first thing they do is de-nounce taxation, huge budgets, and deficits. Once this charade is over, tax bills are designed in such a way as to distract attention from the proceed-ings. Since old taxes are usually considered more palatable than new ones, the goal is to increase either the base and/or the rates of the familiar taxes and to do so in minute ways that escape immediate attention. Still, an an-nual increase of even 0.01 percent can add up to a hefty sum over the years. If taxes can be levied on unpopular activities and persons, so much the better because sin can ostensibly be discouraged while the coffers expand. Gasoline and liquor taxes are prime examples. And if tax increases must be enacted, it is best to do so during crises (particularly during popular wars), as happened with the enactment of the income tax during World War I and the withholding provision during World War II.

Equally popular from a political perspective are taxes levied on the rich or on giant, impersonal corporations. Taxing corporations is especially val-ued because of the widespread misperception that companies rather than their customers pay taxes. Tax increases also seem more widely acceptable when they are accompanied by tax reforms allegedly designed to simplify and rectify past inequities or unfairness. Although genuine tax reform is rare, many important alterations are adopted. Introducing "technical" changes designed to conceal new privileges is the favorite strategy for "cor-recting errors" in tax codes. Local and state governments find it highly useful to earmark certain taxes for specific purposes because this practice enables them to gain the approval of those who make extensive use of the facilities and activities supported by the earmarked revenues. For example, certain tax increases may pay for a cultural events center or a sports fa-cility. Since the income tax is a major source of federal revenues and in-come is taxed directly, taxpayers are quite sensitive to alterations and espe-cially increases. In order to appease all concerned, including the tax collector, revenue-maximizing legislators take special pains in revising the income tax. Although progressive rates are a political necessity, they are often illusory. The government has two rates, the legal, or nominal, rate and the real rate. The real rate is the nominal rate minus the value of tax exemptions and loopholes that apply to each taxpayer's individual circumstances. Thus the nominal rate is much higher than the real rate. With the aid of an accountant, the taxpayer is able to reduce his tax bill by substantial amounts. At the same time, the taxpayer has only the vaguest notion of how the loopholes affect others and appears at least partially satisfied that the rich must be paying much more; how much more remains a mystery to all but the rich. Because they are hidden, these tax breaks are politically more acceptable than outright subsidies of the same amount.

Note too that the government forces the employer to collect the income tax and collect it not once a year but at every pay period, thus assuring or stabilizing the continuous flow of revenues. Automatic deductions make the sacrifice of payment and the inconvenience seem somewhat less onerous than they would be if the payment had to be made in cash in person every week or every month. And the automatic format is a cheaper and more reliable means of collection. Much the same logic of collection is incorporated into other payroll taxes, including the most important one—Social Security.

Social Security suggests still other political considerations, including the very name of the tax itself. Unlike the income tax, which is so labeled on our salary stubs, the Social Security tax is identified by an acronym that baffles all—F.I.C.A. (Federal Insurance Compensation Act). To this day, the founders of the program and its administrators have preferred to call the tax a "contribution" or "premium." It is neither and cannot be so; it is an involuntary payment—a tax. Still, the practice of finding euphemisms for taxes continues with such beauties as "revenue enhancement," "tax incentives," "tax expenditures" and "surcharge." Another patent tactic of the tax writers is to levy the tax on two different groups—employers and employees—with the expectation that employees will never realize they are the ultimate payers in both cases. The Social Security payroll tax, which is presumably shared equally by worker and boss, is in fact paid by the worker.

When seeking additional sources of revenue, politicians prefer those taxes that do not disrupt the continuous supply of revenue. In the language of the economist, the politician prefers to tax those goods and services for which the demand is inelastic, meaning that increases in their prices as a result of the tax have less than proportionate effects on sales and, therefore, tax revenues. Many so-called sin items fall into this category. The same might be said of taxes on such events as marriages or hunting and fishing, the occasion for which is a happy one and therefore not likely to be canceled or postponed by taxpayers protesting or avoiding the fee.

Since we live in a federal system, we should take note of effects generated by geographical dispersion of power, some of which are quite handy for the tax politician. A favorite practice among politicians is to mandate popular expenditures to be administered by lower governmental units but to force the latter to find the tax revenues to pay for whatever good is to be accomplished. Similarly, local politicians like to receive federal grants-in-aid with no strings attached and levy taxes that fall largely on nonresident taxpayers. Hotel and motel taxes are ubiquitous at the local level because the nonresident taxpayer is unable to vote in the tax-levying community. Of course, taxing nonresidents creates incentives for the taxed to avoid visiting and doing business in the tax areas. Since convenience and necessity usually overrule the added cost of seeking pleasure or doing business, such taxes seem a small deterrent to most tourists and business travelers.

Although important to locals, the above considerations pale to insignificance when compared with the two major means of financing government during times of inflation. We refer, of course, to borrowing and money creation. Although there is no mechanical connection between these phenomena, it is quite clear that over the long run significant relationships hold. Because politicians prefer to tax by those means that lose the fewest votes, they resort to running deficits, borrowing, and making use of the progressive income tax. Richard E. Wagner and Robert D. Tollison (1982) explain it as follows:

> The political gains from deficit finance vary in direct proportion to the degree of diffusion of the costs of budget deficits among the population. A cost of $10 billion spread over one hundred million people will generally provoke less opposition than the same cost spread over only one million people. To the extent that budget deficits are financed by genuine government borrowing, the costs of deficit finance will be concentrated upon the investors who are crowded out. In contrast, money creation will diffuse the cost among the population. Therefore, since deficit finance accompanied by money creation will diffuse the cost more generally, it will evoke less opposition than deficit finance in the absence of money creation. (p. 11)

Deficit financing and creating money can be complemented by using inflation as a tax on nominal income, as it was during the 1970s. During this period, inflation sent more and more people into higher income brackets and therefore into higher tax rates. No formal increases in income taxes were enacted by Congress, but the automatic progression of income-tax rates enabled the government to obtain greater revenues. Since most citizens are barely aware of the tax implications of democratic financing practices, they can easily blame inflation on convenient scapegoats (Big Business, Unions, OPEC). That only government has the authority to print money and the political incentives to choose politically optimal strategies of spending and taxing is a difficult lesson for most people to master. The fact that government might abuse its sacred trust to establish and maintain a stable monetary system seems as obscene and unlikely to the ordinary citizen as it does to the Keynesian.

Implicit in much of our analysis of spending and taxing proclivities has been the recognition of two major sources of conflict in the polity: conflicting preferences among citizens for different expenditures and the other and often more severe problem—disagreements over the allocation of tax burdens. Since expenditures on public goods generate spillover benefits for all or nearly all citizens, such spending is not apt to produce all-out conflicts. Not so with taxation. Taxation is something of a zero-sum game: If one taxpayer obtains a reduction, another will have to pay more. Taxpayers conflict to a far greater degree than beneficiaries. Should we be surprised that tax hikes are viewed by politicians as more costly in votes than expenditure reductions? Is it any wonder that tax rebellions occur? The wonder is that there are not more, especially when governments engage in policies that can only exacerbate the situation. The case for constitutional fiscal constraint rests on just such considerations.

The historic tax reform of 1986 may seem to contradict much of what we have written, but such a judgment would derive from only a superficial analysis. The enactment of rate reductions, elimination of loopholes, and simplification of rate schedules in fact support our analysis. Congressional politicians have in effect wiped the slate clean so that they may once more "auction" off tax exemptions and other privileges. The marginal value of the thousands of exemptions and loopholes had decreased enormously over the years; with fewer loopholes, their value increases sharply to the advantage of members of Congress, especially those on the tax committees. At the same time, the worth of tax lobbyists has also increased since they are the experts in obtaining a renewal of old loopholes. One may now expect an annual reenactment of tax exemptions and political rewards in the form of increased campaign monies for compliant members of Congress. In fact, that effect began immediately after the passage of the act with the addition of countless so-called "transition rules" to protect those interest groups essential to the reelection of important members of the Senate Finance and House Ways and Means committees. In short, tax reform permits politicians to look for more donors.

Hard-Working Bureaucrats and Nonworking Bureaucracy

In political stereotyping the bureaucrat is usually portrayed as a faceless, lazy, and incompetent nitpicker. Although stereotypes are informed by elements of truth, this particular stereotype is misleading. The fact is, bureaucrats in general, particularly those holding higher ranks, are not only hard-working but dedicated servants and professionals. They are our permanent government. The paradox is that although bureaucrats are hard-working, the bureaucracy is frequently believed not to be working. The paradox is easily resolved when we distinguish at least two levels in the meaning of efficiency. Before getting into technical definitions, however, we shall describe the institutional setting of a public bureaucracy, for without that knowledge we cannot understand bureaucratic behavior and outcomes.

As Max Weber said, a bureau is a formal, hierarchical organization staffed by persons, publicly paid, holding lifetime jobs won in open competition. The bureau's ostensible goal is to provide civic services at zero prices—activities and services financed mostly by a lump-sum budget authorized by a legislative body. Historically, services provided the public consisted mostly of such public goods as domestic order and defense, but more recently, more private goods and income are offered through redistribution or transfer programs. This change in the mix of activities and services is fraught with significance for the bureau as well as for the general public. One result is increased favor-seeking by clients and bureaucrats alike.

Regardless of the particular services provided, bureaus are resolutely nonprofit in their orientation. As a consequence, other—political—criteria help to shape a bureau's major choices: allocations, internal operations, and responses to changing circumstances and innovation. Since the public agency is a creature of the polity, in general, and of the politicians, in particular, its role and activities are suffused with politics, something civil service is supposed to reduce or eliminate but in practice does not fully accomplish. So, bureaus are major political actors.

Although most political scientists care little about the fiscal aspects of bureaucracy, public choice has made bureaucracy a focal point of analysis. Unlike the business firm, which gets its funds from sales of products or services, a public agency gets its funds from elected representatives convened in legislatures. The critical question, then, is how the legislature decides how much money is to be allocated each agency. Although a theory of allocation among bureaucracies entails nothing less than a full-scale theory of public finance, part of the answer can be briefly summarized: All of the major political actors—politicians, voters, bureaucrats, and interest groups—interact to make collective budgets and, incidentally, to insure growth in governmental spending and taxation.

We must not be insensitive to the role bureaucrats play in shaping the demand for their own services or to their power to influence the cost conditions under which they produce those services. Bureaucrats engage most directly and continuously with legislators who serve on appropriations committees and who therefore have authority to recommend budgets to the entire legislature. Such interaction and mutual dependence is certain to guarantee or reinforce powerful tendencies to spend more funds. These committees consist of largely self-selected politicians interested in winning the votes of grateful constituents. Since cooperating with the bureaucratic providers of services generates votes, we can hardly be surprised at joint efforts by politicians and bureaucrats to maintain the supply of services, expand offerings, and, just generally, be helpful to voters. We have then a kind of benevolent conspiracy, or in the popular phrase, an "iron triangle."

The conspiracy may be benevolent but the outcomes are not. These fiscal outcomes, so insightfully analyzed by William A. Niskanen, Jr. (1971), are bureau budgets twice the size of the average budgets for analogous private firms operating under competition and three times the size of those for private monopolies. It isn't that the public monopoly generates superfluous services, although they frequently offer too much of a good thing, but that the outsized budget finances padded costs; in short, the added funds go to overstaffed agencies employing costly procedures, provide higher incomes and unnecessary perks to employees, and underwrite a more pleasant lifestyle than their counterparts in private enterprise enjoy. Still, we get too many services from too many bureaus—too many, given the opportunity costs. In a more perfect world, where we knew the comparative values placed by citizens on government services, the funds could be spent by other agencies providing other, more valued services or, heaven forbid, taxes might even be reduced.

Citizens confront a bilateral monopoly operated by appropriations committees and bureaus constrained only by other bilateral monopolies competing, indirectly, to be sure, for a vaguely limited budget that is in turn conditioned by past budgetary allocations and the generalized constraint that taxation may have some limits in democracies. This somewhat pessimistic account must be softened by the recognition that few bureaucrats are outright thieves stealing public funds; most are dedicated servants disciplined by their professional training, civic duties, legal constraints, which are not to be underestimated, and, of course, by a critical public. Nevertheless, the dedicated public servant wants to do good and that is best accomplished by ever larger, not tighter, budgets; doing more good requires more money.

Since bureaus do not function within the demanding constraints of market competition, their activities must be subject, if responsiveness and responsibility are to be achieved, to detailed oversight by other branches of government and by whistle-blowers from within and without government. Such oversight is a two-edged sword, for it also entails red tape, public hearings, appeal procedures, and tedious legalities few citizens relish. By contrast, the market registers complaints and dissatisfactions through reduced sales and direct action by irate consumers who confront store owners, car dealers, waiters, clerks, and the like. Such action normally brings forth a quick response, unless, of course, the firm is obligated to operate within a vast and costly consumer protection law (see Chapter 8) or maze of regulations.

Given a politically determined budget, the bureau chooses its fiscal strategies of survival and growth. Without the yardstick of profit and information provided by the price mechanism, the bureaucrat acts so as to improve the agency's position vis-à-vis the legislative committee and the citizen-clients of the agency. The preferred strategy is to insulate the agency from annual legislative scrutiny and control by obtaining earmarked funds, establishing uncontrollable benefit formulas for the clients, adding new supportive activities and services, and, as nearly everyone knows, spending all of the annual appropriations. These same bureaucrats will endeavor to convince the public and legislative committees that the demand for their services is greater than anticipated and costs higher than predicted. Supplemental funds are absolutely essential. While fortifying their budget, bureaucrats do everything within their power to avoid making embarrassing errors that might reflect adversely on agency heads and their own mission. Caution is the password.

Problems of internal administration and individual success within the bureau are strikingly similar to those found in large private firms or corporations since neither employs the price system within the organization and all members have their own ambitions and agendas. Without the discipline of prices, bureaus (whether managed by liberals or conservatives) substitute routine for rational economic calculation, which frequently contributes to still further allocative inefficiencies. The need to implement plans and programs, as well as to secure protection from angry clients, leads to an elaboration of procedure, rigidity, and inertia. Instead of removing these inefficient systems or at least inquiring whether it would be better to remove them (see Chapters 6 through 11 for examples), bureaucracies adopt additional controls. They assume, quite rightly, that where there is a plan, there are loopholes, and that loopholes will not go unused. Unlike the private firm, the bureau finds that program failure means success, for unmet needs can be used as a reason for a larger appropriation. Discovering a critical unmet need increases the motivation of the dedicated bureaucrat and provides something for that bureaucrat to do.

There is another distinct difference between the public bureaucracy and the private firm: Competitive firms protect their market share by improving consumer satisfaction, whereas bureaus, at least in the short run, protect their budgets by *decreasing* consumer satisfaction. Since bureaus obtain their budgets from legislators, they must find ways to convince them that their budgets should be protected during times of economic downturn and increased during times of prosperity. Thus, whenever cutbacks in funding are looming over them, bureaus threaten to reduce the most essential of their popular services. Known as "the Washington Monument strategy," this tactic was so named after the National Park Service threatened to close one of Washington's most popular tourist attractions—the Washington Monument—when the Park Service budget was slated to be reduced. Agencies in cities and towns, for example, periodically claim they will need to reduce garbage collection and police protection if taxes are not increased. In the mid-1980s, Yellowstone National Park threatened to close Mammoth Campground, one of the park's most heavily used facilities. Even universities use the strategy. The University of Utah, for example, cut essential, required courses rather than nonessential elective courses in order to comply with a 1986 budget cut.

Our well-meaning public servants live outside the world of supply and demand and in a culture where there almost never is an objective measure of the value of their work. The public firm has the additional advantage of not having to pay taxes, purchase licenses, or post bonds. They can be unfair competitors. Not unexpectedly, they remain inefficient. Without the goad of profit and bankruptcy they cannot be otherwise. Sadly, and all too often, they spend their time not in reducing costs but in rationalizing higher ones.

The Impassioned Organized Interests

Rational citizens in pursuit of private desires quickly learn the superiority of organized groups over individual pursuit of welfare through the ballot box. By organizing into an interest group, voters can pursue their goals with greater efficiency. The interest group provides a division of labor, specialization, and the power of concentrated passion and incentives. Surely, by coordinated effort, two people can lift more than the sum of what each might lift independently.

With more than 17,000 interest groups now actively involved in our political process we can readily appreciate the power of the above arguments; favor seeking, or "rent seeking" (obtaining more wealth and income through political action), as the economists call it, is now a major activity of virtually all organizations. As more and more interest groups discovered that they could do better by working the halls of government than the shops of industry, government became more and more powerful in deciding questions of allocation and distribution; the more the government's power was enhanced, the more active interest groups became. Political competition supplants economic competition when incentives are altered, and they have been altered, probably permanently, in the direction of political entrepreneurship and political competition and conflict. The tragedy is that gigantic short-run gains by individual groups create mostly long-run dangers of economic paralysis and decline (see Olson 1982).

Despite their rhetoric, interest groups are not organized for the intention of improving the workings of the economic order; they form for the sole purpose of increasing their members' welfare and will strive to do so knowing full well that it comes at a cost to others. Interest groups do not, then, seek public goods for the nation but more private goods for themselves that could not be gained in the private economy. To assert the former would be to repeal the free-rider principle and make the group members either altruists or suckers. Although the former may be an endangered species, surely the latter are not. In any event, special interests, especially those representing producers, seek to have income and wealth redistributed to themselves. And because hundreds of billions of dollars can be redistributed, interest groups are only too willing to make political investments of a substantial magnitude.

All of the better-known interests now have headquarters in Washington, D.C., and in our state capitals, and all make contributions to political candidates and play politics every day of the week, fifty-two weeks of the year. Such organizations have impressive bureaucracies and highly paid consultants to devise political strategies for the attainment of their objectives. And although interest groups work on behalf of their members, their staffs have even greater interests to advance—their own.

We do not wish to exaggerate the influence of interest groups because certain notable constraints operate to limit their power. In the first place, competition can serve to restrain their gains, if not their demands. It is also true that organizing groups is not simple, cheap, or easy; interest groups are hardly immune to free riding. Because the groups' claims impinge on others, smart politicians can mobilize those impinged upon into winning electoral coalitions. Finally, the inevitable corruption and abuses that occur in such settings may arouse citizens who demand reform and additional constraints on group activities.

Conclusions

We have described political processes in terms of the rational pursuit of individual ends but have asserted that these processes occur within an institutional setting replete with perverse incentives and costly, biased information. Collective choice is, accordingly, inherently coercive and irrational in the economic meaning of the term, that is, inefficient—a notion to be developed at length in the next chapter. In the promotion of inefficiency, the influences of log rolling and compromise cannot be exaggerated.

Democratic politics are not really government by the people but rather an intense competition for power by means of votes among contending politicians. In that competition, politicians find it highly rational to engage in obfuscation, play acting, myth making, ritual, the suppression and distortion of information, stimulation of hatred and envy, and the promotion of excessive hopes. Voters find it highly rational to be rationally ignorant, to be governed by ideologies, and to abstain from individual political participation. Thus, in collective choice, everyone is exonerated from responsibility.

Bibliographical Notes

A number of scholars writing in public choice theory have made significant contributions to deromanticizing government and the politics of democracy. Perhaps the best essay is still the classic by James M. Buchanan entitled "Social Choice, Democracy, and Free Markets," originally published in the *Journal of Political Economy* 62 (1954), 114–123, and subsequently republished in a volume of selected essays by Buchanan, *Fiscal Theory and Political Economy* (Chapel Hill: University of North Carolina Press, 1960). Another excellent collection of work on government failures, edited by Buchanan and Robert D. Tollison, is *Theory of Public Choice: Political Applications of Economics* (Ann Arbor: University of Michigan Press, 1972). This book offers many empirical applications of Buchanan's earlier theoretical insights. It is also somewhat more difficult to read.

Two small volumes not usually cited as studies in political failure but that are such in fact include Kenneth J. Arrow's *The Limits of Organization* (New York: W. W. Norton, 1974) and Charles Wolfe, Jr.'s, *Markets or Governments: Choosing Between Imperfect Alternatives* (Cambridge: MIT Press, 1988). Both are good on bureaucracy but somewhat deficient because they never come to grips with the political process. Two other slender volumes that deal with politics while taking somewhat different but liberal views on the workings of markets and politics are Arthur M. Okun's *Equality and Efficiency: The Big Tradeoff* (Washington, D.C.: Brookings Institution, 1975) and Charles L. Schultze's *The Public Use of Private Interests* (Washington, D.C.: Brookings Institution, 1977). Although both economists see more virtues in politics than we do, both are marvelously objective and write with extraordinary clarity and even grace. The proper role of markets and politics is best delineated, however, by Milton Friedman in his superb *Capitalism and Freedom* (Chicago: University of Chicago Press, 1962). Again, Friedman was and remains ahead of his time. His book, too, should win a prize for first-rate writing on critical matters of political economy. While not as scintillating, *Free to Choose* (New York: Harcourt, Brace, Jovanovich, 1979), written by Friedman with his wife Rose, is an updated and somewhat more popular version of the earlier volume. The main point of the book is that when government becomes involved in efforts to ameliorate and improve the well-being of humankind, good intentions often produce deplorable results. One of the more deplorable results is that the growth of government itself replaces other policy purposes. This form of government failure is best described by Robert Higgs in *Crisis and Leviathan: Critical Episodes in the Growth of American Government* (New York: Oxford University Press, 1987).

By way of contrast, we must cite Steven Kelman's efforts to spell out a "hopeful" view of U.S. government in *Making Public Policy* (New York: Basic Books, 1987). His vision may be positive but we do not find it very compelling. Although the book is well-written, in no way is he able to negate the public choice analysis. Still, the book should be read if for no other reason than to learn how the Left thinks about U.S. politics.

References

Niskanen, William A., Jr. *Bureaucracy and Representative Government* (Chicago: Aldine-Atherton, 1971).

Olson, Mancur. *The Rise and Decline of Nations* (New Haven: Yale University Press, 1982).

Wagner, Richard E., and Robert D. Tollison. "Balanced Budgets, Fiscal Responsibility and the Constitution," in Richard E. Wagner, Robert D. Tollison, Alvin Rabushka, and John T. Noonan, Jr., *Balanced Budgets, Fiscal Responsibility, and the Constitution* (Washington, D.C.: CATO Institute, 1982).

❧ 4 ❧

Pathological Politics:
The Anatomy of Government Failure

IDENTIFYING THE MAJOR ACTORS, incentives, decisional settings, and basic interactions provides us with a foundation for the remaining diagnostic analysis—the pathology of politics. Setting forth the failures of markets as we did in Chapter 1 is a necessary but insufficient step; we must also identify the failures of the polity and explain how they occur. All this is preparatory to showing why the polity chooses policies that fail to overcome alleged market failures, that are highly inefficient, and that more often than not are patently inequitable. But that is getting ahead of our argument. In this chapter we complete our analysis of government failure by showing how and why the political process is defective. We examine further whether these defects are inherent in politics or in particular institutions that might be altered and improved.

Citizen Sovereignty and Efficiency

A pathology of politics is meaningless without a normative foundation—in this case, efficiency, a much misunderstood and abused term among non-economists. Here it refers to a measure of how well society provides for the material wants of its members. This simple definition is in accord with the more precise one of Pareto, namely, that efficiency depends on whether a given policy, action, or allocation is able to improve the subjective well-being of anyone without diminishing that of others. Such a result is said to be Pareto optimal. A polity or economy producing huge quantities of *unwanted* goods and services even at the lowest cost would not be considered efficient. No one would be made better off, and indeed many would be worse off since the resources could be allocated for more valued uses. So, our chief concern is with *allocative* efficiency and secondarily with technical efficiency, that is, producing something at the lowest cost. We are concerned with how society meets individual preferences and whether it employs resources in their most valued uses.

Despite the importance of individual preferences in democracies, a number of otherwise attractive political features have the unhappy facility of violating Paretian optimality. The two most prominent involve redistribution of income. Redistributive gains dominate efficiency considerations in policy discussions, and democratic institutions encourage this redistributive propensity. In addition, democracy has an unfortunate but distinct penchant for enacting inefficient proposals—proposals that make some better off but at the expense of others, or even worse, that make everyone worse off in the long run. By choosing policies and rules that produce greater costs than benefits and failing to enact those having greater benefits than costs, citizens fail to achieve their highest welfare.

Sources of inefficiency in the political process may be usefully categorized in six ways: (1) perverted incentives; (2) collective provision of private wants; (3) deficient signaling mechanisms; (4) institutional myopia; (5) dynamic difficulties; and (6) electoral rules and the distortion of preferences.

Perverted Incentives

Adam Smith's greatest accomplishment was demonstrating the beneficence of the hidden hand of the market in converting self-interests into collective good. Just how the invisible hand operates has preoccupied economists for more than 200 years. The great accomplishment of modern public choice theory, and of James Buchanan and Gordon Tullock, especially, has been to demonstrate the pernicious workings of the visible hand of politics. The same decisionmakers operating under market and political rules produce quite different results. Although both political and market participants are assumed to be self-interested, the incentives—objective rewards and penalties—differ profoundly. In fact, what the market and polity offer in the way of concrete rewards, encouragements, discouragements, and costs contrast so much that people who have worked in both environments are puzzled at the variations and sometimes exasperated by them. Businesspeople in particular find working in the public sector frustrating to say the least.

In markets, the promise of profits, fortified by the ever-present risk of loss, encourages entrepreneurs to improve their products and services while lowering the cost of doing so. The wealth of customers and entrepreneurs is increased and the improvements spur on competitors who make their own improvements. By serving himself, the producer serves others; by serving others, he profits. It is, in short, an exchange system enabling mutual gains.

Some students of politics, including well-known economists and political scientists, see parallels and argue that politics ought also be viewed as a vast exchange system. One such economist, Roland N. McKean (1968), has referred to the "unseen hand of bargaining" as the mechanism for converting self-interests into public good. The trouble is that politics and government do not offer a full range of profitmaking activities to their participants. In fact, the abuse of authority is feared so much that profitmaking (as distinct from self-seeking) in politics is prohibited by the imposition of extraordinary constitutional, statutory, and ethical limitations on public officials. Their discretion and even goals are carefully circumscribed. In this respect, the U.S. Constitution was designed to be a distinctly negative document. In the first place, government officials are not permitted to sell their official services or goods. And since they must offer them to all at zero or less-than-cost prices, they never learn the precise values citizens place on activities and goods. Without a market, value becomes impossible to ascertain and implement. Since everything in the market acquires a price, buyers and sellers can make comparative efficiency judgments and fairly accurate calculations about the right thing to do. Political actors have no such guidance, and without it efficient choices become, as Ludwig von Mises and Frederich A. von Hayek argued, impossible. At best, government officials and citizens know what it costs them to purchase resources and products; they cannot determine the values consumers place on the government services produced. Thus, it is next to impossible for even the most skilled government economist to construct a valid demand curve for politically provided goods.

When choosing public policies, politicians—who wish to remain in office—must rank the vote impact higher than the efficiency impact of alternative courses of action. Their calculations are at odds with those of businesspeople, their market counterparts. Whereas the latter ask *how much* people want something, the equivalent of asking what they are willing to pay, politicians ask *how many* people want something. Politicians count majorities first and intensity of preferences and beliefs second and indirectly. A firm does not have to win majorities in order to do business; political actors do. Since a vote is weighted the same as any other vote, all votes are equal. But some buyers have more dollar-votes than others and their voices, therefore, count for more. Since equal votes and unequal dollars are fundamental facts of the political economy they provide the crucial bases for debates and conflicts over the redistribution of income, wealth, status, and power. Those who seek equality of outcomes wish to extend the realm of votes, whereas those who prefer uncertain inequality tend to favor the market domain. Ironically, extreme faith in either can lead to paradoxical results.

Separation of Costs and Benefits

Perhaps the fundamental political fact—one rent with inexpedient and untimely consequences—is the separation of cost and benefit considerations.

The fact that few persons are forced to weigh them one against the other before making policy choices enables and encourages people to seek additional gains at collective expense.

As the number of entities seeking favors from government increases, the government finds itself in the difficult position of having to cater to private desires rather than providing the public goods that governments are supposed to provide. The opportunity cost of devoting more time and resources to favor-seekers is that the provision of national defense, domestic law and order, and other genuine public goods is reduced. Recognition of this disparity has led several writers to worry about "governmental overload" or "gridlock" and the consequent frustrations engendered by failure to provide basic services. Some writers claim that much of our alleged civic malaise and even cynicism results from governments attempting to do too many things and doing none well. Such well-known neoconservatives as Irving Kristol, Samuel Huntington, Aaron Wildavsky, Richard Rose, and James Q. Wilson have made this issue a touchstone in their critiques of contemporary America. Although their point is not expressed in terms of efficiency, it is well-taken.

More economically minded analysts would point out that citizens seeking collective provision of their private wants generally seek those goods for which they would not pay in the private market. So long as the goods come free, they demand more of them and thereby misallocate scarce resources from their higher valued uses. In his personal revelations to *Atlantic Monthly* writer William Greider (1982), David Stockman, former director of the Office of Management and Budget under President Reagan, provided a trivial but telling example of misallocation. Stockman told about two tennis courts built by the federal government with federal revenue-sharing funds near Stockman's family farm in Michigan. The local government accepted the funds and built the courts even though almost no one played tennis. It appears that the two elaborate courts were unused and the local government did not maintain them. Furthermore, local officials most certainly would not have erected the courts if they had to spend their own restricted tax monies when other projects were more needed. Local taxpayers would not have opted to increase their taxes to build the facility. But the facility was built, not only because it did not burden local taxpayers but because the expenditure of dollars from elsewhere provided a local contractor with additional work. The government might as well have used the money to build pyramids or simply to have ditches dug and then filled; the economic effects would have been the same. Virtually all vote trading or log rolling is based on a similar concentration of benefits and dispersal of costs.

The pervasiveness of this means of self-aggrandizement is saddening but understandable. How could it be otherwise when to sacrifice private goods in the public interest forces the sacrificer to pay all the costs while others enjoy the benefits? The divorce of costs from benefits not only induces a favor-seeking motive in each citizen but in the long run also turns democracy into a vast celebration of the repeal of what Milton Friedman called TANSTAAFL—"There ain't no such thing as a free lunch." The basic rule in the political process is: Free lunches are always possible in the short run. David Friedman (1989) describes the process in the following parable:

> Special interest politics is a simple game. A hundred people sit in a circle, each with his pocket full of pennies. A politician walks around the outside of the circle, taking a penny from each person. No one minds; who cares about a penny? When he has gotten all the way around the circle, the politician throws fifty cents down in front of one person, who is overjoyed at the unexpected windfall. The process is repeated, ending with a different person. After a hundred rounds, everyone is a hundred cents poorer, fifty cents richer, and happy. (p. 107)

And consider Henry Wallich's (1965) comment that when citizens seek government favors they become free riders:

> But when it comes to accepting benefits, citizen-taxpayers act like a group of men who sit down at a restaurant table knowing that they will split the check evenly. In this situation everybody orders generously; it adds little to one's own share of the bill and for the extravagance of his friends he will have to pay anyhow. What happens at the restaurant table explains—though it does not excuse—what happens at the public trough. (p. 53)

Political Signaling: Votes and Rhetoric

One of the greatest inventions is money, for it is a wonderfully convenient means enabling persons with diverse interests to communicate in simple, precise, and rapid transactions. Without a monetary system, a modern society would soon dissolve into chaos. Without money we would not be able to avoid the double contingency problem of barter, that is, finding a trading partner who wants what you have and has what you want. Barter is extraordinarily cumbersome, imprecise, and inefficient. So are the socialist substitutes for the pricing system—the surrogates that enable planners to play at market competition. Knowing these fundamental facts, however, has not dissuaded many political scientists from finding virtues in political systems that, in effect, employ barter and planning. In democracies, the chief unit of account and medium of exchange is the vote.

But consider the vote itself as an analog to money. In the first place, everyone has but one vote and that vote is indivisible. Accordingly, the vote cannot express a voter's *intensity* of preferences. Without multiple votes or a weighted voting system, voters cannot indicate to others just how much they prefer one candidate to another or one policy over another. All they can say is that they prefer whomever or whatever they vote for over the other options. The vote on the ballot can therefore convey little information and indeed, when counted on election day, votes produce considerable ambiguity. What do the individual votes mean? Both winners and losers can rationalize the outcomes. Is it a strong positive endorsement or merely a negative minimizing of a choice among bad options? As guidance to policymakers, the voting outcome is highly ambiguous. The notion of reducing the mystery and improving elections has inspired many formal theorists of public choice and others to devise intricate reforms of the ballot, electoral rules, and the like. Few of their suggestions are ever adopted.

These problems can be reduced somewhat through the use of vote trading, a form of barter that is better known in legislatures as log rolling. Although a good case can be made that vote trading offers an improvement over nontrading, the argument usually breaks down in practice because the skewed distribution of diffused costs and concentrated benefits dominates the aggregate size of those results. Vote trading will therefore favor projects in which total costs exceed total benefits. In other words, bad projects that would normally be defeated can be enacted into law when votes are traded, making all concerned worse off.

The logic of log rolling at its worst can be seen in the following example. Suppose three voters are confronted with two projects, a jail and a school, and that each project is to be voted on independently and the decision to be made by majority rule. If the voters estimated their respective costs and benefits as shown in Table 4.1, we would expect that both projects would be voted down: In the case of the jail by voters A and C while in the case of the school by voters A and B. Since both projects are inefficient, that is, total benefits are exceeded by costs, it is clear that this election would have produced the correct result.

But consider what might occur if the voters discovered and practiced log rolling. In such an event, voter B would agree to support voter C's school if C would support B's jail. As a result, the three-member polity would adopt two inefficient projects with a total loss of $200. Although B and C must help pay for each other's projects, they would still come out as gainers; their gain, however, would have to be accomplished at the expense of A,

TABLE 4.1   Inefficiency of Log Rolling

	Voter's Net Benefits		
Project	A	B	C
Jail	−$200	$300	−$200
School	−$200	−$200	$300
Net	−$400	$100	$100

who would have to bear $400 of the total cost of $800. We could just as easily construct further simple situations showing the opposite results, but in the real world, log rolling is more likely to confirm our blackboard illustration.

Although vote trading among ordinary voters is effectively discouraged by prohibitive transaction and monitoring costs, the politicians have managed, quite rationally, to impose a form of implicit trading on voters through the use of issue packaging. This practice occurs when individually popular proposals are combined with not-so-popular proposals in a single package—such as in party platforms or, more commonly, through nongermane amendments to bills in legislature. The less popular proposals are attached as riders so that a legislature or a president who wants to reject the dubious rider has to reject the good measures as well. Without a presidential line-item veto, many taxpayers are forced to suffer losses to support the gains of a few.

A variant on this form of vote trading is found in the strategy Anthony Downs (1957) termed a "coalition of minorities." Suppose that three issues entailing subsidies are presented to voters and that in each case 20 percent are in favor and 80 percent are opposed. One might superficially assume that political candidates would quickly announce their support of the overwhelming majorities on each issue and oppose all three subsidies. However, a politician who supported all three minority positions could garner support from 60 percent of the populace, assuming the three 20 percent minorities did not overlap. Furthermore, this majority would be much more likely to materialize and remain stable than a majority from the opposition because the gains afforded individuals are apt to have a greater impact on their voting choices than individual losses. Realistically, we should also assume that some of the taxpayers/consumers who opposed subsidies other than their own would number among those who would gain from one or more other subsidies.

This problem does not arise in the private economy because coalitions and log rolling are irrelevant to making decisions. Each buyer and seller can and does act independently and normally without consideration of others; in fact, they compete not only across but on the same side of the market, consumer against consumer and seller against seller.

The signaling of intentions and communication more generally is conducted in polity and economy alike through the use of everyday language. The acquisition of a common language is a marvelous achievement, one that we may not fully appreciate until we visit a foreign country. But language, as English teachers know only too well, can be used with varying degrees of skill. Some people communicate better than others. Scientists and technicians, for example, are able to employ the languages of mathematics and science with extraordinary precision and economy.

Because voters are rationally ignorant (the costs of gaining particular kinds of information are greater than the benefits since one vote is essentially meaningless), politicians must employ a language designed to evoke emotion—enough emotion to motivate the right people to turn out and vote. Thus, politicians rarely speak with precise meanings, marginal calculations, or logical reasoning; instead they manipulate affect, raw emotions, group identifications, and even hatred, envy, and threats. Because premature commitment to an issue can cause one to end up in a minority position, successful politicians equivocate, hint, exaggerate, procrastinate, "straddle fences," adopt code words, and speak in *non sequiturs*. Understanding the politician is therefore extremely frustrating for those who value precise statements. But note that this problem is not the fault of the politician; it is rooted in the rational ignorance of voters, the distribution of conflicting sentiments among voters, and the nature of collective endeavor.

What all this means is clear: Political communication is rarely conducive to rational or efficient allocation of scarce resources. This does not mean that the individual politicians are irrational in their choice of language and symbolic activities. Waving the flag and kissing babies are practiced because of their tactical value in an activity that is at once a rational game and a morality play; in that conjunction lies the endless fascination and frustration of politics.

Institutional Myopia

Critics of markets often accuse them of being indifferent to the needs of future generations. This criticism has a profound appeal for many people. Since market agents are selfish and shortsighted, how could they possibly pursue conservation goals? "Cut and run" is their guiding precept. It is assumed and claimed that only the political process and governments have the incentive and the ability to serve the future. Horror stories about the exploitation of our eastern and northern woods, wanton killing of buffalo, and callous fishing of streams and ocean are cited as convincing examples and evidence of the failure.

The fact of the matter is that the historical examples are misunderstood and the capacity of governments to enact protective laws grossly overestimated. Markets are governed by persons, both buyers and sellers, constantly and necessarily engaged in comparing present and future values; if they did not make such comparisons we would have a difficult time explaining why many choose to make substantial investments during uncertain times. Profit maximizers serve themselves, but they do so by investing in uncertain future prospects. Thus, through their efforts to determine whether future generations of buyers will buy their wares, they may conserve now or invest in producing more resources for future use. In order to do this they must estimate future demands for existing goods and services and possibly for new ones. If Oregon logging firms, for example, believed that future sales of lumber products were likely to increase (for whatever reasons), they would choose to harvest fewer trees now and even plant more for future harvest; in fact, the privately owned Weyhauser Company and countless smaller tree farmers have done just that with considerable skill and investment. Private timber firms are even preserving wildlife habitat and scenic vistas because of their expected future value. And, as many close students of the oil industry have pointed out, oil companies do not pump oil twenty-four hours a day; market signals dictate the holding of vast inventories of oil in the ground. All resource holders operating in a private property, free-market context are *forced* to consider inventory policy and the future.

But what of the political possibilities? The conventional wisdom is that informed voters and dispassionate but professional public officials will be more far-sighted than corporate leaders. Deprived of making profits, officials are assumed to place higher values on the future than would entrepreneurs, but just why they should do so remains something of a mystery since future voters are either unborn or have yet to register their preferences at the polls. Common sense suggests that citizen-voters deprive themselves of a great deal in casting support for, say, conservation measures when all benefits are conferred on *unknown* future voters with *unknown* tastes. Politicians seem to understand this dilemma because historically they have not been in the forefront of ecological and environmental movements; both are only twenty or so years of age. If government is so omniscient, why did it take so long to protect our environment? Socialist countries, it seems, are even more negligent. We must not forget that for the politician a week is an eternity, especially around election time. The reason for politicians' myopia is simple; voters are also myopic. And voters are shortsighted because most public policies confer either long-run benefits with immediate costs or immediate gains with delayed costs. In the first instance, political systems produce inaction, delay, and caution; in the second, speedy action is undertaken but it is usually ill-considered, excessive, and enacted under the strains of crisis (see Chapters 6 through 11 for detailed examples). Legislation enacted during increasing unemployment may create the illusion of action and accomplishment but always at considerable, real, long-run costs in the operation of free markets. Price controls enacted during inflation are a singular example of such illusory gains and real costs.

There seem to be no compelling reasons why voters, politicians, and bureaucrats should be more future-oriented than selfish buyers and sellers. Removing property rights and the profit motive does not enhance the future's prospects; their absence actually diminishes the time horizons of political beings.

Dynamics:
Uncertainty, Innovation, and Welfare

Facing uncertainty, governments understandably behave in highly uncertain and unpredictable ways. On the one hand, bureaucracies seem lethargic; on the other, legislatures and chief executives seem all too often to bounce from inaction to hyperaction and back again. Private firms appear to be somewhat more stable in their responses. Perhaps the reason for the variances between government and private firms has to do with the existence of profit and its connection with uncertainty in markets and the absence of profit but the presence of uncertainty in politics.

Students of international politics and public planning have long observed that governments are woefully underequipped with vital information and practical theories on which to base their actions. Unlike private firms, governments do not have a single purpose or goal such as profit maximization; instead they pursue conflicting objectives and make "trade-offs." Relating conflicting ends and highly uncertain means is inherently difficult. Economists might phrase it by saying society does not have a "social welfare function" or a single "public interest." Public planners facing this dilemma react with either excessive caution or haste. There are plentiful examples of both responses. Grandiose projects have been authorized overnight without much assurance of success, while promising programs are avoided and delayed. Few reclamation programs, for instance, have positive cost-benefit ratios, yet they have been enacted with disconcerting consistency. And we should expect such misallocations as long as politicians continue to spend taxpayers' money and interest groups can gain private benefits at public expense.

Elected officials respond to changing voter preferences in predictable ways, usually in erratic over-responses, while the bureaucrats held responsible for the implementation of hastily conceived plans behave in less dramatic but equally inappropriate ways, often involving inaction and delay. Among bureaucrats, the costs of errors are thought to exceed the gains from risky choices, so excessive caution or prudence is the norm. The morass of regulation can be used to delay action, for example. Inadequate resources, due-process requirements, competing claims among clients, and fear of legislators all contribute to maximizing time wasted in performance of regulatory goals. Milton and Rose Friedman (1979) caught the paradox of inactivity and frenetic response when they wrote:

> He, the businessman, can begin small and grow. And, equally important, he can fail to grow. . . . Contrast this with the political process. To adopt some measure requires first persuading a majority before the measure can be tried. It is hard to start small, and once started, almost impossible to fail. That is why governmental intervention is at once so rigid and so unstable. (p. 19)

Policies, once adopted, come to have the status of sacred cows, even when they are manifestly inefficient. This paradox, like many others encountered in politics, can be easily unraveled once we understand that inefficient policies can be enacted if benefits are highly concentrated and costs widely distributed. Beneficiaries enjoying benefits have little difficulty keeping their gains because abolishing them would do great damage and confer but small gains on millions of taxpayers. So the latter do not act, while the former can be certain to mobilize enormous resources in defense of privilege. Apparently people will fight harder to keep a certain gain than they will to bring about a greater but uncertain gain. No wonder the Social Security program remains with us. No wonder all the bankrupt farm programs are not only with us but grow. No wonder other subsidies hang on, and worse, multiply and increase.

Inefficient and even destructive policies continue to exist and grow because virtually every policy can be defended as having contributed som good to someone in need. Even those most disadvantaged by a certain inst tution or policy are often among those who defend practices such as min mum wages, equal opportunity laws, and rent control. Ironically, efficiency reforms have few constituents even during so-called conservative administrations; in fact, one might well contend that conservatives are particularly well-suited to consolidating and legitimizing past inefficiencies as well as serving the interests of the better off. Four recent Republican presidents have not diminished the scope of the welfare state. Some wag has said "The Republican party can only promise to do what the Democrats do, only do less of it." If so, innovation in the practical political sense is largely the prerogative of the political Left, and their reforms typically consist of additions to the state's activities and power. Undoing state activities inspires few.

Once again Milton Friedman (1962) has some intriguing insights—this time into the close connection between beliefs about the role of government, time perspective, and policy innovation.

> The liberal in the original sense—the person who gives primacy to freedom and believes in limited government—tends to take the long view, to put major emphasis on the ultimate and permanent consequences of policies rather than on the immediate and possible transitory consequences. The modern liberal—the person who gives primacy to welfare and believes in greater governmental control—tends to take the short view, to put primary emphasis on the immediate effects of policy measures. This connection is one of reciprocal cause and effect. The man who has a short time perspective will be impatient with the slow workings of voluntary arrangements in producing changes in institutions. He will want to achieve changes at once, which requires centralized authority that can override objections. Hence he will be disposed to favor a greater role for government. But conversely, the man who favors a greater role for government will thereby be disposed to have a

shorter time perspective. Partly, he will be so disposed because centralized government can achieve changes of some kinds rapidly; hence he will feel that if the longer term consequences are adverse, he—through the government—can introduce new measures that will counter them, that he can have his cake and eat it. Partly, he will have a short time perspective because the political process demands it. In the market, an entrepreneur can experiment with a new innovation without first persuading the public. He need only have confidence that after he has made his innovation enough of the public will buy his product to make it pay. He can afford to wait until they do. Hence, he can have a long time perspective. In the political process, an entrepreneur must first get elected in order to be in a position to innovate. To get elected, he must persuade the public in advance. Hence he must look at immediate results that he can offer the public. He may not be able to take a very long time perspective and still hope to be in power. (pp. 16–17)

The future is not likely to be well served by government, not even by well-meaning members of government. Private entrepreneurs, however, can serve the future as they pursue their private interests.

Electoral Rules:
Paradoxes and Impossibilities

Although we have examined numerous properties of democracy, we have ignored one of the most important—the impact of formal rules on group decisionmaking and especially rules pertaining to elections in which voters choose candidates and policies. According to such famous theorists as Kenneth Arrow, Duncan Black, Charles Plott, William H. Riker, and a host of lesser-known formal analysts, rules matter. Because their work is highly technical, accessibility is achieved only by considerable translation and oversimplification.

Much formal political theory, but hardly all, is based on the pathbreaking work of Kenneth Arrow (1951) and Duncan Black (1958), the former a Nobel Laureate in Economics. Our discussion is based mostly on their efforts. For those who see little fault in democracy, Arrow's results are earth-shaking because he proved that no democratic voting rule can satisfy five basic conditions—perfectly reasonable ones—simultaneously. One or more must be violated in the effort to arrive at collective results that are consistent with individual preferences. He also shows that majority rule does not function well when voters have more than two options. If three options are offered and each voter is asked to rank the three, it is frequently the case that no one option will win a majority of first-place rankings. And, if they were to consider their three ranked options in pairs, voters would soon learn that voting cycles had resulted, with each option defeating another and no one winning.

All this can be illustrated with the use of the following table in which we suppose there are three voters and three options, which might be policies or candidates. In any event, the voters rank their preferences as shown in the table.

Ranking	Voters		
	A	B	C
1st	a	b	c
2nd	b	c	a
3rd	c	a	b

If each option is paired or compared with each other option, *a* will beat *b,* and *b* will beat *c,* but *c* will in turn beat *a.* Thus, majority rule has some severe problems for each option can beat every other option, with no determinate winner emerging that can claim to be the majority preference. Cycling is the name of this phenomenon. Of course, there are ways out of the dilemma and ways of preventing it, and there is no necessity that cycling will occur. But it is true that as the number of options increases relative to the number of voters, the cycle will occur with increasing frequency. For our purposes it is sufficient to note that the cycle is real, and although it does not prevent our society from employing majority rule it does create difficulties that should not and cannot be ignored. Majority rule is not perfect.

If plurality enables victory we immediately run into the fact that the winning alternative may garner less than a simple majority and that the losers constitute more than a majority of 50 percent plus one. Like thirteen other presidents, Abraham Lincoln won office not with a majority but a plurality. It has also been argued that plurality rules may be affected by the existence of a third option. For example, one's choices are influenced by whether a third alternative is included. And if we employ a unanimity rule, we soon learn that everyone has a veto power. Are we willing to allow vast majorities to be overruled by one or a few voters? Some students of elections have advanced a variety of weighted voting schemes designed to overcome some of the difficulties of political choice, but their proposals do not solve all of them. The big problem is how to weigh the votes, for that determination will affect the totaling of the various scores. So technical ingenuity has yet to resolve all of Arrow's reservations. And we have not even mentioned the agenda problem, or the order in which options are voted upon, a problem that can be solved but only through manipulation.

Of course, American democracy does not operate by any such direct voting as suggested by Arrow's criteria; instead citizens vote directly on a few policy issues and mostly in elections to select among candidates for public office. In the latter, specific forms of electoral institutions operate that are peculiar to different democracies. For example, American presidential candidates are selected through party conventions and primary elections in which delegates to a national convention are chosen. The nominated candidates then compete in a national election consisting of fifty different state elections in which the winning candidate receives all of a state's electoral vote, whether the victory was gained by a substantial majority or by one vote; it is a winner-take-all result. As political scientists know so well, the strongest candidate in the primaries may not be the one who would be strongest in the general election; this is the case because the more committed voters who attend the party primaries tend to select the more extreme competitors. In addition, candidates for the presidency tend to devote more of their attention to states with more electoral college votes and ignore those with fewer votes.

Earlier we mentioned the problem of the geographical distribution of voters and its relationship to final policy choices. Several studies have shown that neither overall majority nor strongly held minority views will necessarily be reflected by majority voting if the legislative body is made up of members elected from separate districts with a winner-take-all rule in each district. These single-member districts can result in a legislature or convention that does not represent the voters. The overall majority position, for example, may win overwhelming majorities in less than half the districts but lose by small margins in a bare majority of districts. The result is that the majority position is in a minority in the legislature. Conversely, the overall minority position may win overwhelming majorities in a handful of districts, lose by small margins in most other districts, and end up placing few representatives in the legislature. Those who win bare majorities in the districts can therefore win a huge majority in the legislature. All this is accomplished under majority rule! It becomes clear why politicians have such fierce fights over geographical boundaries for legislative districts; their own interests are at stake and so are those of voters.

Another consequence of the U.S. electoral system is the frequent honoring of the so-called median voter, that is, politicians tend to adopt positions that converge on the preferences of median voters instead of extreme positions. The logic of seeking voters is said to drive candidates into a "tweedle-dee-tweedle-dum" situation in which they have no discernible differences. Thus, providing no choice for voters is the best choice for candidates. Of course, minority voters on the far reaches of the normal unimodal preference distribution lose because they are in the minority. At best they gain only vague rhetorical reassurances from the candidates. Since the median voter gets so much attention, it is to the advantage of concerned interest groups to shape voter preferences for one position or another. As Gordon Tullock (1967) argued, the name of the political game is shaping preferences and their distribution. That is why political advertising, including the uninformative, is such an important ingredient in the electoral process. At its worst, advertising tempts exaggeration, deception, and lies. Shaping the options and the agenda become additional subjects of intense scrutiny among activists, for on such factors the outcomes of elections depend.

Since most voting is for candidates rather than issues, and most policy-making takes place between elections, we cannot ascribe much significance to median voters beyond their symbolic value and the few generalized constraints they place on government through elections. In our estimation it is risky to argue that the policies of the center voters prevail. Instead, both theory and empirical outcomes strongly support the notion that most of the distributive policies enacted by government would not be favored by sovereign majorities if the voters were directly confronted in referenda with issues involving tariffs, quotas, makework rules, barriers to entry, and government loans. The only way in which voters might adopt such policies would be through log rolling, but elections that allowed for this practice would be prohibitively expensive. The democratic political process is not, as Robert Dahl (1956) wrote more than thirty years ago, "a majestic march of median-voter majorities but rather the steady appeasement of minorities." If this is true, surely we have a major failure of the polity.

Even a cursory review of a vast and highly intricate, technical body of theory and empirical studies illustrates the extensive perversity of electoral institutions, the cornerstone of democracy. Even if voters, politicians, bureaucrats, and interest groups were all altruistic and informed, their individual policy preferences would be distorted through the workings of the basic rules themselves. These rules create winners and losers and seemingly have no particularly rational or consistent basis. Those who hope for pervasive market imperfections and failures to be properly handled and improved by government are apt to be disappointed. No set of rules can guarantee the achievement of fair and efficient policies. Nor should we assume that politicians and others are indifferent to manipulating the rules themselves; they cannot afford disinterest. Although generations of political theorists have often suspected these results, we could not place much confidence in their suspicions until formal public choice theory enabled us to better understand the actual mechanisms.

Justice and Redistribution

Continual reference has been made to the problem of equity or justice in the context of both markets and democracy but without any sustained analysis. We have alluded to the fact that although government in liberal societies is often expected to rectify "unjust" market distributions of wealth and income, such governments more often than not exacerbate inequalities. Although this problem is addressed in detail in Chapter 10, some preliminary discussion is warranted.

An efficient distribution of income and wealth may or may not be considered just or equitable. If, for example, most wealth were in the hands of a single family and a government proposed to take some away and redistribute it to the less well-off, such a proposal would have to be termed inefficient since the wealthy family would object. Whether a particular distribution is just depends on the criteria we employ in making such judgments. And there is no widespread agreement on the appropriate criteria.

Regardless of one's feelings about distributive outcomes, there remains the positive problem of determining how various political processes will, in fact, decide such issues. Many members of the Left are inclined to believe not only that greater equality should prevail but that under majority rule it will so prevail. We doubt that a good case can be made in defense of the prediction. Our reasoning is as follows:

Suppose that a simple majority of voters is required to pass a redistribution bill and that 100 voters, each of whom has a different income, participate in the decision. Under this arrangement the two median voters (income recipients) will decide the outcome. Those persons could support the choice of the wealthier 49 voters or the choice of the less well-off 49 voters. If they bargain, they may quickly surmise that they can command more of the redistribution by supporting the upper income group than by joining the poorer folk. Or they may reason that they will stand to gain more from the redistribution brought about by taxing the rich. In either case, the median voters will have the power to decide the outcome, and in this case they could exact an outcome that would maximize their share. According to this theory, first advanced independently by Stigler (1970) and Tullock (1988), the middle class profits the most from the redistributive efforts of democratic governments. Whether or not the facts of empirical life support this theory is still in doubt because it is not easy to test; furthermore, it is complicated by the fact that much redistribution takes place within each income class. We do know that welfare programs for the poor cannot be adopted without the support of the middle class, which extracts its rewards by having benefits extended to its own members. More than one study has demonstrated this to be so in such fields as housing, education, transportation, environmental improvements, and health services. And, of course, much tax policy is designed to confer tax benefits on the middle class.

The point is this: The political process not only promotes inefficiency but is skewed to advance the interests of those who are better off. Those who do well in the marketplace also do well in the polity.

Conclusions

The unromantic and pathological properties of the democratic process have been explored in Chapters 3 and 4. The picture is not a pretty one, but readers are cautioned not to draw some easy and superficial conclusions from the examination and comparisons of real and idealistic worlds. Although markets and polities are "imperfect," they are important for individual and collective well-being. But the most important caution we wish to offer is this: Even imperfect democracies have far more to be said in their favor than nondemocracies. Democracies honor individual sovereignty as a goal worth attaining. And whether one citizen likes another's preferences in the market or polity is unimportant compared with the opportunity that both have to give voice to their opinions. But even in this regard the polity suffers by a comparison with the market: Obnoxious political preferences are more difficult to accept than are obnoxious market preferences. In short, the market has fewer externalities than does the polity. Nevertheless, we much prefer living in our flawed democracy to residing in any dictatorship, and this is the context in which our analysis of detailed policy imperfections in the following chapters must be understood.

We might also note at this juncture that tens of millions of people who have lived under communism these past forty-five to seventy years appear to share our enthusiasm for democracy and the capitalistic marketplace. They have truly put their lives at stake.

Bibliographical Notes

In addition to the sources cited in this chapter, one really should consult John Bonner's *Introduction to the Theory of Social Choice* (Baltimore: Johns Hopkins University Press, 1986), a volume that in elementary terms sets forth certain difficulties in aggregating diverse social choices through elections. Bonner summarizes in a very able way the formal complexities of voting schemes and also compares them with market processes. The book is hardly exciting, but it is a reliable source on these arcane and devilishly difficult matters. Written with considerably more literary skill as well as attention to historical cases and data is a book by William H. Riker entitled *Liberalism Against Populism: A Confrontation Between the Theory of Democracy and the Theory of Social Choice* (San Francisco: W. H. Freeman, 1982). Although the book does not deal directly with our concerns, its major messages are quite consistent. Riker shows that voting is no simple mechanism that automatically registers both individual and social choices. No scheme of voting is immune to the pathologies of failure or, at the very least, imperfections. Elections are subject to manipulation, uncertainty, ambiguity, and outcomes that cannot be readily defended as just or efficient. This is not a defense of nondemocracy; instead Riker advances a more sensible, reasonable set of democratic expectations by which to judge political institutions.

Still another volume is that of Hans van den Doel, *Democracy and Welfare Economics* (Cambridge: Cambridge University Press, 1979). Although brief, this book is written more in the style of a text than an extended essay. Nevertheless, the author advances sensible judgments on the nature of welfare, democracy, bureaucracy, representation, majority rule, and what he terms "negotiation." The strengths and weaknesses of these alternative decision processes are set forth with brevity but also insight and clarity.

Both students and professional analysts of public choice should remember that the field was not invented out of thin air. The way was scouted and hints offered by a number of precursors, of whom the best known is surely Joseph Schumpeter. His book *Capitalism, Socialism, and Democracy,* first published in 1942, contains four fascinating chapters on democracy, one of which advances a theory much in the vein of modern public choice. Its chief difference is that Schumpeter did not control his emotions as much as current analysts might, but he uses them to good effect. Still, his images of voters and possibly politicians are somewhat at odds with those of current thinking. Nevertheless, he blames the irrationality of voters on the rules of the game, an analysis very much in keeping with our own. The book was published by Harper and Brothers and is available in paperback editions.

Readers interested in obtaining a summary textbook statement of political failures can hardly do better than consult *Economics: Private and Public Choice* (New York: Dryden/Harcourt Brace Jovanovich, 1992) by James D. Gwartney and Richard L. Stroup. The text is now in its sixth edition. Chapters 4 and 30 lay forth the basic courses of political failure in an admirable fashion. We strongly recommend an early reading of this pioneering textbook, one of the growing number that fully appreciates the workings of a market economy.

References

Arrow, Kenneth J. *Social Choice and Individual Values* (New York: John Wiley and Sons, 1951; rev. ed. 1963).

Black, Duncan. *The Theory of Committees and Elections* (Cambridge: Cambridge University Press, 1958).

Dahl, Robert A. *A Preface to Democratic Theory* (Chicago: University of Chicago Press, 1956).

Downs, Anthony. *An Economic Theory of Democracy* (New York: Harper and Brothers, 1957), Chapters 4 and 9.

Friedman, David. *The Machinery of Freedom,* 2nd ed. (La Salle, Ill.: Open Court, 1989).

Friedman, Milton. *Capitalism and Freedom* (Chicago: University of Chicago Press, 1962).

Friedman, Milton, and Rose Friedman. *Free to Choose* (New York: Harcourt Brace Jovanovich, 1979).

Greider, William. *The Education of David Stockman and Other Americans* (New York: E. P. Dutton, 1982).

McKean, Roland N. *Public Spending* (New York: Mcgraw-Hill, 1968).

Stigler George. "Director's Law of Public Income Redistribution," *Journal of Law and Economics* 13, no. 1 (April 1970).

Tullock, Gordon. *Toward a Mathematics of Politics* (Ann Arbor: University of Michigan Press, 1967).

———. *Wealth, Poverty, and Politics* (New York: Basil Blackwell, 1988).

Wallich, Henry C. "Public Versus Private: Could Galbraith Be Wrong?" in Edmund S. Phelps, ed., *Private Wants and Public Needs* (New York: W. W. Norton, 1965).

PART THREE

Case Studies in the Anatomy of Public Failure

PROTECTING CONSUMERS, the environment, the poor, and the exploited has become accepted as normal democratic politics. In addition, government protects businesses, controls quality, subsidizes research and development, regulates workplace safety and working hours, and suppresses foreign competition. Risks of fire, drought, and flood are covered, medical care is subsidized, income is redistributed, and striking workers are protected from losing income. But at what cost and to what effect does government undertake all these activities? Part Three suggests that the costs often exceed the benefits and the effects are perverse.

Public goods are not easily supplied by government; in fact, private entrepreneurs are far more capable than many theorists have thought of providing goods we often consider to be public. Democratic politics has become, in large part, the political pursuit of private gain by voters, politicians, bureaucrats, and organized interests. Their actions are producing economic instability but political security for Congress and the bureaucracy.

❧ 5 ❧

Politics of Free and Forced Rides: Providing Public Goods

THE DIFFICULTY OF providing public goods through voluntary action has been long recognized. David Hume ([1740] 1975) stated the problem and the conventional response quite clearly in *A Treatise of Human Nature:*

> Two neighbors may agree to drain a meadow, which they possess in common; because 'tis easy for them to know each others mind; and each must perceive, that the immediate consequence of his failing in his part, is the abandoning the whole project. But 'tis very difficult, and indeed, impossible, that a thousand persons shou'd agree to any such action, it being difficult for them to concert so complicated a design, and still more difficult for them to execute it; while each seeks a pretext to free himself of the trouble and expense, and wou'd lay the whole burden on others. Political society easily remedies both these inconveniences. . . . Thus, bridges are built; harbours open'd; ramparts rais'd; canals form'd; fleets equip'd; and armies disciplin'd; everywhere by the care of government. (pp. 538–539)

The common assumption is that public goods will be undersupplied by markets and better provided by government and better financed by taxation. But to turn to government to fund and supply public goods does not easily solve the problem of free riding and, in fact, raises some unanswerable questions. Governments cannot readily and accurately measure how much of a public good is demanded, nor can they eliminate free riding.

Government funding and provision of public goods is subject to all the ills described in Chapters 3 and 4. Prices do not direct actions; politics do. Thus, some outcomes will be entirely arbitrary; others will reflect the desires of the best-organized and most lavishly funded interest groups. Efficient choices and means of provision will be rejected in favor of inefficient ones; demands will be exaggerated; citizen perceptions will be manipulated by the officials who are supposed to be serving the public; and deception will be prevalent. One result is that some publicly supplied goods will be oversupplied and others undersupplied. Few will be provided efficiently.

There are ways to reduce perversity in the provision of public goods. Recognizing that government provision is no more likely to produce optimal outcomes than leaving provision to markets provides some impetus to searching for and experimenting with those possibilities. Also, there are few true public goods. Hume's examples—bridges, harbors, ramparts, canals, fleets, and even armies—are not pure public goods since they allow for excludability, which means that they are amenable to market pricing. Technological advances are also reducing the "publicness" of many public goods: Just as the invention of barbed wire enabled open-access grasslands to become private property, many public goods can be transformed into quasi-private goods.

How Much to Supply

In markets, the interaction of supply and demand determine how much of a private good will be supplied. Prices coordinate the actions of individual suppliers and consumers, and they, as well as society in general, achieve mutually beneficial outcomes. Instead of prices, the polity relies on political processes to decide how much of each public good to provide citizens. And unlike private goods, which can be provided in varying amounts to individual consumers, public goods must be provided in a *single quantity* that will be *equally* available to all citizens regardless of individual preferences. Unlike consumers of goods produced in the market, each citizen of the polity "receives" or "enjoys" the *entire* amount produced.

Agreeing on how much of a public good to produce when everyone proposes different quantities is a challenging task for economists, legislators, and voters alike. Economists have determined that given revealed demands, the optimal quantity is that amount at which total marginal benefits equal total marginal costs. The payments should be allocated so that each citizen's marginal benefits are equaled by his or her respective marginal tax costs. Although the formal conditions of optimality can be identified precisely, they are practically impossible to implement because differential tax payments based on each taxpayer's valuation of the public good would then have to be enacted. And if taxpayers knew they would be taxed on how much they claimed to value the public good, they would have a powerful inducement to understate their valuations. In contrast, if they had to pay equal taxes, some would be upset because their own tax payment would exceed the benefits they received. Clearly, institutions that enabled or required people to be honest in their valuations would be valuable, but such institutions would be difficult to implement. People would accept them only slowly, and perhaps grudgingly.

Free Riders and Forced Riders

Because public goods are offered in single quantities and at fixed tax rates, some citizens receive more than they want; they are forced riders paying for quantities unwanted at the price they are forced to pay. Others receive less than they want and would be willing to pay more; they free ride off the contributions of others. With private goods, each consumer adjusts the quantities purchased, or when faced with a fixed quantity pays more or less depending on the quality. The polity offers neither of these adjustment possibilities to the citizen. Thus, the same citizen can and most likely will be undersupplied with some public goods and oversupplied with others. Figures 5.1 and 5.2 illustrate this situation.

The situation of diverse preferences for both public and private goods is depicted in Figure 5.1, where voter X and voter Y are considered to have

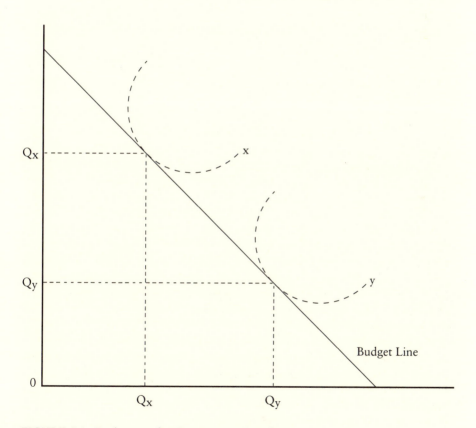

FIGURE 5.1 Preferences for Government Spending

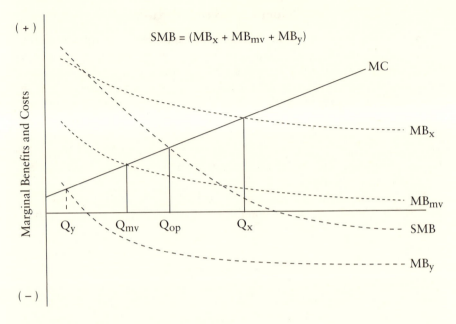

FIGURE 5.2   Preferred Amounts of Welfare

quite different preferences for government spending on welfare and defense. The indifference curves display these preferences by showing X's and
Y's respective rates of substitution for these two goods. Given a fixed budget line, their preferences are irreconcilable. Irreconcilable differences do
not prohibit a political decision from being made, however, and the outcome will depend on the voting rules. This principle becomes clearer when
we include more voters. With additional voters, a simple-majority voting
rule, and everyone voting, it is quite likely that the "median" voters—those
with as many voters preferring positions above theirs as voters preferring
positions below theirs in a preference distribution—will decide the respective quantities of welfare and defense spending. Even though such a decision may be the best choice under the conditions, both X and Y will be
unhappy with the outcome.

  X's most preferred combination of defense and welfare spending is
shown at Q_x on the vertical scale and Q_x on the horizontal one; these points
indicate a distinct preference for more than twice as much spending on welfare as defense. Y's preferences (Q_y) indicate a preferred ratio of twice as
much spending on defense as welfare. Of course, each would prefer that his
or her positions be adopted and may wish that it were feasible to supply
even greater amounts of the more preferred good. The budget limitation, of

course, makes that impossible. It is also entirely possible and likely that while X would like to see the budget expanded (the line moved to the right), Y might well complain that it is too large and should be further reduced (moved inward to the left). In politics, the budget line is as subject to varying preferences as are individual indifference and demand curves.

With the use of another bit of elementary geometry, we can make the point still more vivid. In Figure 5.2 we extend our analysis by showing the preferred amounts of welfare spending among three voters—X, Y, and MV, a median voter. The optimal quantities for each voter occur at those junctures where MC = MB, just as in the case of markets offering private goods. Unfortunately, each voter is unable to simply purchase preferred amounts as they could in markets; only one quantity can be supplied by government and that prevents any easy and exact matching of individual MBs and MCs. For example, Y's MC exceeds the MB Y receives from welfare expenditures at all quantities beyond Q_y. In contrast, X's MB exceeds X's MC at every quantity up to Q_x. Whatever quantity is finally selected, some people will experience MB > MC while others endure MC > MB.

In Figure 5.2, the socially optimal quantity of welfare is Q_{op}, which results from adding, vertically, the demands, or MB curves, of the three voters (such a curve states the collective willingness of voters to pay for each quantity of the good) and finding the quantity at which the cost of provision is equaled by willingness to pay—thus, the Summed Marginal Benefit (SMB) curve. Since Y's negative attitudes toward welfare outweigh the positive views of the median voter and X's views, the SMB curve falls below X's curve for most quantities. But if all voters must share in taxes for welfare, the optimal quantity, that is, where MC equals the SMB, occurs at Q_{op}, an amount that does not correspond to the amount selected by anyone, including the median voter, since he or she would rather have less spent on welfare. Alternatively, neither the median voter nor Y are willing to demand the same amounts as X at the prices X is willing to pay. X's demand curve is much higher at all prices, and at any given price X prefers more than the others.

This condition of diverse and poorly satisfied preferences for public goods is inherent and universal. Although each person is dissatisfied with the amount offered, no one is in a position to make adjustments in personal consumption or alter the overall supply, unless, of course, he or she places so high a value on the "correct" amount as to be willing to pay the costs of political action to change the overall allocation of resources. Not many individual citizens are willing to do so.

Since public goods usually confer their benefits over long time spans and the taxes levied to finance them are felt immediately and continuously, many theorists predict that the public supply of these goods will be suboptimal. Certainly the logic is correct; the question, however, is whether citizens actually perceive taxes and benefits in these ways. We do not always know. Still, it makes sense to assume that variations in these expectations and perceptions should be found and that they are not trivial. It would hardly be surprising, for example, to find that attitudes toward national defense differed from those pertaining to mosquito abatement, which in turn differed from preferences for fire protection and law and order or justice. We may therefore conclude that some of these public goods will be supplied in amounts that are (more or less) further away than others from the optimal quantity. Much will hinge on the degree of the good's publicness and the instruments of finance. If the degree of publicness is widely and accurately perceived and the means of financing is closely connected with the provision of the service, we should expect more optimal supplies. Conversely, the more distant the benefits and the more indirect the tax, the greater the disparity between actual and optimal supplies. Given the problems of distant or dispersed benefits and indirect taxes, it is impossible to predict whether markets or politics will depart further from providing optimal amounts of public goods.

Provision in excess of optimality will be encouraged by certain citizens who place higher values on having more of particular public goods, not because they enjoy consuming the goods, but sometimes because they supply resources purchased by the government to provide the goods. National defense offers the most conspicuous and costly example of the vested interest of suppliers—the armed forces, labor and management in defense industries, stockholders—and of those who worry greatly about some foreign power. These citizens gain substantially by having larger defense budgets. Furthermore, they have the advantage of superior political resources for enacting larger budgets. As the suppliers of defense, they can shape the demand curve for their own services to a considerable degree—a power not often granted or obtained by private suppliers operating in private markets. And the coalition of interest groups, the Pentagon, and congressional committees—what journalists and political scientists call the "iron triangle"—is able to inflate budgets and allow cost overruns that nearly defy the imagination. A $9 hammer costing the government hundreds of dollars is only one of many dramatic examples of outrageous defense billing. But more important than shocking technical inefficiencies are the welfare losses—losses that go beyond the legalities of pricing and contract oversight to fundamental decisions on how much is enough defense.

Misallocation through excessive expenditures on defense is hardly the only form of waste; others include misallocation in the mix of defense programs and resources. Given pressures for increased expenditures, it is likely that too many people will be hired and that they will have time on their hands. It is also likely that personnel skills will not be neatly matched with job requirements—a phenomenon that occurs all too often, as every veteran knows and laments. Although a powerful tendency exists to spend more on "hardware" than on salaries, positions will be upgraded and oversupplied. The size of current U.S. forces is about one-third the size of the forces during World War II, for example, but there are many more officers of general rank. In short, citizens paying for more defense are getting less than might be desired and expected.

Even if society could somehow eliminate incentives that exaggerate demands for public goods, it would still be faced with the persistent problem of discovering institutional arrangements that accurately aggregate individual demands into a collective choice. No matter which decision rule or institution is employed, problems will arise affecting the actual amount of the good to be offered. Regrettably, not much is known about the relationship between decision rule and output. Some suggest that if simple majorities prevailed, supply would tend to be excessive. Extra-majority requirements should reduce those excesses. Others contend that if elected representatives were charged with determining the quantity of public goods, they would opt for more than voters would in direct referenda. Still others maintain that even if the supply of a public good were decided by median voters, the median preference need not be optimal. Some theorists assert that the nature of the alternatives, that is, the competing amounts to be supplied, influences the outcome. If, for example, voters had to choose between some proposed amount and a much smaller amount or nothing, the former would win.

Elementary fairness dictates a recognition of the incredibly difficult problem of knowing how much is enough in the provision of public goods. Informed individual preferences are dependent on information pertaining to efficient choices of means for, say, the achievement of defense, that is neither readily nor cheaply available. We simply must face the fact that in a world of free-willing decisionmakers people cannot ever attain fully reliable knowledge. There is a certain irreducible unpredictability in human affairs. One cannot fully understand a past that cannot be removed or fully grasp a future that has yet to unfold. Of particular poignancy is the fact that preferences for public goods are not fixed as they are in the models of public choice; instead they are always in the process of being formed and reformed, often by the very public servants who have been entrusted with the responsibility of reflecting citizen wants. So preferences for defense, roads, justice, and so on result in part from suppliers competing in a messy process.

Defense, the classic public good, would seem susceptible to rational choice, but the fact that one nation's defense rests in part on its assumptions about the conflicting choices of other nations is unsettling. Intentions and resources of possible opponents are always partly unknown. Under such conditions, knowing what to do, when to do it, and with what supplies and personnel cannot in any remotely scientific sense be done with certainty. Faced with unpredictable responses and conditions, decision-makers and citizens alike are more apt to permit their fears to reign and envisage the worst of all happenings—the armageddon of nuclear holocaust.

Until practical means of ascertaining informed demands for public goods become available, society shall be cursed with the inherent problems of achieving optimal supplies of public goods. Short of institutions that effectively reveal demand at low cost, there is still hope that lesser gains can be realized by taking advantage of various technological improvements in pricing as well as by taking stronger measures such as adopting user-fees, privatizing certain types of goods and services, and simply putting greater reliance on private institutions. Some of these reforms have already been accepted and have provided significant improvements in the provision of civic services.

Technological Gains and Public Pricing

A few inventive public choice theorists have devised means that hold some promise for improving demand revelation and the supply of public goods. Even more exciting are certain technological improvements that may permit the offering of more publicly provided goods through the pricing system and enable greater welfare gains through more efficient choices by individual citizens.

One such invention involves the use of computer chips for pricing streets in Hong Kong. Street, highway, and parking problems have long defied rational choice; that is no longer the case. During Hong Kong's experiment, auto and truck users were charged according to their use of the streets and time of their usage. Computer cables were placed across certain streets and highways to collect information on who used which streets, how much, and when. Drivers were provided price information on conveniently located electronic billboards. When costs are internalized the auto user is more likely to take account of these costs in deciding how much and when to use streets. Under such a system, traffic jams may not be eliminated but will surely be lessened, and users rather than nonusers will pay for the streets. Equity gains are likely to be substantially greater than those realized under the present crude system of differential license fees and gasoline taxes. Needless to say, the unfamiliarity of computer pricing of streets and highways shocked some people. Furthermore, we expect those who object most to be those who benefit most from current transportation subsidies and systems of taxation. Groups have mobilized to delay and prevent further adoption of this eminently sensible means of financing a traditional public good.

In the United States, electronic systems collect tolls on 563 miles of Oklahoma turnpikes, two New Orleans bridges, two Houston roads, and a portion of Denver's beltway. They are planned for thousands of miles of roads across the country by 1995. The method is called automatic vehicle identification (AVI) technology. Tolls are recorded by scanners reading credit-card sized windshield tags, and users receive a monthly bill, much like a telephone or utility bill. With AVI, road and even city street use is transformed into a quasi-private good provided by markets.

The same objections raised by Hong Kong residents against pricing city streets are also raised whenever proposals have been advanced for the U.S. government to divest itself of even small areas of the public domain. "Selling the public parks" and airports is for many ordinary citizens and especially liberal intellectuals an unthinkable idea. Nevertheless, proposals to turn garbage collection over to private competitors seems sensible to many citizens; so, too, with fees for library use, admissions to parks, tolls, tuition fees for public colleges, and so on. Where benefits are clearly personal, voters recognize the rationality of market-pricing principles in the allocation of publicly supplied services. But whenever the rent gains of keeping services publicly supplied are substantial, people are reluctant to accept the notion of privatizing institutions and laws.

Sharing the Burden of Public Goods

Thus far we have considered various problems associated with quantity decisions; except for the examples of privatization, we have yet to face the problem of paying for whatever amounts are provided. Unlike the market, where the dual questions of how much to consume and pay are answered simultaneously through the interaction of supply-and-demand forces, the polity divorces these choices. The committees of Congress that decide how much defense to provide are not the same committees that decide how to pay for defense or any other service. There is no attempt to relate who gets how much benefit from defense with payments for those benefits. It is assumed that since all benefit from a public good, all should pay, but that assumption leaves open the questions of who should pay how much, when, and how. The fact is, government makes no attempt to relate defense benefits and costs at the "consumer" level. Instead society has accepted the notion that those who receive more income should pay higher percentages of their income and therefore larger amounts of income tax. The rationale for this policy is sometimes based on the idea that the better-off should pay more because they have more to lose. Because the subjective worth of defense to the wealthy is not known, that position cannot be sustained. In fact, some wealthy people do not like defense and view it as a negative expenditure.

Many theorists suggest that society would achieve more optimal supplies of public goods if it adopted what is known, after its inventor, as Lindahl pricing. In effect, under this system citizens would be charged according to the marginal value they place on varying levels of provision. Since each citizen's income and tastes differ, citizens would be likely to prefer different amounts of the good and to pay different prices (taxes). Unlike the pricing system for private goods, each citizen would be paying a different price for the same quantity of the good.

But charging citizens different prices for the same quantity of the same good poses all sorts of ticklish and persistent problems. In the first place, the government would have to know the marginal benefit schedule of each individual taxpayer, that is, the demand curve for each public good. But these schedules are not in any way directly observable and they are, in any case, noncomparable. Furthermore, the government cannot deduce marginal benefits from a knowledge of income levels. Given each citizen's understandable desire to minimize taxes, there would be a powerful incentive to deceive the government. One does this by claiming less benefit from the good. Since every citizen would soon perceive this compelling free-rider possibility, total demand for the good would diminish and quite possibly everyone would be worse off.

Prices serve very different purposes in the market and the polity. Prices for private goods in markets serve to allocate resources because they enable each buyer to individually determine how much is enough. Since everyone consumes the same quantity of a public good—all of it—"tax-prices" in the polity cannot serve this same function. Once the quantity of the good has been decided, no one can be excluded. Accordingly, the only task that tax-prices can perform is that of enabling taxpayers to share the financing of public goods; the polity still has to determine just how the tax burden will be spread among the taxpayers. In short, theories attempting to apply market pricing to efficient provision of public goods confront challenging obstacles.

Publicness and Free-Rider Arguments Questioned

Our discussion shows that turning over the production of public goods to the polity is no guarantee of optimal results. Persuasive reasons were offered for this sad but necessary conclusion. Much of the wrongheaded rationale for public-goods provision might have been averted had conventional analysts been somewhat more discriminating in their classifications of goods; mostly they relied upon a simple contrast of pure and public goods but failed to include some intermediate ones better described as "toll" and "common-pool" goods. The latter enable individual consumption decisions but few means of excluding nonpayers, while the former enable exclusion but entail a good deal of joint consumption. Fish in the sea are a prime example of a common-pool good; a rock concert may be best understood as a toll good. Definitions of pure public goods can be confusing because such goods are almost impossible to find in complex societies. Most so-called public goods are "impure," that is, they admit of certain private-good properties. For example, as more people use the good, the benefits of consumption are reduced through congestion—for example, roads and swimming pools. Consumption becomes rivalrous after some threshold of use has been reached. Second, as with private goods, the amount of consumption by individuals varies. So there can be congested public goods without variability of use as well as congested public goods with variable use. These possibilities strongly suggest that financing these different combinations pose quite different problems.

While most economists will agree with these observations, some will raise other considerations. For example, Richard Musgrave (1959) coined the term "merit wants" to classify still another form of good in need of public provision. Merit wants are those items people *ought* to consume but do not or cannot when left to the whim of market provision. Such goods include, according to Musgrave, cultural events, school lunches, environmental amenities, low-cost housing, and free education. Musgrave also suggests that there are goods that ought to be discouraged, including illegal drugs. He concedes that these merit wants entail interference with consumer sovereignty and that elites will decide what is and is not meritorious. He admits, too, that the reason for public action is to "correct" individual choice. He claims that none of these goods or wants can be efficiently rationed by price, so public action becomes mandatory. His examples are not all well chosen since all such goods can be, have been, and are sold in the market. We conclude that most so-called "merit wants" are the wants of elite intellectuals. The argument that market failure provides an irrefutable rationale for government provision of public goods is demonstrated to be fallacious by recent research and theory; the argument is based on both faulty and incomplete reasoning. Equal access to an alleged public good may be converted into selective access by technological improvements, as in the case of Hong Kong streets.

Applying the elementary law of demand to public goods produces a devastating answer to Galbraith's (1958) and Downs's (1960) contention that public goods are always in short supply. Their vivid and dramatic illustrations of shortages of public parks, education, environmental amenities, law and order, and so on are based on the assumption that citizen demand is unconstrained by price. Obviously, any rational citizen-consumer of such services will demand more when the price is arbitrarily reduced or eliminated and less when market-clearing prices are charged.

The conventional wisdom about free riders and public goods has some difficulty in accounting for some current and possibly oversupplied publicly provided goods. One reason is that there are exaggerated demands for greater amounts of publicly provided private goods. Deception in this instance really pays off, since the benefits of the private good are by definition confined to the few using the good while the costs may be passed on to innocent others. Worse, the costs may even be defended as legitimate sharing in the financing of a good with positive externalities—a claim often advanced in advocacy of greater welfare budgets. Since everyone, rich and poor, is supposed to benefit from fighting poverty, welfare is considered to be a public good.

Public Goods and Decentralization

Demand revelation and Lindahl pricing may not actually provide the best way for dealing with public-goods provision. Simpler and more politically acceptable ways include decentralization and the greater use of privatization. Decentralization enables much greater variety of choice, whereas privatization encourages competition among suppliers, thus widening choice as well as serving to reduce costs. To the extent that education is considered a public good it seems clear that public financing is desirable, but the consumption of education should be viewed as a private good. Under present arrangements far too many citizens are denied their preferences as to quantity and type of education. We therefore oppose further consolidation of school districts; in fact, we go further to advise both increased privatization and decentralization of schools.

Large, consolidated, monopolistic school districts frustrate all those families wishing some other type of education as well as those who, despite approval of the type of financing, must finance amounts they do not approve of. The latter situation is depicted in Panel A of Figure 5.3, in which nine voters, who have quite diverse preferences for quantities of education, must accept the choice of the median voter (Q_B). More preferred amounts could be realized by all if the district were reorganized into three districts consisting of three groups of voters whose preferences were less divergent. This resolution of the problem is shown in Panel B of Figure 5.3. Voters in District B face an unchanged situation, but those in Districts A and C now obtain educational services that are much closer to their most preferred quantities. That result would seem highly desirable. Note that such differences among school districts are only possible if state legislatures and state boards of education allow the districts to respond to the preferences of voters.

An alternative to choosing among school districts is allowing students and parents to choose among individual schools. The easiest method is to simply fund the students just as the GI Bill funded veterans who went to

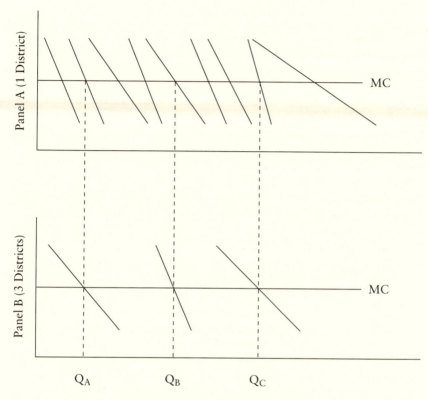

Voter Preferences for Quantity of Education

FIGURE 5.3   School District Realignment

college. Because of fears that students will choose to attend private schools or will choose a school for racial reasons, a system of outright vouchers is generally rejected out-of-hand by legislators. But many states and school districts are now implementing systems of choice and competition in which the public schools compete with each other to attract students. New York's East Harlem District may be the most extreme case to date. There, school administrators have closed schools that failed to attract students and allowed new schools to emerge to compete with the existing schools. They have pioneered a "school-within-a-school" system in which different schools occupy the same building, just like competing stores occupy the same mall. Parents are more involved, principals and teachers work harder to meet parents' and students' concerns, and test scores and graduation rates are up dramatically.

Conclusions

The problem of getting free riders to contribute to providing public goods has caught the attention of and fascinated a great many political scientists, economists, and even sociologists and social psychologists. It is an attention we view as excessive and improperly employed in normative theory and policy choice. Far too many analysts have used the free-rider problem as a means of justifying the state and extending its activities. They assume that the market is inadequate to the task of supplying public goods and that therefore, the state must do so. We do not believe that markets and other private institutions are so helpless; as we have seen, it is quite possible to change the nature of alleged public goods as well as to make greater use of private initiatives to supply public goods. Furthermore, political systems face many problems related to the provision of public goods. Demand revelation, for example, is a universal problem whenever political processes are used to determine optimal supplies of goods. But in those instances where the polity must determine supply, society should be able to use better decision rules and obtain different, superior results.

Bibliographical Notes

Questions involving supply and demand of public goods have been at the forefront of public choice since its beginnings. Much of the work is highly technical and probably beyond the analytical grasp of our readers and, indeed, ourselves. Still, the basic questions can be easily stated in simple terms and the basic principles understood in basic English. After all, we experience public-goods problems in our own personal, everyday lives. But the explanations are not experienced and can therefore be easily misunderstood.

Virtually every modern economics text includes a chapter on public goods if only to show that markets have difficulties stimulating their production. In any case, the single best introduction—and a classic rendition—is that of Mancur Olson in his 1965 book, *The Logic of Collective Action* (Cambridge: Harvard University Press), a book available in paperback. In 1971, Norman Frolich, Joe Oppenheimer, and Oran Young published a book based on Frolich and Oppenheimer's joint doctoral dissertation at Princeton under the title *Political Leadership and Collective Goods* (Princeton: Princeton University Press). Their book supplied a missing element in the Olson thesis, namely, the concept of a political leader who would offer to organize the production of public goods. Just as markets require entrepreneurs to organize and distribute private goods, so, too, is the political system in need of a similar person and function. Most of the book is straightforward and easily understood.

An even earlier volume, by James M. Buchanan, *The Demand and Supply of Public Goods* (Chicago: Rand-McNally, 1968), sets forth a theory of demand but not really of supply, despite the title. The book is a bit heavy-going, not because of any formal or mathematical analysis but because of its closely reasoned argument about a seemingly abstract matter. No bedside reading here.

Another closely reasoned volume is that of Russell Hardin, a University of Chicago political theorist, entitled simply *Collective Action* (Baltimore: Johns Hopkins University Press, 1982). In this book Hardin critically examines three different theories—public goods, prisoners' dilemma, and game theory—to explore various collective actions. His is a philosophical critique of the ability of these three constructs to make sense of collective existence. He is much less the economist and more the caring philosopher who sees human motives as considerably more diverse than does the typical economist working on public choice problems. The book is not only closely argued, it is very scholarly and sometimes eloquent, a book well worth the effort.

References

Downs, Anthony. "Why the Government Budget Is Too Small in a Democracy," *World Politics* 13 (July 1960), 541–562.

Galbraith, John K. *The Affluent Society* (Boston: Houghton Mifflin, 1958), Chapter 18.

Hume, David. *A Treatise of Human Nature,* edited by L. A. Selby Bigge (Oxford: Clarendon Press, 1975; originally published in 1740).

Musgrave, Richard A. *The Theory of Public Finance* (New York: McGraw-Hill, 1959).

❦ 6 ❦

Political Pursuit of Private Gain: Producer-Rigged Markets

PROFIT SEEKING IS a perfectly normal activity in markets; in fact, it provides the motive power of the capitalist order. Since those who earn profits unintentionally attract competitors for those profits and those who lose money go out of business, society benefits from the more efficient use of resources and increased productivity.

This benign portrait is not without blemishes, however. Some producers will note that they could be better off if competition were moderated or eliminated. Such a move could be accomplished through private collusive activity; that is, by the relevant sellers agreeing to restrain production, increase prices, and thereby enjoy higher than normal earnings. The costs of cartels include social welfare losses engendered by the lost production and the transfer from the cheated consumers to members of the cartel. All this is depicted in Figure 6.1.

The restriction in production (Q_r) and the increase in price (P_r) that producers are able to extract from consumers creates the rectangle labeled "Transfer." Because of the transfer the consumers' surplus has been reduced from the large triangle ($P_c P_a$) to the smaller one (SWL). In addition, lost production imposes a cost signified by the SWL triangle, that is, the lost production that consumers would have purchased at the competitive price (P_c). The original consumer surplus—the larger triangle—has now been reduced to the smaller one by the sum of the transfer and the social welfare loss.

All this has been known for some time; what has not been generally recognized is that a good deal of the transfer from consumer to producer is dissipated because the producers have to pay rent-seeking costs in order to reduce supply. In theory, cartels could be arranged by private agreements among the producers. But since producers are tempted, like all of us, to free ride, private agreements among profit maximizers are costly to forge and maintain and, indeed, may be impossible to implement. Market critics who assume that businesses have no problems with free riders might consult the coffee cartel, OPEC, and other such attempted but ineffectual collusions.

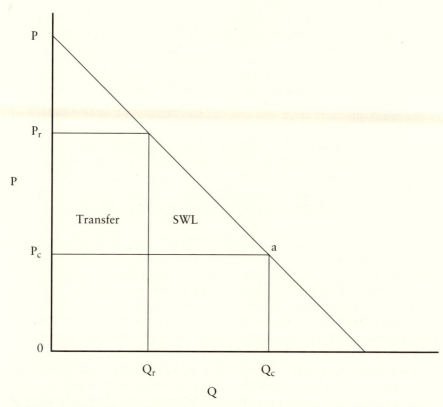

FIGURE 6.1 The Costs of Cartels

Self-discipline is costly. Perceptive cartelists will quickly learn, however, that discipline can be achieved if the cartel simply persuades the government to become the cartel administrator or enforcer. And the government will be eager to provide the service—for a reward. So there are costs to seeking the services of government, and they must come out of the expected profits. Persuading the government to adopt the correct policies for restricting production takes time, energy, and other resources. In addition, opposition to the cartel adds to the costs. Then, too, the politicians and bureaucrats must be continually monitored and "compensated."

Once some producers have obtained privileges, others are, of necessity, forced to participate in the rent game as well. At the present time, there are about 3,200 trade associations in Washington, D.C. They employ an estimated 100,000 people, or 186.9 for each member of Congress. The chief executives of leading corporations now spend several days each month visiting the nation's capital. And they do not visit monuments or museums. They are rent seekers and protectors. They have become so because simple majority rule enables and encourages exploitation. From this rule stems log rolling and thence a transfer society in which short-run gains prevail over long-run general losses.

Welfare Losses from Rent Seeking

Although economists have worked out the theoretical underpinnings of rent seeking, they have been less successful in providing reliable estimates of actual welfare costs. It is particularly difficult to determine the aggregate costs of protectionism and the like for an entire society. Still, some fairly good estimates are available for particular programs during specific years. The figures are disturbing, to say the least, and we may readily assume that an overall "guesstimate" would be mind-boggling.

Costs of Protection

Take the case of tariffs. The deadweight loss to society of protectionism has been estimated to range from 1 to 6 percent of the GNP, translating into tens of billions of dollars each year. Michael Munger (1984), for example, calculated that total costs to consumers of tariff legislation are in the neighborhood of $70 billion. Some of these costs must be understood as transfers from consumers to producers, but other costs are, when the long run is considered, deadweight. They include fewer jobs, lower profits, reduced innovation, reduced investment and growth, and growing instability of the world economic order—an instability that may move from trade to shooting wars. And, of course, protectionism leads to serious misallocation of scarce resources not only within but among nations.

Although estimates are tricky, some solid evidence does exist not only on amounts devoted to particular subsidies but also on the entire subsidy effort. Congress is reluctant, for understandable reasons, to sponsor inquiries into subsidies, but on two occasions it has done so and the results are flattering neither to Congress nor to the subsidized organizations. During the late 1970s and early 1980s the federal government spent more than $250 billion annually on subsidies and subsidy-like programs. In the maritime industry, for example, the income gains were substantial: Every employee in the industry was made better off annually by about $16,000.

The automobile industry negotiated a wage settlement with the United Auto Workers that increased wages by more than twice the average negotiated amount in all other industries. This settlement was on top of employment costs that were already 60 percent higher than those operating in other manufacturing industries. The auto industry was able to make such agreements because it was and remains highly protected under "voluntary" quotas enacted as "stop-gap" aid in 1981.

This protectionist device has come at a tremendous cost to the American people. Robert W. Crandall (1984) of the Brookings Institution calculated that the few jobs that were saved for American workers (26,000) came at the cost of about *$160,000 per job per year.* The protection afforded domestic automobile companies caused car prices to be more than $4 billion higher per year than they would have been without the protection. Another result is that Japanese cars were then $1,000 more than they would have been otherwise, mostly because under the fixed quota the Japanese auto makers have rationally chosen to export their more expensive cars, loaded down with extras. At the same time, the real average price of an American car went up about 5 percent, or $400, per year. Besides paying more for cars, consumers had fewer choices, especially among Japanese models. Once again, protection comes at a high price, as Detroit is sheltered from competition (Bovard 1989). Not so paradoxically, under U.S. quotas the Japanese have earned more profits than they did before the quotas were instituted. And, not so paradoxically, a president noted for his commitment to the free market—Reagan—had little trouble supporting the protection and its extension. His successor—Bush—saw fit to "bash" the Japanese even as he promoted free trade in North America.

Our farm policies provide a particularly poignant lesson in the perversity of governmental efforts to control markets and stabilize income (see Bovard 1989 and Pasour 1990). As is well known, farm crops, including wheat, cotton, feed grain, tobacco, peanuts, dairy products, and others, have long been subject to price controls and, in several instances, to crop acreage restrictions. Acreage removed from production by government programs now totals 60 million acres. Price supports, intended to both increase and stabilize farm income, have come at a high price to the consumer-taxpayer and, worse, have failed to stabilize income. Not only are consumer prices substantially higher than they should be but so too are taxes, which provide a substantial portion of farm income. To these increases must be added costs of transportation and storage of surpluses. And lest we forget, consumers would, in a free market, consume vastly more of the subsidized crops if lower market prices prevailed. These higher costs do not include the high cost of storage and waste of perishable commodities.

Since surpluses pose a number of difficulties, government farm experts decided that the way to resolve them was to place restrictions on output. Doing so, however, soon created a new set of economic and political problems. Although it is true that reduced surpluses can be achieved at less cost through acreage limitations than through price controls alone, there remains the problem of farmer responses to acreage controls. A farmer confronted by an acreage restriction can meet the restriction *and produce more* by applying more fertilizer and labor to the reduced acreage. If a single farmer were to do this he could earn more market income as well as receive government subsidies for honoring the acreage limitation. Since every farmer applies the same logic, however, acreage is reduced but total production is not reduced proportionately. And worse, the cost of producing this additional supply has come at a high price. The farmers are encouraged by government policy to employ their resources too intensively; in other words, the restrictions have produced another government-sponsored inefficiency.

Compounding the farm tragedy are the seemingly intractable perversities of redistribution. The vast sums spent on only 1 percent of the population neither solve the productive problems nor improve the situation of less well-off farmers. Countless government reports and scholarly studies (again, consult the Bovard and Pasour volumes) have repeatedly documented the skewed distribution of agricultural subsidies. In 1984, for example, 51 farms each received at least $1 million in crop subsidies, including free payment-in-kind (PIK) commodities in return to idling crop land. Thirty-one of these recipients are located in one state—California. In 1983, 47 farms received more than $1 million each under the same program. While more than a million farmers shared in PIK benefits, most received less than a few thousand dollars. As might be expected, farmers were paid to idle the land that they would have left fallow anyway in response to changing market conditions. That the least productive acres were retired came as no surprise; farmers are not irrational.

One of the major effects of agricultural subsidies is the unintended devastation wrought on farmers by the capitalization of valuable subsidies into the prices of farm land and buildings. Because potential subsidies are so large, those who wish to sell their farms can command far higher prices than they could without the subsidies. That is, the value of the subsidies get amortized into the value of the farm. This means that young farmers hoping to purchase a farm or additional land find themselves unable to raise the necessary funds, especially when interest rates climb. For them, the future is a bleak one. Originally designed to assist the less well-off, subsidies leave the poor farmer still poorer and the better-off farmer still better off. Although it has been clear for many years that the traditional family farm was likely to become increasingly obsolete, subsidy programs have expedited the process and made corporate farming the dominant production system.

Political Costs

More than 4,000 political action committees (PACs) now ply the legislative halls of the federal government seeking influence over policy and government personnel (U.S. Bureau of the Census 1993). Because the average U.S. senator must raise around $10,000 per week for reelection campaign expenditures for each week of his or her six-year term, money and PACs have acquired appreciable importance in politics. Even at the state level the figures are impressive. For example, more than 500 lobbyists spent more than $12.5 million in 1987 to influence Washington state's legislature. With 147 legislators, that amounts to $85,000 per member. In the state of Oregon, which has a population of only about 2.9 million citizens, lobbyists spent more than $1.6 million in 1989 on workers' compensation legislation alone.

These examples illustrate that vast sums are spent in the political process because it is now an unavoidable cost of doing business, just as purchasing raw materials, paying employees, and so on are regular costs of running an enterprise. We believe it is regrettable that so many scarce resources are devoted to this process, but it is understandable, once the rent game begins. Those who do not participate fail to reduce the scope of the game but pay the costs of not protecting themselves. Instead of hearing applause, they are deemed suckers because they must pay for the gains of those who do play. In any event, tens of thousands of lawyers and others devote their time to shifting money from one pocket to another and make good money doing so.

Rent Seeking: A Precarious Future?

The thrust of our analysis is clear: Rent-seeking interests are exceedingly powerful and rent seeking is costly to society. Nevertheless, all is not hopeless. As in all economic situations, there are contending forces that change and erode gains. When we emphasized the power of various protectionist interests, we neglected to indicate that for every dollar gained by such groups, others suffer—and the burdens are not confined to helpless consumers. When the steel industry is protected from foreign competition, domestic automobile producers pay higher prices for steel and are thereby disadvantaged in their competition with foreign auto manufacturers. Of course, as a cost minimizer, the auto industry seeks to reduce its consumption of steel through building smaller, less safe cars or by substituting less expensive metals and plastics. In the long run, protecting the steel industry most likely will have perverse effects—such as reductions in steel consumption and revenues.

Protectionists everywhere confront consumers whose interests are opposed by protectionist policies; fortunately, many of these consumers are big and powerful industrial organizations that push back when pushed around. In addition to the obviously powerful consumers of goods from protected industries are industries dependent on exports that suffer vital reductions in their own competitive capabilities through protectionist prices. American agriculture must export its products, but if its production costs are increased by a protected steel industry, farmers lose sales. And the same can be said for the internationally competitive airlines and producers of electric power machinery, precision instruments, pharmaceuticals, photographic supplies, telecommunicators, and other highly specialized, high-technology products. Fearful of their reduced competitive capacity, industrial leaders also fear the possibility of trade wars initiated by other countries.

Labor unions in adversely affected industries quickly identify their own security with that of employers and join in political action designed to minimize damages. At the same time, free trade has its own less self-interested but no less ideological supporters, including economists, politicians, and State Department bureaucrats worried about U.S. foreign policies. A Department of Treasury concerned with the overall U.S. trade position and the impact of that trade on domestic money markets must also be considered an ally of free trade. Clearly, there is no monolithic business interest dictating government policies. Many Reagan and Bush administration actions, while far more protectionist than Reagan's free-trade speeches would imply, nevertheless showed a certain sensitivity to the complexity of contending interests. Providing some protection for selected industries, Reagan and Bush reduced subsidies for others and reshaped the support programs in still others. Not all industries will get all they want or had grown accustomed to receiving. Politicians cannot simply grant unlimited protection to everyone; a dollar gained for one interest costs more or less than a dollar for others.

Although self-interest can provide a check on others' self-interest, there are numerous occasions when it does not. In markets, some interests may gang up into bilateral monopolies and take advantage of third parties. And, lest we forget, in legislatures operating under majority rule without a balanced budget constraint, log rollers honor rather than resist one another's subsidies and one business supports another out of fear of retaliation for nonsupport. The political constraints on these ever-present and powerful incentives stem from the facts noted above, namely, differential political power among industries. During the 1984 presidential campaign, the Reagan administration granted some assistance to the steel industry but not to copper producers. Larger users of steel, apparently, either outnumbered users of copper or were better organized and better located with respect to deciding the presidential election; that is, voters sympathetic to steel were located in states with large electoral college vote totals. Arizona's electoral college vote (7), for example, hardly matches that of Pennsylvania (25).

Conclusions

The larger the number of sellers, the more difficult it is to establish and maintain cartels and collusive action. Likewise, those who produce a non-homogeneous product also experience difficulty in maintaining collusion.

There seem also to be greater costs involved in maintaining collusions among industries with excess capacity, which means mostly the older, stagnant ones. Since much of our industrial sector is not terribly old and without excess capacity, that bodes well, at least for the short run. These several conditions suggest that collusion is both costly and unstable; they do not suggest that it is impossible. Indeed, as this chapter has shown, the existence of such conditions only encourages industrialists to seek the aid of government as the most effective way of dealing with their persistent market problems.

Finally, some economists maintain that while rent seeking is, from a social perspective, largely inefficient, there are political forces at work serving to encourage legislators to opt for the less inefficient policies. As yet, this theory has not been adequately tested. But it does have some logic.

Bibliographical Notes

The brevity of this chapter is not due to scarcity of materials; quite the contrary, the enterprise of interest-group scholarship is not only large but burgeoning. One might well contend that it is the main focus of current public choice theory. The basic article is by Gordon Tullock, who in 1967 published "The Welfare Costs of Tariffs, Monopolies, and Theft" in *Western Economic Journal* 5 (June 1967). It is a truly landmark piece. Tullock developed his insight in subsequent investigations, many of which are found in James M. Buchanan, Robert D. Tollison, and Gordon Tullock, eds., *Toward a Theory of the Rent Seeking Society* (College Station: Texas A & M University Press, 1980). Some twenty-one papers by a variety of scholars are also printed in that volume. We call attention especially to papers by Richard A. Posner, Anne O. Krueger, Dwight R. Lee and Daniel Orr, Harold Demsetz, and Edgar K. Browning. Another outstanding collection is *The Political Economy of Rent Seeking,* issued by Kluwer Academic Publishers in 1988. Charles K. Rowley, Robert D. Tollison, and Gordon Tullock are the editors. This collection and the previous one noted form much of the Virginia School approach to rent seeking; as such, both books provide essential ideas and research.

Another book worth reading has an intriguing title—*Black Hole Tariffs and Endogenous Policy Theory* (Cambridge: Cambridge University Press, 1989)—and is written in a most unique manner by Stephen P. Magee and William A. Brock. Some parts of the book are very elementary and others will test one's professional skills and knowledge. The book ranges, too, from the purely analytical to the normative judgments of its authors. Rent seeking in these pages is not the antiseptic thing it is in the hands of a Gary Becker. Rent seeking is, pure and simple, highly inefficient and exploitative. The authors make a powerful case not easily countered.

Once again, Mancur Olson becomes relevant but in quite a different way than with his 1965 book on the logic of collective action. In *The Rise and Decline of Nations* (New Haven: Yale University Press, 1982), Olson takes up the matter of the consequences of a rent-seeking society, and they are not good. Economic growth is stunted, stagflation sets in, and a variety of social rigidities are created and maintained because of rent seeking. The logic is quite as good in this work, as is the evidence presented; the only problem is that Olson studied only the demand for, not the supply of, rents from the polity.

Another effort by a political scientist who would not be at all sympathetic to the views of this book is Benjamin I. Page's *Who Gets What from Government* (Berkeley: University of California Press, 1983). Although the analysis is incorrect, the data and examples are good, even if dated. An analysis more in keeping with our own is that of Thomas Sowell, *Preferential Policies* (New York: William Morrow, 1990). The beauty of this book is the international perspective it provides. It is also written for the so-called educated layman, not technical experts.

We end by citing two other volumes, both aimed at the layman and both consistent with public choice perspectives, although the term is never mentioned. Robert Leone's *Who Profits: Winners, Losers, and Government Regulation* (New York: Basic Books, 1986) is highly readable. Here the perspectives are those of business and government administrators as the author attempts to demonstrate that policy inevitably produces both winners and losers, a point we have also chosen to stress. Undergraduate readers of the book will love its many anecdotes. *Agriculture and the State* (Oakland: The Independent Institute, 1990), by E. C. Pasour, Jr., is an informative and well-written case study of rent seeking in a specific industry—farming. It is a most suitable illustration of much of what we have claimed in a more general way. We commend the book not only because of these virtues but because of its explicit use of public choice models. They are appropriately and skillfully employed by Pasour. The two books cited in the following References by James Bovard are devastating critiques and exciting because of his unexcelled use of ridicule and facts.

References

Bovard, James. *The Farm Fiasco* (San Francisco: Institute for Contemporary Studies, 1989).

———. *The Fair Trade Fraud: How Congress Pillages the Consumer and Decimates America's Competitiveness* (New York: St. Martin's Press, 1992).

Crandall, Robert W. "Import Quotas and the Automobile Industry: The Costs of Protectionism," *Brookings Review* (Summer 1984), 8–16.

Congressional Quarterly, Inc., *The Washington Lobby,* 5th ed. (Washington, D.C.: Congressional Quarterly, Inc., 1987).

Munger, Michael. "Trade Barriers and Deficits: The Hidden Tax of Protectionism," *Policy Report 6* (February 1984).

Pasour, E. C., Jr. *Agriculture and the State: Market Processes and Bureaucracy* (Oakland: The Independent Institute, 1990).

U.S. Bureau of the Census. *Statistical Abstract of the United States: 1993,* 113th ed. (Washington, D.C.: U.S. Government Printing Office, 1993).

❧ 7 ❧

Political Pursuit of Private Gain: Government Exploitation

PRODUCERS, including virulent free-traders and believers in market competition, are among our primary and most successful rent-seekers. Their protectionism is supposed to be mitigated by the policies of an objective government, a government not unlike that described in Chapter 2, the idealized liberal state. However, there is no such state. Worse, the state itself may be counted among the rent seekers. Its members not only take sides in policy disputes among interest groups but pursue their own interests and perspectives, as indeed one should expect. These perspectives on the political world and the interests policymakers and administrators possess are somewhat different and not to be confused with those of other rent-seekers. Nevertheless, the actions of government officials can best be understood through the same theoretical framework as that employed to explain the actions of private individuals and organizations.

Governments may not be and are not all-powerful, but they are surely the single most powerful agency in society. Accordingly, they are protective of their positions, wealth, status, and income. The larger the budget the greater the power of the officials. In the following case studies we document how politicians and nonelected officials are able to exploit the citizenry. We are able, in the abstract, if not empirically, not only to identify the exploiters, or rent seekers, but also to explain whom they exploit, how much they gain, and, of course, their ability to accomplish this task.

Exploitation Defined

To exploit, in everyday terms, means to take advantage of someone. Political exploitation occurs whenever purposive political or rent-seeking efforts increase one's wealth or income at the expense of others. It is important to further qualify this definition by stressing the fact that the exploited have not consented to the deal. Governments and officials may well rest their authority on the premise that, since they are elected or otherwise

111

chosen by constitutional rule, no one is being coerced or taken advantage of. But that is a weak formality. The more important point is that citizens can be exploited by their governments because of two highly important factors: First, decisions can and are taken with less than unanimity, meaning that majorities (including those constituted by transient log-roll deals) are enabled to exploit minorities. There are, then, winners and losers. Second, opportunistic behavior is difficult to counter because of the costs of opposition and exit. Voters usually have to accept their political fates, if not in the long run, at least the short run.

Rent and exploitation can, of course, occur within the private sector. But in the private sector, rent really does get dissipated and profitmaking generates social welfare; political profitmaking does not. The overpayment of public employees, for example, should be regarded as rent inasmuch as it is a payment higher than would be necessary to attract the requisite quantity and quality of labor to the public sector. More on this below.

Finally, what makes rent seeking by politicians and bureaucrats so insidious is the fact that, unlike gainers in the private economy, gainers in public life can camouflage and rationalize their gains with the flag and some purported national interest. The exploiters speak not for themselves but for others whose roles are easily defended in the national interest. Then, too, one's exploiter in the economy is much more readily known than in politics. The widespread ignorance of consequences is the culprit. Those who benefit most from any specific policy are rarely those who have fought for it, and those injured are rarely those who opposed it or even know they have been injured. And, of course, the unborn cannot possibly oppose their masters.

We begin with the most fundamental coercive act of government: taxation.

Official Exploitation of Citizens: Taxation

Recent work by both Marxists and neoclassical theorists has shown the importance of the state in shaping the basic rules of society (including property rules) and in determining economic growth as well as the distribution of income, the allocation of resources, and of course, political power itself. Since predatory behavior has been a prominent aspect of the historical development of the state, that fact is prominent in much of this literature. Some analysts, including Douglas North (1981) and Margaret Levi (1988), have maintained that constraints on the state's capacity to exploit develop even in nondemocratic states. Rational rulers concerned with maximizing their revenues from taxpayers pay due attention to incentive effects. As with the Laffer curve, rulers learn that tax rates have important effects on the GNP. Since the curve shows two rates generating the same revenue, the rulers have a choice to make. If they adopt the higher rate they run the risk of destroying the tax base, whereas if they adopt the lower rate they can not only increase revenue but also bring about a larger GNP and tax basis for the next period.

Nevertheless, short-term exploitation by the state is a distinct possibility because politicians tend to be myopic in their pursuit of votes and reelection. In Figure 7.1 this possibility is shown by the dotted line, which may be termed the short-run as distinct from the long-run Laffer curve. Since private economic agents, particularly investors, are unable to adjust their behavior rapidly, it is possible for the politicians to enact higher tax rates that generate higher revenues in the short run even though in the long run the negative incentive effects dominate and the state's revenues diminish.

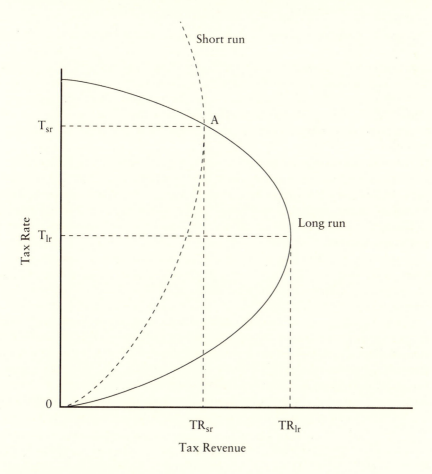

FIGURE 7.1 Laffer Curves

Even in the short run there is some constraint on tax rates and therefore on the amount of exploitation.

Once at point A, politicians are caught in a dilemma; they can understand that a rate reduction will produce more revenue, but the increase can only eventuate in the long run. They can also perceive that a rate reduction will cut into current revenues and necessitate a reduction in social programs, an increase in deficits, or both. Vote-maximizing politicians resolve the dilemma by opting for short-run choices and camouflaging them as best they can. In any event, helpless future citizens are exploited in the interests of the current generation. Our Social Security program may be viewed within this context.

Bureaucratic Exploitation of Citizens

Practically everyone has horror stories to relate about bureaucracies; some become novels or sociological treatises. Economists working within the public choice framework have detailed the fiscal activities of bureaucrats to show that bureaucracies produce excessive budgets, wage costs, perks, and services and that all this waste drastically reduces the citizens' welfare. Moreover, bureaucracies have preferences regarding their own mixes of equipment and personnel and these mixes do not necessarily make the citizen clients better off.

The best known of the bureau models is still that of Niskanen (1971). His concern was to demonstrate that the typical bureau could opt for and probably receive an outsized or excessive budget. On the assumption that total costs must be covered by total benefits, the bureau opts to maximize its budget at that point rather than at the smaller one in which marginal costs are equated with marginal benefits. What Niskanen accomplished so neatly was to show the limits of the bureau's budget, and therefore the inefficiency that we maintain is exploitation. The limit was determined by the size of the consumer surplus under competitive conditions, as shown in Figure 7.2.

Once the agency knows the sponsor's demand and its own cost curve, it is able to calculate the size of the sponsor's "consumer surplus," and that information enables the agency to decide the maximal size for a budget that can gain the sponsor's approval. In the diagram, the triangle beneath the MC line must not exceed the size of the consumer surplus area located above the cost line. The added budget and production of services amounts to "too much of a good thing," thus wasting the tax dollars of the taxpayers but increasing the returns of the agency and its clientele.

Niskanen explained inefficient budgets in terms of an asymmetric information relationship between the legislative sponsor and the bureau with the latter having most of the advantages. Citizen-taxpayers are in an even worse position and can therefore be readily taken advantage of and ex-

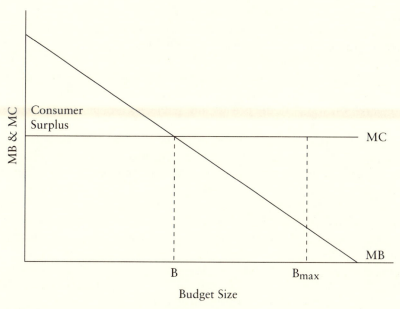

FIGURE 7.2   Exploitation by a Niskanen Bureau

ploited. Whereas bureaucrats continue to benefit from too much of a good thing, taxpayers incur a net loss. The opportunity costs of their taxation or excess burdens are not inconsiderable. They could enjoy having their taxes reduced or having the excessive budget spent on other, more preferred public programs. But neither option is likely to be adopted, and as a result, taxpayers are taken advantage of. Voting with one's feet or exiting is usually too costly a response, and protesting is both costly and unlikely to succeed. Consequently, affected citizens are exploited. In the long run, they may obtain some relief from competition among bureaus, that is, competition over shares of the budget. Unfortunately, bureaus and the budget-writing legislators can choose to log-roll rather than compete over a fixed budget.

Although not derived directly from Niskanen's theory of the bureau, a good deal of research on the wages of public employees supports his main contentions (Borjas 1988). Overpayment of such employees seems well documented. Such overpayment has a variety of consequences—all costly—for society. For example, generous rewards have attracted a surplus of applicants seeking public employment. This being the case, some way must be found to choose among them. In the real world a surplus would lead to a lower wage and reduction in job seekers; not so in the public sector. One frequently used allocative device is the civil service exam. Since the examination is more often than not a general rather than a job-specific

test, it sorts out candidates who are overqualified for the jobs to be performed. One result is that, at the margin, rents have been competed away;
in other words, public employees obtain no higher returns than they could
in the private sector. At the same time, they are overpaid for the type of work
they do in the bureaucracy. Of course, only those workers who obtained their
jobs before the increase in standards will have received a windfall.

Research on wages in the private and public sectors has tended to show
that money wages are fairly similar in the private and public sectors but
that the public sector receives far more in the way of fringe benefits, perks,
and the like. Public employees, especially at the federal level, receive as
much as 23 percent more compensation than employees doing similar jobs
in the private sector (Bellante and Long 1981). This is so because unlike
private employers, politicians are able to increase these wages without unduly disturbing taxpayers. The political cost of increases in fringe benefits
is less than those attached to direct wage increases. Thus, retirement programs for public employees are usually much more attractive than those for
private-market employees. Furthermore, government employees have considerably more job security than their private counterparts. Their lower
quit rates reflect this particular job attraction. At current wage rates there
is a persistent queue of qualified applicants, suggesting not a chronic shortage but a surplus. Obviously, there cannot be underpayment.

The public bureaucracy is overstaffed, overpaid, overqualified, and well
protected. Much of it also enjoys and wields far more power than that
envisaged by the Founding Fathers or that would seem desirable in our
time. Although many bureaucrats are highly dedicated and work hard,
the bureaucracy within which they labor does not work well. Without
the guidance and constraints of the competitive market, it could hardly be
otherwise.

Manipulating Median Voters: Agenda Control

Little did Downs know that his median voter theorem would lend itself to
explaining exploitation of voter-taxpayers by government officials. Romer
and Rosenthal (1978) surely demonstrated that possibility in their justly
famous model based on Oregon school district referenda.

They considered a simple situation in which bureaucrats prepare a proposed budget to be placed before the voters for approval or rejection by
simple-majority vote. The hooker comes in with a "reversion" budget if the
proposal does not pass. The reversion level is set ahead of the election
by some means exogenous to the model; that is, it is simply assumed by
Romer and Rosenthal.

The bureaucrats must offer a proposal they think will be acceptable.
Voters will understand this proposal in terms of the reversion budget, and

clearly, voter information will influence the outcome. In addition, strategic thinking on the part of the school board will affect the proposal. Aside from the empirical details, the model can be set forth in the forms shown in Figure 7.3 (A and B).

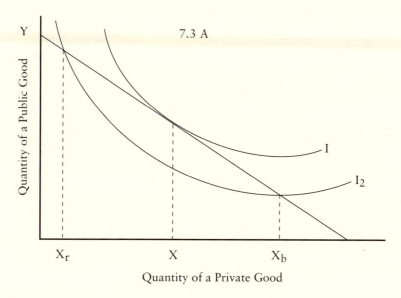

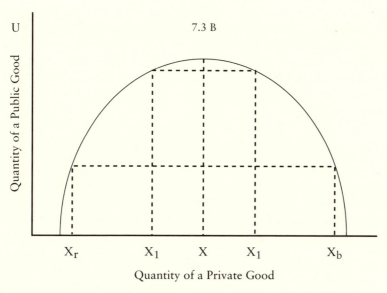

FIGURE 7.3   Romer-Rosenthal Exploiters

Figure 7.3A depicts a representative voter whose choices between a private good (Y) and the bureau's budget (X) are shown as being optimal at budget X. The budget line represents the voter's tradeoff between X and Y, and its slope is the negative of the taxpayer's tax-price for X as determined by the financing plan in effect. If the reversion level is X_r, then clearly that voter prefers a larger budget because the reversion level places him on a lower indifference curve. The question is how much larger a budget that voter will accept rather than be forced to live with the reversion level. The answer is simple: She will, despite her preference for X, accept budgets beyond that level up to one that generates the same utility as the reversion level, and that is X_b on the same indifference curve. The same analysis is set forth in Figure 7.3B, which shows a utility curve for the voter and the range of choices as the reversion level differs. Ironically, the lower the reversion level, the larger the budget the officials can extract from voters. Avoiding the lower reversion level comes at a high cost. Of course, if the reversion level were less threatening, the capacity of the bureaucrats to increase their budgets would be considerably reduced. Contrast X_r with X_1.

Even if the reversion level were above that of the median voter's, the bureaucrats could still prevail and obtain the higher levels of expenditure. Apparently, the best situation for the bureaucrats is a reversion level of zero, since virtually all voters will prefer an excessive budget to none at all. Again, it appears that the officials have a superior strategic position compared to voters. However, one must also know how the reversion level is chosen. In the Romer-Rosenthal model it is a given.

It is clear that the reversion level is all-important, but whether and how much exploitation takes place is dependent on whether the median voters' preferred supply is itself efficient. And that may not always be the case. However, if the median voter's preferred level of expenditure is greater than the optimal level, the outcome will be even more inefficiently high and bureaucratic exploitation of taxpayers still greater.

Profscam and Price Fixing
at State Universities

"Profscam" is a neologism taken from the title of a recent book by Charles J. Sykes (1988). Readers of this book may be amused by it or brought to the point of despair. It details exploitation, or in popular terms, a "scam" operation, that takes place on college campuses. What gives it its bite is the fact that so many citizens and academics regard themselves as dedicated members of a profession seeking to serve rather than profit. Sykes provides countless examples of profscam, most of which refer to private institutions of the Ivy League. He does not deal much with state-owned and -operated institutions, and worse, he does not really set forth a rigorous and well-thought-out analysis of why this exploitation takes place and the extent to which it does. Fortunately, we can explain profscam using some simple models from the rent-seeking literature of public choice as well as from recent work on nonprofit organizations.

A state institution of higher learning is an organization, like most others, bureaucratic and complex in its ways. It produces goods and services and is financed by means other than the market. It must deal in markets but clearly it is not a firm. Its property-rights structure is quite different from that of organizations seeking profits. Following James M. Buchanan and Nicos E. Devletoglou (1970), one might say that it combines students as consumers who do not buy with faculties or producers who do not sell and taxpayers or owners who do not control. With this peculiar structure one obtains behavior that is quite rational on the part of all participants but irrational in outcomes. The structure permits a great deal of rent-seeking—successful rent-seeking—on the part of both faculty and administrators.

Although professors and administrators are fond of claiming they are paid less than their counterparts in other professions and much less than they are "worth," the facts are that they do quite well. On average, doctors and lawyers are better paid but put in far longer hours and have far less freedom to allocate their time and energies. And the consequences of their work are far more serious. Tenured professors usually teach but a few hours a week at times of their own choosing. They can quite literally work but five hours a week in the classroom and do that for but a total of twenty-eight to thirty weeks of the year for a grand total of, say, 150 hours. Add to that the time required to grade examinations and the total is, depending on type of examination and number of students, another fifty hours. Then add a few hours of departmental committee work, and we find that a professor can work just over 200 hours per year. At most, the tenured professor can work an amount of time equivalent to not more than one month of full-time employment for other professions.

Obviously, a great many academics work much longer and harder than these casual estimates suggest, but such work is either the product of a workaholic or a free choice, rarely imposed by the requirements of the job. In addition to these basic considerations, the academic profession affords considerable social status and a more or less monopolistic position within one's department and certainly in the classroom.

What enables all these political achievements? Not so ironically, this favored profession has been the product of highly successful rent-seeking. Figure 7.4 is helpful in understanding the process. If universities were genuine competitors in a free market, enrollment would be S_c and the price paid by students would be P_c. State universities, however, do not participate in free markets (although they do compete); instead, state schools offer highly subsidized educations paid by taxpayers and controlled by state officials.

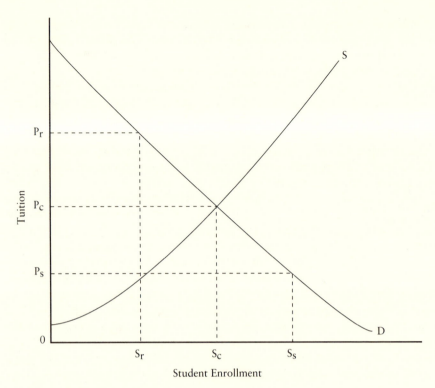

FIGURE 7.4   Profscam at State Universities

The typical student pays but one-fourth to one-third the cost of his or her education, unless, of course, the student is a nonresident, in which case he or she bears nearly all of the cost. The fact that students pay less than full cost means that demand for admission exceeds the supply of "seats."

As is true of any price-controlled good, holding down the price enables the suppliers to decide who will obtain the good. And thus we have the beginning of exploitation. Universities are now in a better position than ever to decide whom they will admit. Admission is valuable and much sought after, thus enabling universities to impose more stringent entrance requirements as well as more demanding standards for graduation. We should not be surprised that such institutions will select those students who appear to be easiest to teach and least likely to disturb the professors' daily lives. In fact, admissions officers will select those able and compliant applicants who can perhaps further the careers of the professors, thus enabling a certain amount of exploitation, particularly at the graduate level (Steindl 1990).

In Figure 7.4, an enrollment of S_r enables rent amounting to the difference between P_s and P_r. This is so because the students are willing to pay up to the higher price rather than go without the education. Ironically, the lower the tuition fee the greater the rent for professors. The difference between the two prices consists not of money exchanges but of real costs paid by the students to the chief beneficiaries—the faculty. The students pay in the form of having to meet standards set by the professors, show proper deference, accept the monopolist role of the professor in the classroom, take exams, and perform menial but important work for faculty. Again, ironically, if the free market prevailed the money cost of tuition would be higher but the amount of rent lower. In Figure 7.4, contrast P_c with P_r and P_s. The amount of rent is cut by half.

Since the slope of the demand curve is all-important in determining the amount of rent, we can readily appreciate why rents are higher in Ivy League institutions than in state universities and thus why the Ivy League professors enjoy substantially greater opportunities to exploit their situation. A more elastic curve discourages and limits exploitative tendencies.

This analysis also enables us to better understand the connection between rent seeking and the numbers game played on most campuses. Since departmental budgets are set by politicians attuned to voters, most of whom are more interested in teaching than in research achievements, the legislators tend to tie budgets to enrollments. So, although the professors would like to limit enrollment, especially to the better students, the legislative preference must be honored. But how?

The answer is simple. The professors counter the increased demand for their teaching time by providing "guts" for the less motivated and able students, courses to be taught by obliging teachers and/or poorly paid graduate students. The easy courses and requirements are not aberrations; they follow logically from the professorate's desire to expend as little time and energy in the classroom as possible. And so the tenured professor has his precious little seminar of three students, his kind, while the untenured teach the mass "mickies" or "guts."

The discussion, thus far, suggests that academic rent comes in the form of real benefits rather than monetary returns. Although much of the rent assumes these real forms, some of it is pure income. Given the fact that professors' salaries are determined within a bureaucratic-political process and the fact that the output of the university makes marginal productivity measurement difficult, salaries may all be excessive, that is, more than necessary to retain the services of the professors. Even the salary of the least able faculty member may be higher than the salary he would earn in his next best employment possibility.

Given the fact that salaries vary and that the politics of salary determination enable a great deal of discretionary behavior on the part of authorities, it is quite possible, and indeed highly likely, that competition among faculty for rents will ensue. It is also possible and quite probable that the most rent may be obtained by the less able professors (Frank 1985). This leveling tendency is abetted at the state level by the legislative practice of authorizing across-the-board salary increases. Those who remain at the same institution for lengthy periods increase the base of future increments beyond what one might regard as a just reward. Those who have the lowest reservation prices have the greatest rents, and those who have the highest professional status usually earn more but obtain less rent (Brennan and Tollison 1980).

Less able faculty also have a distinct advantage in the fact that the replacement costs of obtaining a superior person can be high, not only in additional salary costs but because of the uncertainties that inevitably accompany hiring a new person. Even those with well-known reputations can turn out to have quite different skills as teachers and colleagues, once installed in the new position. Dealing with a known liability may be preferable to an unknown potential. Finally, the employment of a "star" may also generate invidious comparisons and upset existing but acceptable inequities.

Thus, rents exist and are unequally divided among the academy members. Nevertheless, opportunity costs paid by the professors are relatively low since most would rather work in the halls of ivy than apply their skills elsewhere. In fact, many professors could not offer much in the labor market. Their intellectual assets are neither readily transferrable nor of much value to the average employer. Their social skills may be even less valuable. From the point of view of the academic, alternative positions are not very attractive. One might therefore conclude that professors are in a weak bargaining position vis-à-vis the administrators, and indeed that is probably true.

Professors whose opportunity costs are high, such as those in law, engineering, and business, are exceptions. Their skills are in high demand among nonacademic employers and command much higher salaries. Among social scientists, only the economists appear to have that advantage.

One form of rent needs some elaboration: tenure. This lifetime guarantee has enormous benefits for the professor holding it but at great cost to students, younger faculty, and society. Tenure enables monopolistic power, which in turn means that positions for others possibly more talented are reduced. Tenured professors have a power over students that could not be maintained in a continuously competitive market for teaching. The tenured person is simply beyond the control of the students and taxpayers. And, if desired, the tenured professor can become the ultimate free-rider in his department. The professor-monopolist decides what to teach, how to teach it, when, and under what conditions. Although dedicated, student-oriented, humane, and so on, the professor remains a monopolist and a potential free-rider. Unlike regular consumers, students have little sovereignty and few rights to vote with their feet. Exiting from one class means moving into another monopolist's classroom.

A last word on tenure. Whereas this venerable practice once protected the deviant intellectual, or at least was designed to do so, that purpose has been subverted. The tenured now use it as an instrument to keep the deviants from being hired in the first place. Tenure "enhances" the scholarly environment by ensuring there will be only amiable colleagues instead of challenging but possibly abrasive individuals who are, to say the least, unsettling. Tenure should be abolished and replaced with, say, five-year renewable contracts.

We end this discussion of the academic as a rent seeker by noting but not developing an analysis of college price-behavior, including price-fixing and discrimination, both examples of collusion and monopoly in America. The Justice Department is currently investigating the practice of price fixing among forty of America's most prestigious institutions of higher learning. They may be in violation of the Sherman Anti-Trust Act. In addition to sharing information and making agreements on tuition and other costs, these universities, like many others, engage in a number of other anti-competitive practices including mandatory room-and-board contracts for nonlocal freshmen, and of course, the cartel behavior of the NCAA in suppressing wages (Siegel 1990). Academic regulation of sports is indeed unsavory.

Perhaps, the most pervasive and well-known form of price fixing—and the one that people object to the least—concerns tuition, that is, the practice of discrimination between in-state (i-s) and out-of-state (o-s) residents. The latter are charged far higher rates because they have a less elastic demand than in-state residents. As shown in Figure 7.5, price discrimination maximizes profit for the university. The same may be said about the common practice of charging the same tuition to students majoring in different disciplines. In this case, cross-subsidies are involved because students in the nonsciences subsidize those in the sciences. Surely, the cost of educating a political science major is less than that of training a science major who must use expensive equipment and facilities. Yet both pay the same tuition.

Our age-old depiction of the university as a hallowed, disinterested searcher for truth and exemplar of altruistic values must be subject to the same careful analysis we accord business firms, political parties, interest groups, and other organizations.

Limits on Exploitation

The power of states and various groups within them cannot be easily exaggerated. In the first place, whenever a state emerges to offer public goods such as law and order and defense, it has a natural monopoly and possesses

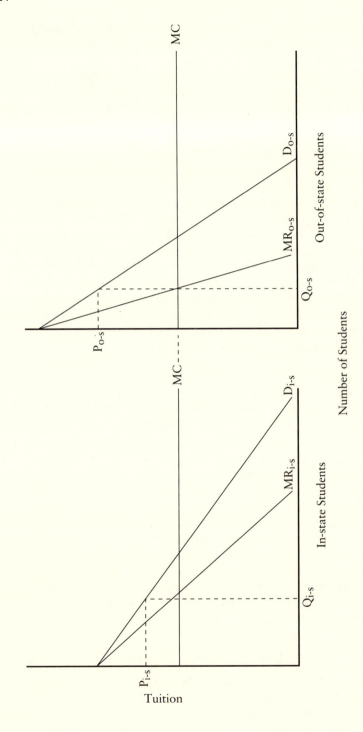

FIGURE 7.5 Price Discrimination at the University

all the market advantages of such systems. One is the monopoly over violence. If successful in providing these goods, the state gains credence and a position enabling it to discourage competitors.

While the state has a monopoly of force, its power is not unlimited, as we are now discovering as we learn more about "totalitarian" societies. As with all monopolies, an increased rate of exploitation will lead eventually to a decrease in the number of consumers. The demand curve, it should be remembered, slopes downward and to the right even for market monopolies (Brough and Kimenyi 1986; Bloch 1986).

Exploitation is limited in the first place by the self-interests of the exploiters; as we see in the Laffer curve, optimal tax rates can be low. This same self-interest on the part of officials may serve to alert them to the possibilities that their subjects can, under majority rule, supplant them. Subjects may also emigrate or vote with their feet in federal systems. More likely, citizens will engage in various forms of cheating the government through tax evasion and resistance. They may also enact more limitations on the taxing power than the officials would prefer (Brennan and Buchanan 1980). Although exploitation cannot be eliminated, it can be countered in democracies, but only with a realistic understanding of the advantages possessed by government.

Bibliographical Notes

We recommend four books on the state as an exploiter. The first and most technical is *The State as a Firm* (Boston: Martinus Nijhoff, 1979) by Richard Auster and Morris Silver, two economists with a firm grip on both economics and the nature of politics. The authors are able to cast new light on the state by viewing it as a special type of business firm and then comparing it with how real firms operate. A far more eloquent and perhaps profound study is that of Anthony de Jasay, *The State* (London: Basil Blackwell, 1985), a rare treatise both highly original and wise. The book is a beautifully written and genuine masterpiece. His insights come from an original if simple question: "What would you do if you were the state?" Readers will learn much from his answers to this question.

Another highly relevant volume is that of Margaret Levi entitled *Of Rule and Revenue* (Berkeley: University of California Press, 1988), which is less profound but more in keeping with conventional scholarly practices than the de Jasay book. Levi attempts to combine questions of a macro-sort about states with the logical apparatus of public choice and economics. She wishes to know the optimal mix of revenues from the point of view of the state. Since the author once pursued Marxist thinking, her command of that material is sound, as is her understanding of public choice. The book is also quite clearly written and argued.

Our final notes pertain to a quite differently argued book, one of the many written by Murray N. Rothbard, a prominent libertarian scholar. In paperback it is titled *Power and Market: Government and the Economy,* and it was published in 1970 by the Institute for Humane Studies, an organization presently located at

George Mason University in Virginia. Rothbard pulls no punches in his character-ization of the state as an exploiter. He deals with both state expenditures and taxation as well as regulation or intervention in the marketplace. Readers who like forthright language are especially encouraged to try this book. It is both logically argued and clearly stated. We have gained much from our readings of it over the years.

References

Bellante, Don, and J. Long. "The Political Economy of the Rent-Seeking Society: The Case of Public Employees," *Journal of Labor Research* 2 (Spring 1981).

Bloch, Peter C. "The Politico-economic Behavior of Authoritarian Governments," *Public Choice* 51 (1986), 117–128.

Borjas, G. J. "Wage Determination in the Federal Government: The Role of Con-stituents and Bureaucrats," *Journal of Political Economy* 88 (December 1988), 1110–1147.

Brennan, Geoffrey, and James M. Buchanan. *The Power to Tax: Analytical Foun-dations of a Fiscal Constitution* (Cambridge: Cambridge University Press, 1980).

Brennan, Geoffrey, and Robert D. Tollison. "Rent-Seeking in Academia," in James M. Buchanan, Robert D. Tollison, and Gordon Tullock, eds., *Toward a Theory of the Rent-Seeking Society* (College Station: Texas A & M University Press, 1980), Chapter 21.

Brough, Wayne T., and Mwangi S. Kemenyi. "On the Inefficient Extraction of Rents by Dictators," *Public Choice* 48 (1986), 37–48.

Buchanan, James M., and Nicos E. Devletoglou. *Academia in Anarchy: An Eco-nomic Diagnosis* (New York: Basic Books, 1970).

Frank, Robert H. *Choosing the Right Pond* (New York: Oxford University Press, 1985).

Levi, Margaret. *Of Rule and Revenue* (Berkeley: University of California Press, 1988).

Niskanen, William A., Jr. *Bureaucracy and Representative Government* (Chicago: Aldine-Atherton, 1971).

North, Douglas C. *Structure and Change in Economic History* (New York: W. W. Norton, 1981).

Riker, William H. *Liberalism Against Populism* (San Francisco: W. H. Freeman and Co., 1982).

Romer, T., and H. Rosenthal. "Political Resource Allocation, Controlled Agendas, and the Status Quo," *Public Choice* 33 (Winter 1978), 27–43.

Siegel, Alexander Hollander. "College Price-fixing: Collusion and Monopoly in Academia," *Campus: America's Student Newspaper* 1 (Spring 1990), 10.

Steindl, Frank G. "University Admission Requirements as Rent-seeking," *Public Choice* 65 (1990), 273–279.

Sykes, Charles J. *PROFSCAM: Professors and the Demise of Higher Education* (Washington, D.C.: Regnery Gateway, 1988).

❦ 8 ❦

Political Pursuit of Private Gain: Consumer Protection

ONE REALM OF government policy that has direct daily importance to all consumers and workers is that comprising governmental interventions in markets designed to advance their interests. Before we can make much sense of the new learning in this area we must expand on the discussion in Chapter 1 to examine not only how theorists view markets but also how ordinary people view them. Strangely, the market is subject to some unusual stereotyping; great myths have arisen that are exceedingly difficult to dislodge. We might call it agoraphobia—a fear of the marketplace.

Agoraphobia

As buyers and sellers, most people participate in markets virtually every day, but general knowledge of market operations and interpretations of their meaning are neither profound nor notably consistent. Part of the reason is that attending to the details of price, quantity, and quality has distinct payoffs while obtaining an intellectual grasp of the overall economy does not; worse, gaining an intellectual grasp is actually enormously costly since highly disciplined thinking and reliable information are prerequisites. Average consumers and workers, however, consistently believe that market exchanges are what the jargon of game theory calls "zero-sum games" in which the gain of one person necessarily matches the loss of another; in other words, gains equal losses. Several implications are widely thought to follow from this basic principle: Whatever competition prevails is cutthroat; most prices are too high; the seller has all the advantages; labor is weak, exploited, and even impoverished; monopolies pervade the economy; profits are unconscionable; markets are impersonal and ungiving; advertising is all-powerful but wasteful; and the consumer is helpless. Given these widespread and deeply held opinions and beliefs there is little wonder so many call upon government to protect consumers and workers.

This portrayal of the market is decidedly one-sided in that it conveys the views of only the rationally ignorant consumer and worker. They are not the only citizens fearing competition in the market and who therefore seek shelter from its vicissitudes; capitalists, managers, and producers, more generally, have solid rational reasons for fearing competition. They, too, can entertain the possibility of greater gains by reducing or restraining competition and "stabilizing" market forces. In short, markets impose a powerful and unremitting discipline on sellers. Although all sellers have a vested interest in maintaining rivalry among their suppliers (a public good), no supplier desires greater competition among his competitors (a public bad to existing suppliers). Recognition of this dual nature of the market has led Milton Friedman to complain, somewhat defensively, that he is not a friend of business; instead, he maintains a consistent *promarket* "bias"—a fundamental distinction not widely understood or appreciated.

Since markets are neither well understood nor appreciated it is nothing less than remarkable that they survive and even prosper. The dilemma is that although everyone gains from markets, everyone is also tempted by a powerful short-run motive to engage in actions that in the long run make them worse off. In seeking greater security, everyone is led to seek special protection and gain through politics. We must, therefore, be suspicious of and opposed to claims for safety nets and other protectionist policies that reduce efficient market competition but necessarily increase inefficient political competition.

The Market as a Positive Game

In modern market economies, markets of all sorts exist and competitors come and go as do new products. Creative destruction is the basic fact of market life. But the main point is simple: Markets, even those possessing some monopoly power, offer all participants the possibility of making *mutual* gains. A buyer goes into a market to obtain a good but must make some sort of payment for that good. Although the seller wishes to maximize that payment, the buyer not only has power to resist but usually ends up with the product. We know many highly educated academics who complain about "plastic societies," materialism, inequality, "obscene" profits, and monopoly while somehow managing to purchase the latest electronic equipment, sports cars, outdoor recreational gear, cameras, and so on, possessions evidently cherished. Still, they believe consumers are usually "taken." If they are, why return to be taken again and again? And they refuse steadfastly to acknowledge the ability of capitalism to provide us with a steady flow of pleasurable and useful material goods and a high and increasing standard of living. All that is taken for granted and need not be explained. Like many people, our friends want everything at a lower price. They confuse relative gain with their personal notion of a "just" price.

Judged by these contradictory criteria, no transaction can possibly be good for both parties. Dissatisfaction with market results would seem then to be based not only on the belief that everyone but sellers should gain absolutely from exchanges but also on the notion that they should gain relative to others. We cannot have it both ways.

On the basis of these fundamental ideological commitments, some people believe that monopolies pervade the economy, that the only way workers can protect themselves is through powerful unions, and that consumers require the continual guidance and assistance of a benevolent government. Oddly, the alleged monopolists and oligopolists must constantly advertise to create demand for their offerings. But if their power to compel consumption is indeed so great, one must wonder why the advertising is needed. This myopic but widespread view is at glaring odds with economic reality. Unfortunately, much of our analysis is counterintuitive, as, indeed, is an appreciative understanding of the beneficial workings of the market economy.

Monopoly: Sources, Power, and Welfare Losses

If the term "monopoly" means a sole seller of a particular good or service, there are no monopolies in the United States except the government itself. All sellers face downward-sloping demand curves they cannot control, and although they may be price-searchers they still must pay attention to supply constraints (costs) and demand. They cannot simply impose their own preferred demand and supply curves. Close substitutes are always available or becoming so. Bus companies compete with one another but their major source of competition comes from automobiles, trains, airlines, and even bicycles and, yes, walking. Paint manufacturers must compete not only with other paint producers but also with suppliers of wallpaper and wood paneling. Wine competes with other wine as well as with wine coolers, hard liquor, soft drinks, beer, water, and drugs. The potential monopolist has a hard row to hoe. Monopolies in unregulated markets tend to erode rather rapidly, and long-lived monopolies persist only when protected by government. Without the coercive power of government, monopolies could not survive. In fact, monopolies generally cannot be formed without political assistance. The one exception seems to be those industries such as utilities in which long-run average cost continues to decrease over substantial ranges of production. And then, of course, public ownership or regulation are the preferred political modes of control. Finally, monopoly profits attract outside competitors who expand production and thereby lower prices and dissipate profits; the monopolist can win, but not for long. Hardly any of 1994's largest Fortune 500 corporations even existed fifty to seventy-five years ago. What happened to the largest companies of the 1920s?

Of far greater importance than outright monopoly are industrial cartels created and administered by government. Because of the free-rider problem, few private cartels survive for protracted periods. Without an enforcement agent, cartels are doomed to a short existence. Free riders, incidentally, should be commended for violating cartels because by doing so they advance the cause of competition and the welfare of the consumer. But even if the free rider could be controlled, it would have to be by court decree, and courts are reluctant to uphold collusive contracts. But democratic governments will gladly maintain cartels and justify them as being in the public welfare.

Cartel management, or as it is better known, "regulation," comes about as a result of demand on the part of producers to reduce and manage their own competition and the willingness of politicians to supply appropriate regulation. The interaction of economic demand and political supply sets the "price" that must be paid for mutual gains to be realized. Producers demanding regulation want competition made more livable, that is, they want entry to their market strictly controlled so that the market is stabilized for the fortunate few in the industry. Detailed regulation of supplies, prices, quality, and entry are all important ingredients of cartel management and success.

The politicians and bureaucrats who provide the supply of regulation collude because of tangible and substantial gains provided them by the industry. Regulators gain more positions with more authority, higher salaries, and more status; the politicians gain votes, campaign monies, possible positions in the regulated industry once they retire or resign, income from the industry lecture circuit, and, perhaps, bribes. Obviously, the consuming public loses from all these cozy arrangements: They suffer reduced supplies, increased prices, and higher taxes. In fact, regulation itself may be considered a form of taxation in the sense that the cross-subsidies some consumers gain, as they did under regulated airline and telephone service, are paid for by other consumers whose fares and prices are increased. The airlines were permitted to charge higher than cost prices on long-distance flights in order to finance the below-cost tickets on short hauls to Podunk. First-class postage has usually subsidized third-class mail, and long-distance telephone charges have often made up for unlimited local service. In other words, those who paid the higher charges were being taxed to support services to those paying below-cost prices. Cross-subsidies is one name for this practice; regulation as taxation is another. The regulated firms complain publicly about all these practices, but regulation is the price they pay for greater stability and profits in the industry. Apparently they have been willing to pay, since few have shown any ardor to be deregulated and those few who have clamor to regain the benefits they once knew. Cartels cannot be maintained without firm control; government offers industry the best if not the only legal deal.

Welfare losses from monopoly and imperfect competition are relatively easy, in theory, to identify and measure but exceedingly difficult to estimate in practice. They are particularly easy to describe in terms of a graph if one deals with the short run. Figure 8.1 depicts the situation in typical textbook fashion. The triangle ABC constitutes the welfare loss to society, and the box P_rP_cBA indicates the magnitude of the transfer of income from consumers to the monopolist or cartel. This rectangle depicts not simply a zero-sum transfer but rather additional social loss, because some portion, if not all, may go to payments incurred in privilege or rent seeking. In fact, rent seeking is a billion-dollar growth industry. The total loss to society, then, may approach the entire area of trapezoid P_rACP_c. When the long run is introduced, measurement is dubious. Welfare losses are manifested in less than optimal supplies and temporarily higher prices, but since monopolies do not exist for a protracted time, losses have been estimated at

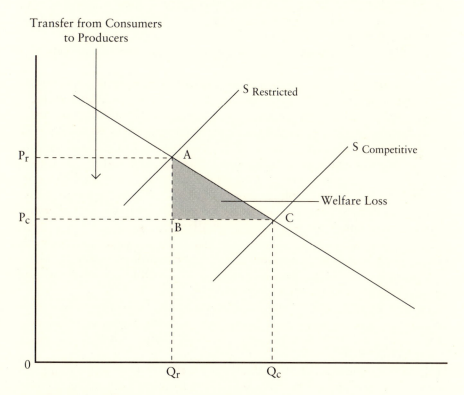

FIGURE 8.1 Welfare Losses from Monopoly

not more than 3 percent of annual GNP (Harberger 1954). But others (Cowling and Mueller 1978) believe the losses total up to 12 percent. In contrast, some analysts have contended that monopoly may even confer some long-term benefits. The less perfectly competitive firms are also thought to confer similar gains in the form of greater willingness to innovate; however, other theorists have suggested that the monopolist wishes nothing more than quietude.

Government-sponsored cartels are everywhere: in agriculture, the professions, some transportation, and even local trades such as barbering, building, communications, and public utilities. Consumer losses would not be great, or at least they would be tolerable, if but one or two industries were regulated, but when all are, costs mount rapidly. At best, rent-based regulation is a poor substitute for market competition. Much regulation not only favors the regulated but is costly in and of itself. In the first place, regulation is inherently difficult to design and carry out even in the hands of "experts" and moralists. The purposes of regulation may be vague or contradictory, and every situation in regulation is in some respect unique. Every violation of the regulation calls for another more detailed regulation. And regulation is expensive. Some estimates of regulatory costs range in the neighborhood of $2 billion annually for administration and more than $100 billion in compliance costs paid by businesses. And it is unlikely that the taxpayers are better off for having made these expenditures.

These obvious costs entailing sacrificed welfare for society and costly administration constitute but a portion of the total losses. Although technically not a welfare cost, there is also substantial transfer of gains from consumers to producers in the form of artificially high profits. Society may not lose but the consumers do while producers fortunate enough to have monopoly advantages gain. Perhaps more important are the rent-seeking costs paid by producers for governmentally mandated privileges. The cost of obtaining political advantage is a deadweight cost; interest-group efforts to gain the benefits generate social waste rather than welfare. Otherwise productive resources are employed in an attempt to gain rights to governmentally created scarcity. And once a costly political gain has been realized, it must be maintained against the competing efforts of others to share in the profits as well as against those who may wish to do away with the rights. Eternal vigilance is the price of rent seeking.

Even though the strictly based welfare costs may be as low as those estimated by several Chicago economists, these estimates represent only a portion of the total costs of monopoly. Less output and higher prices reduce consumer surplus, but the greatest loss may well be in the enormous rent-seeking costs engendered by the political search for gain. Once more, we take note of the curious fact that whereas market competition leads to inadvertent social welfare, political competition generally leads to social waste.

In dealing with rent seekers and monopoly we have but six options: live with them; buy back from the holders; auction off monopoly rights for a specified term to the lowest bidder; slowly dissolve rents; regulate; or reduce governmental intervention in markets. At various times the United States seems to have practiced all of these, excepting, perhaps, the second and third options. We believe that the antitrust laws have had some effect on industry but that the consequences of enforcement have been mostly bad for the general public. Such protection has been mostly redundant and therefore wasteful. And sometimes it has been perverse. The market is far more demanding and resilient than the trustbusters ever dreamed. Living with temporary market-based monopolies is a small price to pay for maintaining market institutions. Far more consequential would be a policy of buying back monopoly privileges. Compensation seems in order for those who, like the cab drivers of New York City, have had to invest up to $130,000 for a license to operate a cab. Since the government in collusion with the original industry imposed this requirement on drivers who did not create the restrictive practice, we think medallion holders should be compensated for the inevitable losses of freeing entry to the cab industry. In other industries, we are less sure that compensation should be given, mostly because the current holders of privilege, such as the doctors and peanut growers, may be able to make the transition with less sacrifice than cab drivers. In any event, antitrust laws ought to be eliminated and more industries deregulated. Let us deny exclusive franchises that create barriers to entry and legal monopolies. Let us reduce regulation so that the regulated will not be forced to seek control of their regulators.

Consumer Protection: How Much Is Enough?

Until the age of Ralph Nader, one might have believed that consumers and workers either did not care about their own safety or were forced by monopolists and oligopolists to accept defective products and hazardous work situations. Although this view is mostly false, it is true that both workers and consumers have become increasingly conscious of safety during the past decade or two. Just why preferences on these matters have altered is not a simple question with a simple answer. Regardless of the answers, the fact is that although safety is now more highly valued it is still not thoroughly or widely understood. One result has been a rash of crisis legislation mandating immediate action; the Occupational Safety and Health Administration (OSHA) is but one manifestation. Ironically, government first creates monopolies and is then forced to protect consumers from monopoly abuses.

Safety, whether in products like automobiles, kiddy-cars, ladders, and prescription drugs or in the workplace, is an attribute that affects demand. In a sense, then, safety is no different from any other object of demand; it comes at a price, is subject to individual preferences, and has a market. Accordingly, we can best understand consumer protection if we apply the laws of supply and demand, as shown in Figure 8.2.

Individual demand varies as benefits and costs change. Accordingly, some people will prefer—all else remaining equal—to have more safety while others prefer less—and some even a good deal less. As price varies so our demand varies, inversely. Both of these choices are illustrated in Figure 8.2 by different downward-sloping demand curves for consumers preferring more and less safety. For any given quantity of safety, the risk-avoider is willing to pay more than is the risk-taker. At the same price, the risk-taker prefers less safety than does the risk-avoider.

In Figure 8.2, the two consumers show preferences such that one, the risk-avoider, will buy more safety and be willing to pay more for it than will the other, the risk-taker. For example, some auto purchasers buy Volvos because they are thought to offer more safety or protection than other cars, and such buyers do in fact pay more for their Volvos than they would for other cars. The owner of a Volvo is not necessarily more rational than the buyer of a much cheaper automobile. Given their respective in-

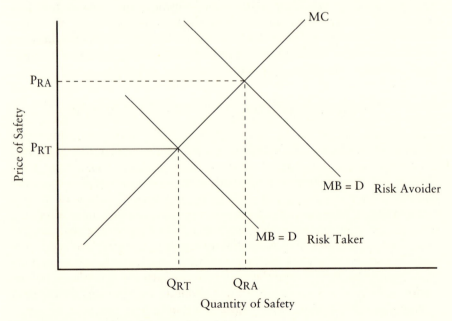

FIGURE 8.2 Supply and Demand for Safety

comes, the prices of the autos, their tastes for other features in cars, and, of course, differing preferences for safety, the chooser of a Yugo is every bit as rational as the Volvo fancier. The nice thing about competitive markets is that both buyers can be satisfied. The problem with government-mandated safety or protection is that the policies enacted often violate consumer preferences. A seat belt or air bag costs money to build and install and affects an automobile's price; as a result, either or both of these features may confer, at given prices, more or less safety than a particular driver prefers.

The example of auto safety is worth pursuing further. An air bag is estimated to cost somewhere between $1,300 and $2,200. This amount is a significant addition to the cost of an auto even at today's prices. If air bags are mandated, it is entirely possible that some buyers will not purchase new autos and will instead opt for second-hand cars without air bags, a somewhat perverse result. Other rational responses might include purchasing still less safe modes of transportation including motorcycles, bicycles, and so on; at a less dramatic level one can understand why consumers might choose an entire array of less costly, presumably less safe products.

Even when a good case can be made for increased safety, some distinction must be made between safe products and product use. Users' choices, as police and insurance people know so well, may leave much to be desired. Young male drivers have notably greater accident rates than other drivers. Many people insist on climbing mountains, some without proper training or equipment; some people pilot motor boats without adequate knowledge of boats and water and its dangers; and some people insist on flying hang-gliders without formal training. We feel that everyone should have the right to endanger themselves, but not at the cost of others. Improving the safety features of autos, boats, and table saws rarely compensates for recklessness. In fact, as research has shown, added safety not only complicates product use but all too often emboldens users to take further risks, a phenomenon known as a "moral hazard." Moral hazards are not fictions conjured up by the greedy insurance agents. Better tires, auto bodies, safety belts, and highways make some drivers willing to assume greater risks because these features appear to lower the cost of risk. And, indeed, they do when cost is socialized among the innocent.

Analyzing the demand for consumer protection does not provide all the answers to these problems. Polemicists of consumer protection usually claim or imply that business will not provide safety because it is costly and reduces profits. The logic is no better than the historical record assumed in such arguments. The fact of the matter is that sellers invent and adopt safety features as a means of creating and increasing demand. Long before Ralph Nader, U.S. automakers continuously offered automobiles that were safer than previous makes. Nader did not invent or mandate more reliable engines, steel-belted tires, better lights and air circulation, better brakes, more reliable windshield wipers, rear view mirrors, door locks, steering mechanisms, shatterproof glass, roll bars, and so on. Competing oligopolists marketed these improvements without the force of law. They not only responded to changing demand but invented new means of safety as a method of competition. One must assume that in the absence of regulation automakers would have continued these profitmaking activities.

Not all consumers will choose all of these or other auto safety improvements, but many will. People will always want to protect their own health and safety and that of their children. Moreover, life will never be risk-free. Recognizing these truths should enable us to better understand why much legislated airline safety is redundant. Neither passengers nor airline employees want to risk their own limbs and lives unnecessarily. Few if any pilots can be coerced into flying planes carrying hundreds of people knowing full well that a safe journey is not very probable. Stunt and test pilots may fly themselves around at greater risk, but that is their own private concern. Any airline that gained a reputation for unsafe flying would soon be out of business. In the meanwhile the stock market devaluates the stock of airlines suffering plane crashes. A prescription drug company would face the same fate if its products were deemed unsafe.

We find it odd indeed that consumers of private goods are assumed by Naderites to be incapable of assessing their own risks but highly capable of voting for public officials who can assess those risks for others. Of course, consumers need information about product safety in order to make wise consumer choices, and it too comes at a price. Many private sources of information, however, are available to users. Consumer guides are available at low prices at virtually all newsstands. And, although society may choose to socialize risk, the best way seems not to coerce individuals into purchases they do not want but to supply them with relevant information and allow them to make more informed choices. And if they choose not to be informed, and many will, there is a limit to what the protective state should do, and indeed can do, to protect people against themselves. "We have met the enemy and he is us."

How much safety is enough is best decided by the person most interested in the question—the buyer. In the case of children, those who are senile, and the mentally retarded, reliance seems best left in the hands of their families and other private protectors. Where none are to be found, then obviously some private organization and/or the state must assume some responsibility.

Perverse Regulation: Setting the Speed Limit

In 1974, Congress responded, predictably, to a media-generated crisis of highway accidents and death as well as the incipient energy crisis by enacting the 55-mile-an-hour speed limit. The goals were noble: to stop the "slaughter" and "irrational" energy consumption. The means were simple: a speed limitation. With gasoline apparently in short supply and highway deaths numbering more than 50,000 annually, the case was plausible even though deaths per million vehicle miles driven on highways had been dropping since the mid-1960s.

But as many researchers have shown, the anticipated results were not attained. Unfortunately, the supporters of the law were not particularly informed about the nature of the transportation system and focused, therefore, on the least important element without reference to costs and alternative ways of saving lives.

In the first place, speed is not the primary cause of injury and death; most traffic deaths occur at speeds of less than 55 miles per hour. In California, where drivers are not only numerous but seemingly pursue speed as a natural right, it has been learned that speed could not have caused more than 30 percent of all traffic deaths in that state. More crucial were risk-prone drivers, errors in judgment, unavoidable accidents, and highway conditions. Even so, considering the number of autos and the miles driven each year, the fatality rate was extraordinarily low even before the speed-limit law was enacted, and it was declining. Technical improvements invented and sold by the auto industry over the past seventy-five years had much to do with this.

Traffic deaths continued to decline after the speed-limit law was imposed on the states. The proponents of the law claimed the reductions were attributable to the lower speed limit and used these statistics to justify keeping it in place. Even if the reductions were truly caused by the new speed limit, it is questionable whether the human lives saved justified the high costs of enforcing the law. In 1978, Charles A. Lave calculated the opportunity costs of the law and decided the law was not a bargain. The value of all the additional time that police officers spent on the highways was worth more than $6 billion, and that estimate was based on a conservative hourly wage rate. In short, the estimated 4,500 lives that may have been saved per year cost taxpayers $1.3 million, or 102 years of highway patrol staff time, *per life* purportedly saved. Lave argued that we can find cheaper ways of saving lives, including smoke detectors in every home. Such devices cost $50,000 to $80,000 per life saved.

What is more, the speed-limit law cannot be credited with saving the 4,500 lives annually that its proponents point to. The number of deaths per million vehicle miles was falling at a faster rate prior to 1974 than after the law's enactment. The too-tempting conclusion is that the 55-mile-an-hour limit cost lives instead of saving them. The safe conclusion is that the speed limit contributed little or nothing to the ongoing reduction in fatalities.

Saving lives was one goal; saving gasoline and oil another. Here, again,

Lave showed that the law was not a good bargain. Most driving is necessarily done under conditions that do not permit speeds in excess of 55 miles per hour because it is done in cities, on bad country roads, or on hilly terrain; moreover, many people simply have a personal preference for slower driving. At most, not more than about one-sixth of all vehicle miles are subject to the speed limitation. Assuming total compliance among those people driving these miles, savings amount to a little less than 2 percent of all gasoline consumption. The case of large trucks is even worse because such rigs may perform most efficiently at speeds over 55 miles per hour.

Moreover, relatively few drivers honored the law when driving on freeways. Apparently they did not fear arrest and citation. And, of course, the greater fuel efficiency of the newer small cars enabled drivers to travel faster at a lower cost. If our goal is to save fuel, we should do what President Carter did—allow the price of gasoline to rise to market-clearing levels. The increased gasoline prices encouraged drivers to purchase more fuel-efficient vehicles and to drive fewer miles. Another option for saving fuel is to abandon the older gas-burners and subsidize the purchase of new cars. Perhaps those interested in income redistribution should consider having the government buy all older models from the poor and replace them with free or below-cost cars. Such a policy would cost less than the 55-mile-per-hour limitation, save fuel, and redistribute income.

Even if our claims were less well-founded, those who rely upon the government to protect consumers should pause to wonder about their faith. The Department of Transportation, at the direction of Congress, sets fuel-economy rules for automobiles. Analyses by Robert Crandall and John Graham (1984) at the Brookings Institution show that these standards kill an average of 3,000 people per model year. The excess deaths occur because people are forced into smaller, less safe cars.

Because of the fuel-efficiency standards and Detroit's unwillingness to adapt to a competitive world market in automobiles, throughout the early 1980s American consumers had to choose between slow, clumsy American cars and peppy, agile Japanese cars. The Japanese cars were chosen at such an alarming rate that American manufacturers sought import restrictions to reduce the competition; in 1981 President Reagan obliged by persuading the Japanese government to limit imports. Robert Crandall (1985) estimated that by 1984, "the import prices for Japanese cars rose by nearly $2,400 due to the quotas, even without extra dealer markups." The quota-generated price increase for imported cars allowed American automobile manufacturers to increase their prices as well—by $500 to $1,500 per car. By 1985 that amount accounted for almost all of Chrysler's profits since its reorganization. Protection from competition and gouging the American consumer may account for Chrysler's recovery. Governmental protection is a two-way street or, to mix metaphors, a two-edged sword. Consumers ought to be wary of their benefactor.

Vehicle Safety Inspection Laws

In a comprehensive examination of federally mandated vehicle safety inspection programs administered by states, W. Mark Crain (1980) discovered that such programs have had no discernible effect on highway safety. Through the use of standard statistical analyses comparing states with and without such systems, he was able to demonstrate quite convincingly that in view of the costs and the relative lack of benefits the programs ought to be reevaluated and perhaps terminated. He compared different inspections, frequency of inspection, inspection by state-owned and privately operated systems, spot and periodic checks, and the like. The deadweight welfare costs were estimated to be in excess of $300 million in 1976, when 76 million vehicles were inspected. In addition, the rent-seeking costs of obtaining an inspection license were estimated to approach $200 million annually.

Crain claims that this highly inefficient program of safety is actually a rent-seeking operation by the operators of inspection stations and the auto parts industry. We know of no study contradicting his findings or analysis.

Protecting Citizen-Consumers: The Case of Government Goods

Galbraithians who worry about private monopolies seldom seem equally concerned over the real monopolists, our 80,000 governments that simultaneously oversupply some services and fail to provide for many other important daily wants. Each day drivers traverse poorly designed and maintained highways and streets. People routinely must deal with an inefficient postal service, slow-moving bureaucracies, and ineffectual schools. Parks and other public facilities are poorly maintained, and the adequacy of the national defense is questionable. Although increasing numbers of retired people find the Social Security system a bad deal, each payday young workers discover increasing payroll taxes have been deducted to maintain the Social Security program—possibly the world's largest Ponzi scheme. Every year homeowners confront an increased property tax—a tax most taxpayers regard as excessive and unfairly allocated. Governmentally supplied services generate many of consumers' most critical current concerns. But if consumers wish to sue government for unkept promises, poor service, or damages, they must await governmental consent; government, it seems, does not readily honor consumer sovereignty.

Alcoholic Beverages: State Liquor Stores

One particular example may serve to illustrate the continuing failure of government in its relationships with citizens; the case involves the Oregon Liquor Control Commission (OLCC), the state agency that holds monopoly rights in the distribution of alcoholic beverages within that state. In Oregon, wine and beer are sold by private wholesalers, wine stores, and, of course, privately operated nightclubs, bars, and restaurants. Hard liquor is sold by state-owned but privately operated liquor stores. The commission itself is made up of appointed individuals, many of whom seem to come from careers in the ministry and the military. The commission makes all the critical decisions concerning the number of retail stores (it has a population formula to guide its choices), the requirements for potential store operators, the location of stores, business hours, prices, displays, and brands that can be offered for sale. In short, they make all the decisions, and most if not all of these work against the consumer's interests, unless, of course, one is a teetotaler.

The stores are few in number, inconveniently located, and have highly inconvenient hours. The prices on nearly all brands are among the highest in the country. Consumers with special tastes must place orders for their preferred brands and they must usually purchase a minimum of an entire case and then wait several weeks for delivery. While the commission has loosened some of its practices during recent years, the business is not run as a competitive industry might be run, as it is in other states. Clearly, the commission wishes to maximize two partially conflicting goals: It wants to discourage drinking and make exorbitant profits that can be used, in part, to finance alcohol treatment programs. In one sense, the commission is quite rational: The high real costs endured by drinkers tend to discourage consumption, and high bottle prices do provide large sums for the treatment of alcoholics. However, changes in drug as well as liquor prices have led many young people to greater consumption of substitutes—beer and wine as well as pot, speed, crack, and so on. It is clear that the commission monopoly does not honor consumer sovereignty. Unfortunately, like many appointed governmental bodies, the commission is not terribly responsive to changing public preferences.

Oregon's state liquor monopoly has had another perverse consequence, namely, encouraging Oregonians to illegally import substantial quantities of alcohol from California, where prices, despite a stiff sales tax, are much lower. Then, too, moonshiners still operating in the Oregon hills provide not only private drinkers but also private taverns with sometimes lethal booze. Bars have been known to mix the cheaper home brew with the commercial product to enhance profit margins. Again, governmental action leads to unintended results, including greater immorality, cynicism, and bodily damage. And higher prices have not reduced consumption by addicts; instead, moderate users are penalized.

Government Schools and Mediocrity

State legislators are told at every legislative session that education at all levels is in short supply. Education is popular among politicians because it is a good with positive externalities verging on being a genuine public good. The important policy implication is that public schools are an essential service. Since all social benefits beyond those going directly to the student are underestimated by the market, some means must be adopted to permit the broader social gains to be reflected in prices and quantities of education supplied. The policies can range all the way from educational subsidies to outright government ownership and control. The latter is better known as public education. We believe a more accurate designation is "government schools."

In examining the alleged shortage of education, critics are apt to ignore the thousands of private schools that offer instruction in everything from aviation mechanics to gourmet cooking and ballroom dancing. They also ignore such renowned colleges and universities as Harvard, Yale, Princeton, Chicago, and Stanford. Actually they don't ignore them; they attended them and sacrifice greatly to enroll their own children in the leading private secondary schools and colleges. But the more important point is that, while education has external benefits, its primary ones redound to the advantaged and usually are better provided by highly competitive, private suppliers.

This fundamental fact is only now being appreciated by ordinary people who, in increasing numbers, have come to demand an end to the public school monopoly. Polls now show that a solid majority of Americans favor allowing parents a choice of where to send their children to school. And, interestingly but hardly surprisingly, this demand is emanating mostly from lower income families. They are the ones who suffer the failures of government schools. Higher income groups have the best of the public schools and, when that is not good enough, send their offspring to the expensive private boarding schools. Less affluent academics living in college towns make certain that they reside in that public school district having the best schools in town.

Ending the government-school monopoly can be accomplished in various ways, including school vouchers, tax reductions for those attending private schools, privatization of the government school system, or measures permitting parents to send children across public school district lines. There is nothing like a little competition to sharpen up the offerings of the competitors.

But the effort to demonopolize education will not proceed in a costless manner: School boards, administrators, teacher unions, and liberal intellectuals will all resist and do so with considerable resources, many of which are provided by the public itself (see Lieberman 1989). Having much to lose, they will not surrender gracefully. Instead, they will contend that the federal government must take a more active role in controlling government schools; the increased administration costs should be financed, of course, by taxing the wealthy. "Social justice" will dictate the solution. Nevertheless, the citizens of Minnesota, Wisconsin, Utah, Indiana, Illinois, Iowa, Arkansas, Nebraska, Ohio, and Oregon have all adopted various policies that serve to decentralize schools and make them more responsible to the students and their parents. If the newly liberated schools produce mediocrity, at least it will be by the explicit choice of informed citizens. More likely, parents will demand a higher quality of education.

State Systems of Higher Education

Thus far, we have concentrated on failures of public education at the primary and secondary levels, ignoring the vast state university system consisting of nearly 2,000 institutions. Our criticisms of this enterprise are voiced with the knowledge that the system is, without any question, the finest in the world. Scholars and students alike seek to enter it by the tens of thousands. But the fact that it is the best serves to remind us that the others represent an advanced case of inefficient state ownership and control as well as rent seeking (Steindl 1990). We should not wish to emulate others.

Within the U.S. school system, students—as consumers—get much less than they might if institutional arrangements were different. Some consumer protection is desirable but that protection is best provided by applying market principles in the provision of education. As things now stand, students are consumers who do not buy from professors who do not sell. Equally bad, taxpayers, who bear most of the burdens, do not control; that is done by administrators. The result is massive inefficiency. Students choose, but within a highly bureaucratized setting full of constraints set by those who hold monopoly power—the professors, deans, and curricula committees. Schedules are often arranged to suit not the needs of students but for the convenience of the faculty and through the power of the university administrators.

Insofar as education may be considered a "good" and students consumers of that good, we must conclude they are not treated as sovereign consumers. In part, of course, this limitation stems from the institutions of choice presented students. Students are treated as immature, uninformed, and in need of considerable guidance. Thus, many of their course requirements are prescribed within the parameters that professors deem essential or find convenient to teach. The typical university catalog is replete with exotic courses, duplication, and minute requirements that the average professor does not even pretend to know. Four years of study are imposed when a carefully thought-out curriculum would surely not require more than three. Students are required to take esoteric topics and learn tools of thought having little relevance in the real world.

As rational humans, students soon learn how to survive and flourish within the educational system. They learn all the shortcuts, both ethical and unethical. They learn not to attend class in those courses in which attendance has little bearing on their grade. They learn how to write exams that will pass. They learn how much reading is really necessary. In short, they learn that scholarship is secondary to learning how to work the system. For many, the most valuable learning in college comes not from the intended lessons of the professors but from the unintended experiences of having to associate with all sorts of people on campus. There they learn about sex, sharing living quarters, paying rent each month, having fun, and meeting a few deadlines. Much of the academic knowledge they pick up lasts but a short time and is promptly forgotten, and deservedly so.

Students do not typically complain a great deal and for two simple reasons: One, they do not know what education could be, and second, since they pay such a small portion of the total cost of their formal education the cost of inefficiency is low. But if they had to bear 100 percent of the formal cost of education they would think more carefully about whether they were getting their money's worth. At the average state university, the student pays but one-fourth the costs of a college education. No wonder so little value is attached to the classes and work assignments. No wonder there is so little complaint about having to stay four years. No wonder they demand so little from their teachers.

Higher education will become more responsible and responsive only when its monopoly powers have been diminished and its officials and professors required to behave in more market-like settings. We urge a more thorough use of the pricing mechanism throughout academia; that is, complete elimination of subsidized education, greater use of variable prices for different courses, greater use of charges for use of facilities, including payment of rent by professors for their offices and laboratories, and the like. Only with the use of campus pricing will efficiency be improved. We believe, also, that when this objective is accomplished, resources will be rationally allocated. The overall price of education will decrease as waste is eliminated.

If the voters wish to subsidize certain groups, they should do so with vouchers or with straightforward grants to students rather than with grants to administrators. Vouchers would provide the low-income but able student with educational funds that could be used anywhere his qualifications permitted. Pricing would also revolutionize teaching practices and reward the able teachers, something that is not currently done. Professors would learn, like enterprisers, to respect consumer sovereignty or find another trade in which to ply their wares.

All these reforms will be resisted bitterly by administrators and academics because much is at stake. The monopoly position of the traditional academic will be threatened as never before. Professors will have to sell, a task most regard as crass and demeaning to their self-image as selfless, sophisticated, dedicated seekers of truth and bearers of culture. We envisage a new academy resembling the real world of diversity not only on individual, privately owned campuses but across campuses. Liberty will be genuine, and liberals will have to compete with conservatives and libertarians and give up the monopolistic hold they have enjoyed over the past sixty years. Universities will no longer be enclaves designed to advance and protect the privileges of the tweedy class.

Bibliographical Notes

Most of the better work on consumer protection is found not in books but in journal articles and specialized monographs. Much of that literature is treated under the label of "regulation," meaning regulation of producers, including drug manufacturers, airlines, automobile companies, providers of medical services, and so on. But very little of it deals with the government as producer of consumer goods and services, except, of course, education, about which far too much has been written.

One classic paper that should be read by serious students is George Akerlof's "The Market for 'Lemons:' Quality Uncertainty and the Market Mechanism," printed in *Quarterly Journal of Economics* 84 (August 1970), 448–500. This is another of those germinal articles that begins with some simple observations of the real world and discovers some nonobvious implications. Read it.

On the matter of governmentally provided goods we recommend two books. The first is Alston Chase's *Playing God in Yellowstone: The Destruction of America's First National Park* (Boston: Atlantic Monthly Press, 1986). The main title indicates the nature of the consumer good while the subtitle suggests how the government has provided the good. For those who cherish the National Park system, the book will be a revelation, or is it an expose? Another equally devastating investigation pertains not to a single park but to national water policy and its history and consequences: Marc Reisner's *Cadillac Desert: The American West and Its Disappearing Water* (New York: Viking, 1986). This volume documents the interbureau conflicts between the Bureau of Reclamation and the U.S. Army Corps of Engineers as well as their respective client allies. One result has been the overbuilding of dams and, worse, the waste of water resources. The pork-barrel, log-rolling processes of Congress are shown in dismaying detail. This book is a stunner.

With respect to education, one of the better books is that of James M. Buchanan and Nicos E. Devletoglou, *Academia in Anarchy: An Economic Diagnosis* (New York: Basic Books, 1970). In academia, students are consumers who do not pay;

faculties are producers who do not sell; and taxpayers are owners who do not control. It is a most revealing analysis. A new book edited by John W. Sommer, *Academy in Crisis: The Political Economy of Higher Education* (New Brunswick, N.J.: Transaction Publishers, 1994) is also revealing. It asks the question, "Where have all the educators gone?" and uses property rights and public choice theories to provide disconcerting answers. Still another excellent but different sort of book on education was discussed in Chapter 7: *PROFSCAM: Professors and the Demise of Higher Education* (1988) by Charles J. Sykes, a son of a professor. Regnery Gateway of Washington, D.C., is the publisher. Unlike the previously mentioned authors, Sykes devotes most of his words to documenting the demise of higher education and rather less to gaining an understanding of why the demise has occurred. Read along with the volume by Buchanan and Devletoglou, the documentation makes considerable sense. The source of the problems are the institutional arrangements that do not permit costs and benefits to be internalized in the decisionmakers, a point we may have pounded into the ground. Anyway, repetition is the foundation of pedagogy.

References

Cowling, Keith, and Dennis Mueller. "The Social Costs of Monopoly," *Economic Journal* 88 (December 1978), 727–748.

Crain, W. Mark. *Vehicle Inspection Systems* (Washington, D.C.: American Enterprise Institute, 1980).

Crandall, Robert. "Assessing the Impacts of the Automobile Voluntary Export Restraints upon U.S. Automobile Prices," paper delivered to the Society of Government Economists, New York, December 1985.

Crandall, Robert, and John D. Graham. "Automobile Safety Regulation and Off-Setting Behavior: Some New Empirical Evidence," *American Economic Review* 74 (May 1984), 328–331.

Harberger, Arnold C. "Monopoly and Resource Allocation," *American Economic Review* 44 (May 1954), 77–87.

Lave, Charles A. "The Costs of Going 55," *Newsweek* (October 23, 1978), 23.

Lieberman, Myron. *Privatization and Educational Choice* (New York: St. Martin's Press, 1989).

Steindl, Frank G. "University Admission Requirements as Rent Seeking," *Public Choice* 65 (1990), 273–279.

❦ 9 ❦

Political Pursuit of Private Gain: Environmental Goods

IF THE VOLUME OF legislation and political rhetoric is a good indicator, we might dub the 1980s the Environmental Decade. Never before were so much attention and so many resources devoted to "saving" the environment, reducing pollution, preserving wildlife, creating more environmental amenities, keeping fit, vacationing in the wilderness, and purchasing fashionable hiking shoes, backpacks, bicycles, and ski equipment. Morally enraged attacks on industrial polluters and obscene profiteers were and remain fashionable in dinner table conversations. Humans, we are told, do not live on bread alone; poetry, the mind, and environmental amenities must also be cultivated in civilized societies. In short, what economists label as externalities, social costs, or neighborhood effects have become a staple of daily conversation as well as of modern textbooks.

This new-found concern over the amenities of life is made possible, paradoxically, because of the tremendous economic growth engendered by capitalism. As material goods have become more plentiful, their marginal value has, as the law says, diminished; at the same time, the "quality-of-life" attributes have increased in value, posing further allocative choices. The problem becomes one of determining that combination of material and quality-of-life goods we wish to consume. For example, poor people place higher values on scarce material things, whereas those who take high incomes for granted seek the less available, more costly amenities. But any sacrifices from preserving environmental amenities are expected to be shared by all.

Public opinion polls do show continuing support from all income classes for the government to "do something" about environmental degradation and to protect environmental amenities. But the methods government officials have chosen and continue to choose, as the analyses of Chapters 3 and 4 would predict, are often failures. Some policies create the illusion of creating improvement while actually making things worse. Others succeed at protecting or improving environmental amenities but at costs that are greater than the value of the amenities.

146

A Primer

Ever since Paul Samuelson first wrote about public goods in the 1950s, political scientists and policy analysts have asserted that voluntary collective action in large groups and markets will fail to produce the socially optimal level of those private goods having external costs or benefits in production and/or consumption. As explained in Part One, the market overproduces a good when external costs exist because not all costs are incurred by the producers and consumers of the good. In effect, consumers of the good are subsidized by the damaged third parties. Conversely, the market underproduces a good whenever external benefits exist because all benefits are not captured by market demand for the product. In competitive markets, especially those consisting of large numbers of people, there will be little or no incentive for individuals to voluntarily do anything about negative externalities; everyone is induced to become a free rider. On the basis of this argument, the standard approach has been to apply extensive and forceful governmental action to remedy the situation.

This discussion will gain in precision if we consider an elementary graph that will enable us to pinpoint the nature of the problem and locate possible solutions. Consider Figure 9.1. Let the line ABC represent the marginal spillover costs of an industry and the line DBE$_m$ the marginal costs of

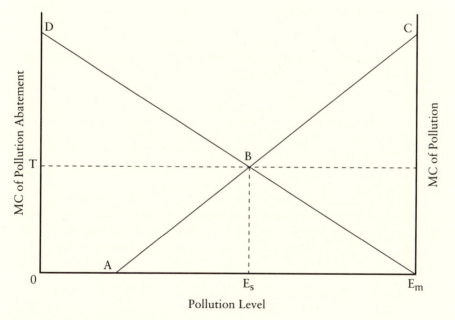

FIGURE 9.1 Controlling Pollution

abatement by the industry. In an uncontrolled market the industry will emit a total of OE_m units of pollution even though the socially optimal level is OE_s where the two sets of marginal costs are equal.

The standard approach suggests two responses. The first, preferred by most environmental groups and politicians, is to mandate OE_s. This approach, known as "command and control," is characteristic of most of the environmental legislation enacted during the past two decades. The second response is to tax the industry by the amount of OT or BE_s. A tax will encourage the industrialists to produce the correct combination of products and pollution. Each firm will reduce its level of pollution until the marginal cost of abatement equals the tax rate. Any further reduction of pollution would be more costly than paying the tax, so OE_s is the optimal level. Presumably, the marginal cost of abatement will be equalized for all firms minimizing the costs of pollution control.

Economists tend to favor the taxing scheme because enforcement costs are lower and innovation encouraged. But taxing an undesirable or even "immoral" activity is seen by many environmental activists as a social statement of indifference to environmentally destructive behavior. Taxing an activity fails to stigmatize it the way prohibiting or controlling it would, at least in the minds of the environmental elite. Both schemes are bound to be highly inefficient. Choosing taxes or command-and-control policies is dictated in the first place by an incorrect diagnosis of the sources or causes of externalities and second by political considerations honored by politicians and bureaucrats.

The analyses presented in Chapters 3 and 4 need not be repeated except to say that faith in government's ability to raise social welfare through cost-benefit analysis and adopting command-and-control or tax policies is unwarranted. It is unwarranted because environmental problems must be understood more as failures by government to specify property rights than as offshoots of private profit-seeking. Most politicians and many welfare economists do not agree with this argument, however, and instead view private property and profits as the culprits and imply that if government restricted or controlled them, society and the environment would be better off.

We emphasize the elementary but crucial fact that externalities, both good and bad, are *unintended* consequences of *useful,* purposive actions. Polluters do not go into business in order to pollute; they go into business to make money by satisfying consumer demands. Private firms as well as individual citizens take account of their own direct business costs in making decisions; they do not often take account of social effects. As a consequence, the prices attached to products reflect only the former and not the latter costs. That is what economists mean when they write of divergences between private and social costs. The market does not require such accounting because the environment is, in effect, a free garbage dump. If the environment is owned by no one, it pays to reduce costs by dumping; if the environment is owned by another private person, charges for dumping can be demanded. Since commonly owned property is owned by no one, the results are clear—it will not be cared for as well as private property. Everyone has a powerful incentive to dump and few have sufficient incentives and power to prevent others from dumping. A resource owned by everyone is treated as if it were owned by no one. That is why we notice litter on public streets and sidewalks. Smokers find it convenient to drop their cigarette butts on the ground, and no one wishes to incur the costs of thwarting them. Wherever streets and sidewalks are kept clean, it is because cities have employed a street-cleaning department and/or rely on private businesses whose potential customers seem to value ready, clean access to their shops.

Choosing Inefficient Policies

Efficiency dictates that if property rights to the environment were better defined and enforced, private transactors could more effectively control one another. Nevertheless, politicians, bureaucrats, and many voters tend to prefer highly complex but often inefficient regulations, taxes, and subsidy schemes. Unfortunately, each of these policies places a heavy burden on our capacities to gather and process information and multiplies the administrative costs of supervising polluters. At the same time, command-and-control or taxation solutions ignore the incentives and capacities of private parties to bargain with one another.

Politicians may prefer direct controls because controls enhance their own power and because many voters mistakenly believe that regulation through law is the simplest and most effective way to discourage antisocial behavior. Since politicians must honor electoral myths, passing a law seems to demonstrate their deep concern and forcefulness in attacking outstanding problems.

Whenever large numbers of people are involved in polluting, politicians are notably reluctant to enact tough antipollution legislation. The Oregon state legislature, for example, summoned up a great deal of courage and imagination in devising statutes to limit the number two polluter in Oregon, the wood-burning stove. The law permits people to use existing inefficient stoves and does not mandate costly improvements for them; however, manufacturers of new wood-burning stoves will be required to meet the higher standards beginning several years in the future. Needless to say, most homeowners will not voluntarily pay for more expensive but less polluting stoves. Old stoves will, accordingly, command a higher price in the second-hand market and pollution will not be reduced for a decade or more. Now politicians claim to have "done something," yet the net costs imposed on present voters are minimal.

Likewise, politicians are reluctant to make drivers the culprits in auto pollution and traffic accidents. Industry serves as a convenient scapegoat. And many politicians of the highest rank blame drug abuse not on users but on suppliers, foreign producers, and disreputable local pushers.

Bureaucrats, too, prefer environmental controls over market solutions; controls provide them with something useful to do and give them a ready claim to larger budgets to meet further unmet social needs. When they institute controls, they may be seen as dedicated servants of the public, hard-working officials protecting the environment; that they restrict the choices and behavior of others is of lesser concern. And, although their activities may be costly in the long run and, worse, ineffectual, few people notice the long run. Since higher costs of abatement appear to fall on the wealthy, corporate "malefactors" rather than the small taxpayer and consumer, politicians and bureaucrats gain support among voters.

In addition to the political attractiveness of illusory control policies, conventional approaches ignore the technical problem of identifying the optimal level of pollution. Without this information, it is impossible to calculate what amount of tax or level of control will best succeed in bringing social costs and benefits into line. Moral suasion on the part of government presents even more problems, for it calls for nothing less than an ethical revolution. Besides being impractical, such a government policy is devoid of a mechanism to achieve the optimal level of pollution. Still, governments resort to moral suasion where enforcement is impossible (littering) or where immediate action is required in brief emergencies (temperature inversions in Los Angeles). Outright bans may be more reliable than moral suasion so long as they are limited in scope. But outright bans cannot work if the ban affects nearly everyone, as is the case with pollution from internal combustion engines. In any event, such prohibitions are unlikely to achieve the optimal amount of the externality—unless, of course, the optimum is zero pollution. In general, risk-averse governments have chosen the ban when the cost of discovering the optimum level was in itself prohibitive and they had to choose an arbitrary level between zero and unchecked, highly dangerous pollution.

Setting standards seems to be the most popular environmental policy, at least in the United States. Whether the standards pertain to resource inputs, emissions, or ambient standards, all have a serious drawback; they are likely to be extremely costly and, for the most part, unnecessarily so. Since it is inordinately difficult for governments to catch, prosecute, and convict violators, administrative costs are high. And compliance costs are also apt to be high because standards must be tailored to the special circumstances of each polluter. Governments faced with this administrative nightmare therefore enact uniform standards but enforce them selectively.

Governments may also use a variety of subsidy instruments, including income-tax credits, accelerated depreciation privileges, low-interest loans, and exemptions from various taxes to purchasers of pollution-abatement equipment. These are only partial bribes and are therefore highly ineffective in encouraging installation of the equipment. A substantial private sacrifice on the part of the polluters is still required. Such programs also introduce a powerful bias toward the use of control equipment that may not be the least costly.

The Clean Air Act of 1970 and its 1977 amendments provide a useful guide to the politics of environmental protection. Prior to 1970, coal-fired generating plants produced about one-half of all electric power generated in the United States and, according to Environmental Protection Agency estimates, produced 65 percent of the sulfur oxides emitted. Sulfur oxides (sulfur dioxide—SO_2—in particular) are the pollutants believed to be the major cause of acid rain, so reducing their production was a major goal of the clean air legislation. In fact, the act required that SO_2 emissions be reduced to no more than 1.2 pounds of SO_2 per million BTU of energy produced.

What the act did not specify until the 1977 amendments was how the reductions were to be attained. Utility companies could install flue gas desulfurization mechanisms (scrubbers) in their smokestacks, wash crushed coal to remove most of the sulfur-bearing particles (coal washing), or burn coal with a lower sulfur content. The least effective and most costly of the alternatives was scrubbing, and the least costly was burning low-sulfur coal.

But burning low-sulfur coal presented a political problem because most of the nation's low-sulfur coal is located in the mountain states. The East and Midwest have mostly high-sulfur coal. If utilities shifted to low-sulfur, western coal in order to meet the clean air standards, jobs would be lost in the eastern coalfields where the United Mine Workers Union's membership is concentrated. Thus, the Clean Air Act amendments of 1977 became a legislative battle over regional protectionism.

Environmental groups joined the battle on the side of eastern "dirty coal" interests. The National Clean Air Coalition, the Environmental Policy Center, the Sierra Club, and the Natural Resources Defense Council supported a mandate for scrubbing *regardless of the coal's sulfur content*. Some environmentalists apparently favored forced scrubbing as a means of reducing the amount of strip mining in the West. Another rationale was the belief that scrubbing might reduce emissions below the 1.2-pound target.

Like the Oregon legislation that applied only to new wood-burning stoves, forced scrubbing, mandated by the 1977 amendments, only applied to new plants; existing plants were allowed to continue to emit four or five pounds of SO_2 per MBTU. Since adding scrubbers increases the cost of a new power plant by about 15 percent, old plants were being kept in production far longer than they would have been otherwise. And this "old plant effect" outweighs the extra benefits for air quality of forcing all new plants to scrub.

As modified by the 1977 amendments, the Clean Air Act is a model of political symbolism. Environmental groups won new standards; politicians, notably Senator Howard Metzenbaum of Ohio, appeared to protect the environment; and the United Mine Workers in the eastern coalfields reduced the competition for their jobs. But the air is not cleaner. As Bruce A. Ackerman and William T. Hassler maintained in their book *Clean Coal/ Dirty Air* (1981):

> As far as the West is concerned, scrubbing is an exceedingly expensive way of achieving minor reductions in sulfates; in the East, scrubbing is not only far more expensive, but may be positively counterproductive. Even on optimistic assumptions, forcing new plants to scrub will lengthen the life of dirty plants and may generate increases in emissions of sulfur oxides in the industrial Midwest for the next twenty years. And once a realistic view of enforcement is taken, forced scrubbing may make the sulfate problem worse, not better, for even larger portions of the nation's vulnerable northeastern quadrant. (pp. 77–78)

The cost of such symbolism is not trivial. Paul Portney (1990b) of Resources for the Future, a Washington, D.C., think tank, estimates that by the year 2000 utility companies will have spent anywhere from $400,000 to $800,000 annually for each job saved in the Eastern coalfields. Portney's estimate was generated by comparing the cost of scrubbing with the cost of coal washing and burning low-sulfur coal. Portney points out that the miners could be bought out at their present salaries for less than one-tenth of the cost of the regulation. Instead, the East gets dirtier air and consumers of electricity produced in the Midwest get to pay for dirty air and political symbolism through their utility bills.

These effects of the Clean Air Act have not changed the tactics of the Washington, D.C., environmental community. In fact, the effects appear to have encouraged more of the same behavior. When one of us (Simmons) asked the lead person on acid rain at the Natural Resources Defense Council (NRDC) whether NRDC would promote a form of legislation more satisfactory than the 1977 amendments in its efforts to have acid rain controlled, she snapped, "You must have been reading Ackerman's book. It's easy for him to accuse us from the comfort of New Haven but he was not here needing to get legislation passed!" Apparently passing legislation was more important than the legislation's effects, at least to her. During the Reagan administration, several bills seeking to mandate reduced emissions circulated in Congress. They typically proposed installing more and better scrubbers on new and existing plants. In one version sponsored by Representatives Jerry Sikorski and Henry Waxman (HR3400, 98th Congress), 90 percent of the cost would come from a tax on all consumers of electricity regardless of whether the source of their electricity was coal, nuclear, solar, or hydro plants. The bill's sponsors argued that "a nationwide fee system is necessary . . . to lessen utility rate increases and avoid economic disruption or increased unemployment." The provisions of this bill would increase the cost of forced scrubbing another $70,000 annually per job saved.

The 101st Congress amended the Clean Air Act and, although there are some important improvements, in most instances the new amendments make the same mistakes as the 1977 amendments. Portney's (1990b) analysis is as instructive as his previous analysis. He estimates the annual cost of compliance by the year 2005 at between $29 billion and $36 billion, with annual benefits ranging from $6 billion to $25 billion. He estimates the most likely value of the benefits to be about $14 billion, which is in line with other studies. Thus, costs exceed benefits by almost two to one. Nevertheless, President Bush trumpeted this legislation as landmark environmental legislation.

Pollution by Government Agencies

Pollution is produced by government agencies as well as the private sector. A somewhat straightforward example illustrates governmental externalities and the applicability of economic reasoning to public bureaucracies. The agency is the U.S. Army Corps of Engineers and the activity is the pollution of Lake Michigan. Chicago is linked to the Mississippi waterway system and Lake Michigan by a series of ship and barge canals. These canals also transport sewage away from Lake Michigan. The Corps has been assigned the task of maintaining the canals, including dredging the garbage that accumulates in them. Because the Corps is required to operate within a fixed budget, economies were practiced. Among them was the practice of dumping the dredgings in Lake Michigan. The Corps did this for a simple reason: The cost of such dumping was much lower than any other means of disposal. And, since the Corps was obligated to keep the canals clean but not Lake Michigan, the response was rational. By our analysis, the Corps of Engineers had a kind of "property right" in the canals but not in the lake. A clean lake could not, under the legal arrangements, be an objective. At the same time, no single citizen or organization had any incentive to protect the lake: Why should they bear all the costs and share the benefits with everyone?

One finds the same sort of behavior among other agencies. Similar behavior is documented, for instance, in several recent studies by authors who have impeccable credentials—not the least of which is their dedication to the environment. Marc Reisner, in *Cadillac Desert* (1986), writes in a most compelling and moving way about the public mismanagement of water supplies in the far western states. Reisner's analysis of the roles of the Bureau of Reclamation and the Army Corps of Engineers in the Iron Triangle, while depressing, is familiar indeed. Their sponsorship of dams and other water-control projects displays the usual hocus-pocus of saving the world, concealing enormous costs, including externalities, and exaggerating the benefits for all. In the San Joaquin Valley in California, for example, the bureau charges the typical farmer less than $20 per acre-foot for Central Valley Project water that farmers value at about $50 per acre-foot. The cost to the taxpayers for just the irrigation portions of the Central Valley Project range from $300 to $500 per acre-foot. Such subsidies made those who owned the farmland at the time the project was built very wealthy at taxpayers' expense. A severe depletion of natural water resources has been one consequence; another is the accumulation of salts in the soil, which has killed farmland, created further drainage crises, and poisoned wildlife.

The environmental costs of government actions so eloquently documented by Reisner and others have been somewhat more dispassionately analyzed by economists making more rigorous cost-benefit studies of all sorts of public projects. Among others, University of Wisconsin economist Robert Haveman (1965) has shown that no matter what cost-benefit procedures are employed, most of the 147 water resource projects authorized by Congress during the post–World War II period (1946–1962) were highly inefficient and egregiously inequitable in the distribution of costs and benefits. And even though the Bureau of Reclamation recently announced that it has completed its prime mission since 1902—building dams to make western U.S. deserts bloom—the costs to society of the bureau's continuing to supply water at subsidized prices will exceed the benefits.

Water policy is one area where substantial progress is being made to use property rights to manage a resource. As it has become abundantly clear that eastern members of Congress are unwilling to support more, massive water subsidies for the West, those wanting more water have turned to markets. The Western Governors' Association, for example, has called for an increase in water marketing—allowing water to be bought and sold. Although firm, private-property rights have not been established for water from federal projects, experimentation is under way. The Imperial Water District in California, for example, is attempting to contract with the Municipal Water District to have Municipal pay the costs of lining Imperial's canals in exchange for 100,000 acre-feet of water annually. The water traded is part of what is currently lost to seepage from the unlined canals and is more than Imperial would have gotten if the bureau, or anyone else, had built a new dam.

Water marketing could really begin to allocate and conserve water currently supplied in federal projects if current water allocations were converted into property rights and issued to existing irrigators. Currently, water allocations not used are taken away from the irrigator so he or she has little incentive to conserve or to seek out those who place a higher value on an alternative use of the water. Allowing farmers to sell water at a profit, by contrast, would enforce conservation because it would prevent farmers from wasting water; instead they could sell it and increase their personal income. Municipalities, instream recreational users, other farmers, and transport users could all buy water for their purposes.

Trading Dirty Air:
Markets for Optimal Pollution

In 1960, an English economist at the University of Chicago published one of the most remarkable papers in the history of economic theory—a paper entitled simply "The Problem of Social Cost." In this paper, Ronald Coase shattered previous analyses and offered an entirely new way of approaching social costs and the policies needed to deal with them. The idea, once understood, is fairly simple. Coase claimed that externalities are not caused by markets. Instead, they are caused by a failure to specify property rights so that markets can internalize all costs and benefits. Once such rights are well-defined, if not fully defined, the allocation of scarce resources is accomplished efficiently. As Coase said, the only time externalities can result in market failure, if property rights exist, is when exchange costs are high.

What happens in most pollution situations is this: The polluter emits costly emissions into space occupied by others who have no control over the polluter. Since the persons damaged by the pollution do not "own" the airspace or waterways adjacent to their surface property, they cannot legally claim damages. If they could assert legal ownership to that space, they could either sue for damages or demand a price from the polluter in a regular market transaction. From an efficiency perspective, it makes no difference who is the initial owner of the rights so long as transactions are permitted. If the polluter is assigned the property rights, the pollutee must pay the polluter not to pollute; if the pollutee is given the rights, the polluter must pay to pollute. Fully informed utility maximizers will then arrange a mutually beneficial exchange and arrive at the "correct" amounts of pollution and production. Establishing property rights causes costs and benefits to be internalized and thereby aids in the calculation of efficient courses of action.

Some city governments are creating pollution rights to the airspace above their cities. These rights are also transferable, an important ingredient for their success. In addition to specifying property rights, the government also specifies the maximum amount of emissions that may be generated by polluters. Once these pollution rights are decided, businesses have a powerful market incentive to reduce their own emissions because they can then sell their excess rights to others. A company that closes a plant, reduces operations, or installs more efficient antipollution devices receives emissions credits that may be purchased by new or old firms. The idea is to permit industry to negotiate the prices and details of the tradeoffs as long as the overall level of air pollution in the shed is not increased. When the City of Portland, Oregon, adopted such a policy, businesses quickly learned how to operate in the new market. As might be expected, some individuals soon became brokers in pollution rights. Thus, the traditional function of the middleman has been extended in a most novel way. Companies that propose to build new plants and add to pollution may be established; other concerns are encouraged to reduce their emissions, and everyone is made better off, except perhaps the bureaucrats who might have regulated the matter.

An imaginative restaurateur in Portland, Oregon, who had probably never heard of Coase, applied the theory, in part, to the running of his establishment by offering his patrons a 5 percent discount for not smoking. One of the authors can testify from personal experience that the policy is working well. The owner claims that his business has improved since he adopted the practice: He makes better profits and reduces pollution, and his customers enjoy better dining.

The 1990 Clean Air Act included some innovations along these lines. It allowed polluters to meet SO_2 emissions standards any way they liked, including buying "excess" emissions reductions from other sources able to cut back more than the amount required by the legislation. In this new pollution market, the EPA grants pollution credits to the nation's 101 dirtiest power plants—credits that total just 30 to 50 percent of the sulfur dioxide they now emit. The credits can be swapped or sold. The EPA has chosen the Chicago Board of Trade to run treasury-style auctions in credits that are in addition to those granted the utilities. The auction will be held each March and is open to anyone, including speculators who want to buy pollution credits as investments or environmentalists who want to retire the credits. Portney (1990a) estimates that this approach will save $2 billion to $3 billion annually compared to the amount spent under the 1977 Clean Air Act amendments.

The State of Wisconsin, the City of New York, and Japan have all enacted legislation that enables ownership and transference of airspace rights, and Japan also enacted a sunshine law that guarantees rights to scarce sunshine. New York City's Museum of Modern Art recently helped finance an expansion plan by selling its air rights for $17 million to a developer who will construct a forty-four-story apartment tower above the museum. Again, everyone is made better off—the museum, art patrons, tenants, the developer, and investors in the apartment building. And, lest we forget, the coffers of New York City will gain millions in property taxes.

Market Limitations

Although markets can address water, sunshine, air, and pollution problems, we cannot simply assume that all is well. The Coase theorem has abstract problems that are not easily shed and even if they were the theorem would still face considerable political problems of implementation. At the abstract level, critics have pointed to some highly restrictive conditions, including the fact that transaction and administrative costs must be on the low side. Others have argued that the assignment of the initial rights has profound wealth effects and that everyone will therefore want the original title. The original allocation is also critical because in general the amount that someone will pay to acquire something (say, pollution rights) is often less than the amount we demand to give it up. Who can demand compensation is exceedingly important.

A crucial issue for pollution control is determining the total amount of pollution permitted within the bubble. The decision may and should be influenced by scientific considerations but should not be dominated by such considerations. In democratic processes, citizens are being asked to collectively determine the absolute pollution level. Arriving at a common decision will not be easy, nor is the outcome likely to be optimal. And there have been bitter political battles over attempts to change the levels. These battles, in many instances, spilled over into the rules governing the airshed until the regulations made it nearly impossible for the pollution market to function. Given these public choice problems, we still do not know how effective pollution markets will be.

Even with these difficulties, when compared to the alternatives of taxation, subsidies, and regulation, markets for pollution have much to commend them. One problem with taxation is the obvious one—who will become the tax setters and how will the many tax rates be set? Any such system is bound to become immensely complex and will be subject, of course, to political battles at every session of the legislature or city council. Although a tax system may be efficient in theory, its implementation presents a hornet's nest of logistical problems. Another problem with the tax scheme is its failure to encourage the kind of entrepreneurship and creativity stimulated by property rights.

But the worst consequence of political controls is that they do not get at the heart of the pollution problem; they deal with symptoms. We have argued that the basic problem is that our system incompletely assigns property rights. Markets for pollution provide a way of requiring polluters to pay the costs they impose on others. And by polluters, we mean the ultimate consumers of goods that give rise to pollution. The prices they pay must include the social costs not now taken into account in price setting. Markets for pollution accomplish that end with a minimum of red tape, coercion, and monetary outlays.

Other Environmental Markets

Water markets and markets for pollution are two of the more dramatic applications of property-rights and market principles; there are many others, some of which also test the credulity of conventional thinkers. One example is that proposed by John Baden and Tom Blood (1984) in which they extend these ideas to the preservation and propagation of wild animals. They note that U.S. landowners often support game and other wildlife without compensation and at considerable personal cost. They suggest that such helpful ranchers be rewarded for increasing their conservation practices. This could be done by permitting them to act as wildlife entrepreneurs able to recoup their costs of production by selling their products. Hunting fees should be charged hunters, as is done with conventional private goods. Ranchers and other landowners providing wildlife habitat might be granted tax credits, just as are owners of historical buildings who maintain and refurbish them. "Fee hunting" is being more widely practiced in the United States, especially as the hunting quality on public lands diminishes. But landowners cannot yet sell the animals, although they can sell the right to pursue them, since the animals are owned by the state. Thus, state agencies set bag limits and establish seasons.

Markets for wildlife are widely employed in other nations, including seemingly "socialist" Britain, where private clubs hold fishing rights to certain streams and rivers. The owners of these valuable resources maintain them in far better condition than is usually the case for commonly held properties. Much of Africa's wildlife is threatened with extinction; the wildlife on private game ranches and in a few national parks, however, are the exception. Even Zimbabwe's Marxist regime actively promotes private game ranching as a means of preserving wildlife and bringing in desired foreign currency. In one variation of game ranching, the government granted peasants property rights to wildlife, including elephants, on the communal lands so that they would have incentives to protect "their" animals. Zimbabwe's elephant herds are increasing at a rate in excess of 5 percent per year, whereas Kenya's herds (which are owned only by the government) have become so depleted that they will, in all likelihood, be gone in ten years (Simmons and Kreuter 1989). Zimbabwe and other southern African countries opposed the international ivory trade ban instituted in 1989 because they claimed their programs for moving wildlife into markets was far more effective than programs to remove them from markets.

A powerful example of property rights in action in the United States occurred on the 200,000-acre Deseret Ranch in Utah. The ranch manages cows, sheep, deer, elk, and bison for a profit. Because the ranchers can control the habitat itself and access by hunters, they are able to manage the elk and deer much as they manage the cows, sheep, and bison and charge significant fees for hunting. Although the ranch contains just 0.6 of 1 percent of the elk habitat in the state, it produces 15 percent of Utah's elk. The elk and deer herds have better age-class stratification than those on public lands. The average mule deer buck on the ranch, for example, is a four-point (western count) with a 22-inch spread. On the public lands, by contrast, the average is a two-point with a 12-inch spread.

Baden and Blood note that at present cows are "hardier" than elk; the reason is simple—private-property arrangements. Elk, whales, buffalo, snail darters, and birds will all increase in proportion to the property rights held in them by profit-oriented entrepreneurs. Need we beat the point into the ground by observing that there is no shortage of dogs, cats, horses, sheep, cows, chickens, and pigs?

It has also been proposed, notably by Milton Friedman (1962), that public parks be sold to private investors. Richard Stroup (1990) went one step further and suggested that the national parks be given to "park endowment boards" managed by the leadership of such environmental organizations as the Sierra Club and the Audubon Society. These boards would treat the lands as privately held property. Stroup contends that the parks would be better managed under this arrangement, not because the board's members would care more for the natural resources than the National Park Service does, but because the board would soon adopt such efficient practices as increasing the park fees. Fees would reduce the damages of overuse by the price mechanism, not by fiat. Furthermore, the boards would also begin to "exploit" other currently unused resources found within the parks, including oil and coal deposits, timber, and so on. Revenues from these sales would doubtless be used to maintain and improve the recreational resources and services of the parks as well as to acquire new properties. As the preferences of U.S. citizens move away from plastic goods to natural amenities, Stroup believes, the market for park and environmental services will become a growth industry. One need only note that private entrepreneurs are already in the recreational business: ski lodges, motels, hotels, private lodges, golf and tennis clubs, RV parks, and the like are but a few of the facilities everyone takes for granted.

Why, then, must parks be in the public domain? And why are so many public parks in disrepair, dangerous, and accorded low status? Perhaps property rights have been misplaced. The Nature Conservancy has for more than three decades purchased and protected ecologically valuable properties for preservation and public use. One of the authors has hiked the lovely trails of a Conservancy property located along the Oregon coast not far from Salishan Lodge, one of the top five lodges in the nation and itself a sensitive owner and manager of beautiful forests and ocean beaches, not to speak of restaurants, tennis courts, a golf course, hiking trails, and art galleries. The Nature Conservancy, Salishan Lodge, Deseret Ranch, and Zimbabwe's elephants are just a few examples suggesting that private-property holders can be at least as dedicated as public agencies in protecting the environment and usually can do so more efficiently.

Conclusions

Current environmental policies are based on antipathy for business, support for increasing government intervention and regulation, and a belief that the ecology and economy are conflicting systems. We have suggested just the opposite, that environmental protection would be best achieved by enabling entrepreneurs to hold property rights to environmental resources and relying on market forces. Economy and ecology harmonize when property rights are clear.

From the earlier chapters it should be clear why we believe that only a private, decentralized system can enlist the dispersed knowledge necessary for wise resource management and why we have concluded that a property-rights system is the best way to create the incentives for people to act on that information. The information and incentive problems so easily handled by markets are at the heart of government mismanagement.

Obviously, there are many difficulties with extending markets and property rights that are now controlled politically, but those difficulties are not unique to the environmental arena. And the creative student might attempt to apply lessons from successful privatization programs worldwide to extending property-rights principles to the environment.

Bibliographical Notes

The overproduction of words about the environment is analogous to the externalities environmental activists are so concerned about. Perhaps word pollution should be subjected to the very harsh policies that mainstream environmentalists are so eager to have applied to others, for much of the literature is the policy-equivalent of garbage. There are, however, a handful of works that are valuable, including some famous essays. The first essay is Ronald Coase's extraordinary "The Problem of Social Cost," first published by the *Journal of Law and Economics* 3 (October 1960), 1–44. Without using mathematics or even much economic jargon, Coase correctly diagnoses the nature of externalities and prescribes what needed to be done about them. That essay, plus his 1936 piece on the nature of the firm, garnered him the Nobel Prize. In another essay, "The Lighthouse in Economics," *Journal of Law and Economics* 17 (October 1974), 357–376, Coase examines the claim that lighthouses were public goods and therefore could not be provided privately. He finds that, contrary to conventional wisdom, lighthouse services have been successfully provided by private enterprise. English lighthouses were built, operated, financed, owned, and sold by private individuals whose agents collected tolls at English ports. Coase's lighthouse study suggests that markets may fail less easily than many theorists have thought.

A less famous but most influential article is Steven N.S. Cheung's piece with the intriguing title "The Fable of the Bees: An Economic Investigation," in *Journal of Law and Economics* 16 (1973), in which the Coasean tradition is further refined and applied. Here the externalities—beneficial—of bees and beekeepers are explored in an imaginative exercise of the mind.

A few books and one government report deserve citation. John Baden and Richard Stroup, eds., *Bureaucracy vs. Environment: The Environmental Costs of Bureaucratic Government* (Ann Arbor: University of Michigan Press, 1981), offer fourteen chapters by a diverse set of authors on the harm inflicted on the environment through governmental actions and policies. The subjects range from natural gas policy to the grazing policies of the Bureau of Land Management. Those who assume that governments serve only to correct the externalities of profit-seeking businesses will be surprised and, we hope, dismayed, if not angered, by what the government actually does to our precious environment.

Another extremely interesting and devastating attack on mainstream environmentalism is the book by William Tucker entitled *Progress and Privilege: America in the Age of Environmentalism* (New York: Anchor Press/Doubleday, 1982). Tucker was among the early ones to discover that the environmental movement was not only controlled by the upper middle class but served the very selfish interests of that group. Environmentalists have successfully convinced others not only that the environment is in crisis but also that the resolution of that crisis must assume forms that benefit them. Of course, all this is dressed up in terms of selflessness and the public interest. This phenomenon was earlier documented in a fine case study of how housing policy was shaped in the interests of better-off homeowners and defended in terms of environmental protection. The average prospective homeowner is being hustled by environmental groups protecting their own property. All this and more is richly documented in the case of Marin County, California, by Bernard J. Frieden in *The Environmental Protection Hustle* (Cambridge: MIT Press, 1979).

Terry L. Anderson and Donald R. Leal of the Political Economy Research Center published a short but powerful book on property-rights solutions to environmental problems: *Free Market Environmentalism* (San Francisco: Pacific Research Institute for Public Policy, 1991). Anderson and Leal carefully develop a property-rights approach by examining traditional resource problems and then apply the approach to recreational and environmental problems.

Chapter 9 of *The 1984 Annual Report of the President's Council on Environmental Quality* (Washington, D.C.: Government Printing Office, 1984) provides several examples of far-sighted private environmentalism by for-profit and not-for-profit organizations. Although not at all comprehensive, the chapter is the first published catalogue providing examples of using private-property rights to protect species and enhance habitat more surely and with less confrontation than can be achieved by using the power of government.

References

Ackerman, Bruce A., and William T. Hassler. *Clean Coal/Dirty Air* (New Haven: Yale University Press, 1981).

Baden, John, and Tom Blood. "Wildlife Habitat and Economic Institutions: Feast or Famine for Hunters and Game," *Western Wildlands* 10 (Spring 1984), 8–13.

Coase, Ronald H. "The Problem of Social Cost," *Journal of Law and Economics* 3 (October 1960), 1–44.

Friedman, Milton. *Capitalism and Freedom* (Chicago: University of Chicago Press, 1962).

Haveman, Robert H. *Water Resource Investment and the Public Interest* (Nashville: Vanderbilt University Press, 1965).

Portney, Paul R. "Air Pollution Policy," in Paul R. Portney, ed., *Public Policies for Environmental Protection* (Washington, D.C.: Resources for the Future, 1990a), 27–96.

———. "Policy Watch: Economics and the Clean Air Act," *Journal of Economic Perspectives* 4 (Fall 1990b), 173–181.

Reisner, Marc. *Cadillac Desert* (New York: Viking Press, 1986).

Simmons, Randy T., and Urs Kreuter. "Save an Elephant—Buy Ivory," *Washington Post,* October 1, 1989, D3.

Stroup, Richard L. "Rescuing Yellowstone from Politics: Expanding Parks While Reducing Conflict," in John A. Baden and Donald Leal, eds. *The Yellowstone Primer: Land and Resource Management in the Greater Yellowstone Ecosystem* (San Francisco: Pacific Research Institute for Public Policy, 1990), 169–184.

❦ 10 ❦

Political Pursuit of Private Gain: Coercive Redistribution

THAT MEMBERS OF occupational groups, including well-paid professionals and highly successful businesspeople, seek still greater wealth and income should be no great surprise; they are simply Homo economi, or wealth-maximizing citizens operating in a capitalist and democratic society. That they have a comparative advantage in rent seeking has been shown in some detail. What we have yet to consider are the wealth-maximizing activities of those who have not and are not now doing well in the private economy. Some of these individuals made bad choices; some were born with incurable physical disabilities and never had a chance; some became ill and cannot fend for themselves; some suffer "bad luck"; some are born in hopeless social circumstances; others are improvident; and still others prefer leisure or lower-paying work. In any event, there are some citizens who cannot readily care for themselves. What is to be their fate in a capitalist economy governed by democratic processes?

Most people appear to have some semblance of concern for others, especially those who are close and share a commonality such as family, race, religion, nationality, occupation, class, and so on. Such bonds of potential identification may provide motivation for people to offer care and wherewithal. Altruism is a well-established fact of human existence; its prevalence is easily observed but difficult to count because it occurs in so many private ways. The most prevalent means are so common they are taken for granted; we refer especially to mothers and fathers whose sacrifices are seemingly without bounds. Obviously parents consider a child worth more than the now estimated \$150,000 it takes to raise and see one through college.

At another level, substantial amounts (\$122.6 billion in 1991) are given to charitable causes and organizations, and over 80 percent of that comes from individuals. Although such giving is substantial, it is not likely to identify all those in distress, let alone provide decent care and income to all of them. Much of this charitable funding goes not to the destitute but to civic organizations and activities such as museums, universities, Boy Scouts and Girl Scouts, and the like. That the cost of care for millions of unfortunate people is high goes without saying, but equally important is the public good element in altruism and its concomitant free-rider potential and incentives. Coerced contributions from countless nongivers offers one means of solving the free-rider dilemma. Indeed, and contrary to much opinion, those who initiate redistributive action are not always the intended recipients but rather potential donors. Whereas beneficiaries of redistribution are usually unable to muster sufficient political resources, the well-off donors possess the needed political resources—information, tax incentives, status, and income. By enacting state-directed welfare programs for the less well-off, wealthy donors accomplish two things of immediate importance to themselves: increases in the income of the poor and a reduced personal tax share in providing the higher benefits. State coercion for the good of the less well-off hardly seems an imposition when the donor knows not fellow taxpayers, nor their burdens. And of course, individual taxpayers will hardly know how much they are, in fact, paying for support of the poor. Even if they knew they may approve of the policy and sacrifice because they want to follow a biblical command, fulfill a civic responsibility, or offer the public appearance of doing good.

Expenditures on social welfare programs have grown dramatically for the past three decades. A decent concern for alleviating poverty, even when combined with self-interest, does not, however, exhaust possible explanations of growing welfare budgets. Marxists, as well as some public choice analysts, contend (and not without reason) that state expenditures on the less well-off are rational responses on the part of capitalists to buy off disgruntled and potential revolutionists. Such payments are considered part of the "social capital" of capital economies. Although social unrest may be reduced by such policies, however, we doubt that "the" capitalists in fact consciously act as a group to enact bribe payments. They too face a free-rider problem. Instead, we see other powerful groups that have shared interests in expanding the welfare expenditures of government, including bureaucrats who administer programs, private suppliers of goods and services, politicians who provide public funds, and intellectuals who justify redistribution.

Many of our current social welfare programs were enacted during the New Deal when the normally low unemployment rolls were suddenly increased by millions of otherwise responsible, hard-working people. These working- and middle-class groups did not assume responsibility for their unemployment; instead they demanded that government do something about their plight—a plight not of their own doing. Politicians responded and were rewarded by votes and reelection. Regardless of their ultimate failure in reducing unemployment, President Roosevelt and the Democratic party were hailed for their efforts, commitments, and identification by those whom the party befriended. A new and loyal generation of Democratic voters was created. Self-interest was not only a powerful motivator of voter support for welfare policies; it was also generalized into an ethic for equality based on "entitlements." Subsequent intellectuals of the Left provided appealing arguments for democratic equality to counter the traditional inequality and personal responsibility that are characteristic of the market. Having helped to create the growth industry of redistribution, they increased demand for the use of their scarce polemical skills.

As New Deal and later Great Society redistributive programs proliferated, new agencies came into being and created jobs for those who wanted to do good as well as for those who wished to do well for themselves. Since the taxpaying public will ordinarily not tolerate outright grants or cash transfers, detailed, cumbersome controls were deemed mandatory. And the bureaucrats, even those whose sole motivation is to do good, profit from having to administer the detailed controls and red tape demanded by taxpayers; there is now more good to do requiring still larger budgets. Doing good costs money; doing more good costs more money.

Not all who join government as bureaucrats share the convictions and motivations of their more benevolent predecessors. Some even develop a curious antipathy for the people they serve, and others want nothing more than a secure job and an easy day. Sooner or later, the highly motivated egalitarian ideologue succumbs to bureaucratic routine or is replaced by a self-interested career aspirant. This routinization of benevolence deprives both the do-gooder and the beneficiary of pride, a fact that all reformers ought but seldom respect. Still, we assume that most bureaucrats choose to work in agencies of their preference and that a person who joins the Defense Department prefers to work on defense while a person caring about the problems of the poor chooses to work in a social welfare agency. If this is the case, it confirms the proposition that personal motivations reinforce selfish bureaucratic propensities for enlarging budgets. We are also inclined to the view that most people wish to see their own concerns made into such other-directed concerns that their work becomes socially useful. The mutual reinforcement of these beliefs serves on the one hand to improve employee performance but on the other to increase overall bureaucratic inefficiency, that is, the highly motivated energy of individuals is allocated into socially undesirable projects.

An ideology of equality and entitlement borne of desperate conditions has now taken such hold that even able supporters of effective capitalistic institutions are placed on the defensive. Presidents Reagan and Bush found themselves in the uncomfortable political position of having to justify their actions to reduce overall budgets while asserting that they and Congress had actually increased overall welfare expenditures from $492 billion in 1980 to $956 billion in 1989. They also slowed the rate of increase in federal expenditures to 7.9 percent from 14.6 percent in 1980.

In any case, claims for democratic equality tend to prevail over efficiency and economic inequality. The very wealthy must usually conceal their status, especially if founded on inherited wealth. The birthdays of the capitalists, it should be noted, are not celebrated. Clearly, a person wishing to defend market institutions generating social good not out of intention but from selfish motives has a devilish problem on his hands. Adam Smith's hidden hand provides neither an apparent nor an appropriate way of demonstrating genuine concern. So long as this remains the case, the ideology of capitalism will remain on the defensive.

The Quest for Equality:
Some Inconvenient Facts

The facts about government redistribution from the better off to the less well-off will, ironically, disturb both those who value inequality and those who detest it. As for the facts, one of the most authoritative studies (Hershey 1984) shows that as of 1983, nearly 33 percent of all U.S. citizens received direct benefits from non-means-related programs, mostly from the federal government. Benefits deemed public goods and therefore available to all, such as defense, highways, and education, were not included in the estimates. Most beneficiaries were and remain middle-class citizens entitled to benefits regardless of private income. Social Security, Medicare, railroad retirement benefits, unemployment compensation, educational assistance, and veterans' benefits are the best-known transfers.

In addition, another 19 percent of U.S. citizens were aided by need-based programs more commonly understood as welfare. Here the most prevalent forms of benefits included food stamps and Medicaid. Lesser amounts were spent on Aid to Families with Dependent Children (AFDC) and subsidized rental or public housing. Some 42 million received aid from these programs, whereas nearly 67 million received assistance from the non-means-related benefit programs.

Robert Hershey's data foreshadowed the growth of transfers during the 1980s. The 1991 census data show that 42.2 percent of all families received government transfer payments not including Social Security benefits. One-third of all families having incomes over $25,000 in 1991 received government transfer payments, and more than 50 percent of those making less than $25,000 received transfer payments.

Conservatives are disturbed by these expenditures because they document an extraordinary dependence on government by 40 percent of the nation. Similarly, the figures may disturb both liberals and radicals because they suggest the continual failure of capitalism and a liberal society to adequately provide for its citizens. The latter critics may also contend that although social welfare expenditures are substantial in the aggregate, they are highly deceptive because actual benefits received, especially by welfare recipients, are considered woefully inadequate to sustain a decent life. Although there is truth in both these views we think there are more devastating criticisms to be voiced.

Although social expenditures have increased notably during the past thirty years, little equalization has been accomplished. This inconvenient fact is further buttressed when account is taken of the tax side of the ledger. Although government taxation to the tune of billions of dollars reduces the welfare of those taxed, it does not enhance that of recipients. In short, while vast amounts of money are transferred from one pocket to another, many transfers have the peculiar habit of moving within income groups rather than across them. In other words, members of the same income classes support one another as well as pay the cost of transference.

More depressing still is the "leaky-bucket" phenomenon (Okun 1975); a dollar authorized for the poor usually means they get something worth less than a dollar, with administration, administrators, and suppliers taking the difference. Based on 1991 Census Bureau statistics, it would take expenditures of $50.3 billion to bring the incomes of the 32.5 million living below the government's official poverty line out of poverty. Actual total government spending in 1989 on social welfare totaled $956 million (U.S. Bureau of the Census 1992). The Congressional Research Service estimates that combined federal, state, and local antipoverty spending amounts to $126 billion per year. And Charles Murray estimated in 1984 that since the mid-1970s the total expenditures of all government programs designed to relieve or eliminate poverty had amounted to more than $200 billion per year (in 1980 dollars). No matter whose estimates we use, clearly the welfare bucket has huge leaks.

At this juncture we can make good use of a table and graph, each depicting a somewhat different aspect of the distribution of income and the role of government. Table 10.1 shows the distribution of income in the United States during the period 1950–1990 to have been both highly unequal and persistent; there is virtually no change in the market shares obtained by each quintile.

Figure 10.1, however, demonstrates government's enormous fiscal impact on the distribution of income. When both taxes and transfers at the federal level are examined, it becomes clear that a substantial portion of the population (more than half, probably) profit from their fiscal interactions with the federal government (see Ando, Blume, and Friend 1985). That is, when taxes are subtracted from expenditures, families earning up to about $20,000 per annum (1985) are net beneficiaries. And, interest-

TABLE 10.1   Percentage Income Shares for Families, 1952–1979

| Year | Quintile | | | | | |
	Lowest	2nd	3rd	4th	Highest	Top 5%
1950	4.8	12.0	17.4	23.4	42.7	17.3
1955	4.8	12.3	17.8	23.7	41.3	16.4
1960	4.8	12.2	17.8	24.0	41.3	15.0
1965	5.2	12.2	17.8	23.9	40.9	15.5
1970	5.4	12.2	17.6	23.8	40.9	15.6
1975	5.4	11.8	17.6	24.1	41.1	15.6
1980	5.2	11.5	17.5	24.3	41.5	15.3
1985	4.7	11.0	17.0	24.4	42.9	19.0
1990	4.6	10.8	16.6	23.8	44.3	17.4

SOURCE: U.S. Bureau of the Census, *Statistical Abstract of the United States: 1992*, 112th ed. (Washington, D.C.: U.S. Government Printing Office, 1992), Table 704; U.S. Bureau of the Census, *Statistical Abstract of the United States: 1979*, 99th ed. (Washington, D.C.: U.S. Government Printing Office, 1979), Table 742.

ingly, those who lose are the higher income earners. Those families earning $50,000 or more lose about 25 percent of their income. This raises a most important point: Why do the wealthy permit this loss to occur and why do they apparently approve a transfer to the less well-off? One answer, already given, is that the wealthy may have a sense of noblesse oblige and/or altruistic impulses. Another, also noted above, is that the wealthy are taking out "social insurance" to preserve their position. And still another explanation is based on the notion that the better-off taxpayers are simply minimizing the costs of inevitable redistribution. Unfortunately, motives are not easily attributed. The existing ratios of private and public redistribution and the polity's reasons for adopting certain programs rather than others are important subjects requiring explanation.

Although certain obvious group gains from redistribution have been realized, little progress toward general equality has been achieved. The terrible truth is that most of our antipoverty programs are misplaced and perverse; a poverty class has been perpetuated if not created by a public policy based on being generous. Being politically generous in the short run, however, solves neither the problem of why people are poor nor the problem of why they remain poor. The only realistic policy is one that encourages private economic growth, thereby increasing employment opportunities and real income. But being for growth usually requires public policies that are interpreted by many as initially favorable to the well off. Reduced inflation rates, higher savings, greater investment, improved competitive markets—all provide increased welfare but only indirectly and in the long term. Such policies do not seem to offer immediate assistance to teenaged kids in the

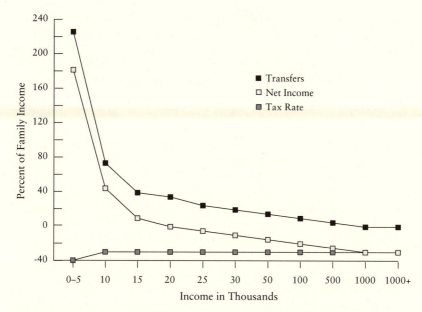

FIGURE 10.1   Taxes and Transfers as a Percent of Family Income
SOURCE: Albert Ando, M. E. Blume, and I. Friend. *The Structure and Reform of the U.S. Tax System* (Cambridge: MIT Press, 1985), Table 2.9.

ghettos, the poor single parent, or the person for whom crime seems a rational pursuit among severely limited legitimate opportunities.

Redistribution in the Real World of Democracy

Our answers to the foregoing questions are really quite simple, and once the basic premises of the analysis are accepted everything follows in a straightforward manner. People make use of government, as they do all social institutions, for the purpose of advancing their own welfare, and this objective is accomplished primarily by demanding special benefits and dispersing their costs among others. Even in seeking more general or essentially public goods they may profit through being suppliers to government of those goods. And, of course, they seek to minimize their share of the tax burden. Since no citizen can achieve these goals alone, coalition partners are sought, partners just sufficient in number to win and sometimes individually "weaker" than the person seeking allies. A small coalition ensures that the costs of the rent seeking will be less than the sought-after gains of income redistribution, and the "weakness" condition maximizes one's share of the winnings. The problem, of course, is that everyone becomes a member of many coalitions and is forced therefore to pay out substantial rent-seeking and protection costs as well as increased benefits for all other coalitions. In short, we all run the risk of having our own benefits out-weighed by the increasing costs of supporting the gains of countless others. But this is a highly uncertain calculation; we simply do not have an accurate public accounting system to handle all the transactions.

It is important to emphasize that, in the U.S. polity, redistribution is accomplished by direct and indirect transfers and most of the latter are unintentional. Even direct expenditures on pure public goods generate unwanted redistribution. Equal consumption necessarily means that some citizens must "consume" more than they wish while others are coerced into consumption levels short of their ideals. Thus, no public expenditure or tax instrument is ever revenue neutral. Private market choices are necessarily affected.

Because all fiscal and monetary policies are redistributive, they are controversial, and because none are ever simple in their workings, redistribution will take place in such a manner that identifying all beneficiaries and taxpayers is most difficult. Accordingly, we should not expect that simplistic predictions about vertical redistribution will hold true. Redistribution may take place along horizontal lines, that is, within a single class grouping, and may proceed upward as well as downward in the overall class "structure." As to the former possibility, cross-subsidies, such as long-distance phone users subsidizing local users, provide a beautiful example. Then, too, an individual may sometimes do very well while at other times not so well. That is one but hardly the only reason why the Congress enacts "transition rules" to ease unexpected burdens resulting from important changes in tax laws. Whenever vast new government programs come into being the consequences are apt to be widespread, consequential, and somewhat unpredictable. And worse, neither the beneficiaries nor the harmed may have any good idea of their fate or how it was decided. The macro or aggregate results summed up by income category in some table or graph are usually not terribly helpful in explaining unique outcomes for individual citizens. Individual situations are usually bewilderingly complex and, of course, special.

Despite these general cautions it would appear that certain generalizations can be made about who gets what. In the first place, most social scientists, and especially political scientists, claim that transfers generally move from the less- to the more-organized citizens. Political scientists who analyze interest groups have long maintained that it can be no other way, and modern public choice confirms that earlier proposition. The argument in support of the idea is the familiar claim that special-interest organizations have all the political advantages, including incentives, organization, resources, votes, and weaker opponents. At the same time, the politician has a powerful incentive to not only comply but positively advance the concerns of the demanders.

But there is one notable fact that cannot be overlooked or minimized when discussing redistribution from the well off to the less well-off; the latter are not normally thought to be politically powerful. If this is the case, how are we to account for vast public expenditures for the advancement of low-income people? Public choice scholars have confronted this theoretical dilemma in a variety of ways but mostly by arguing some version of contractual theory. According to this approach, either risk-averse voters choose to insure themselves over the long period of income fluctuation or the wealthier citizenry attempts to protect their status by using public funds to bribe the discontented. We do not deny the intellectual appeal of the contractual approach, but first of all, it is clear that citizens are never offered such clear-cut voting choices, and second, politicians make partial policies in the immediate context of electoral and legislative struggles. They do not vote directly on overall welfare policy; rather, they confront special welfare programs dealing with specific difficulties facing specific groups.

It is fairly clear that the truly poor do receive substantial benefits but receive far fewer than those immediately above them. Welfare policies deal with specific contingencies such as unemployment; poverty among mothers with dependent children and absent husbands; old age; mental illness. Those citizens who suffer from incurable conditions such as mental retardation or physical disabilities must obviously depend upon the goodwill of others. But even here there are interested persons, including the family and public bureaucrats as well as private philanthropic agencies, wanting additional help. Although obvious altruism is involved, self-interest is not thereby precluded. A welfare industry exists, and it consists not only of the aided and potential beneficiaries but of an entire bureaucratic apparatus— both public and private—to deliver services, income, and benefits-in-kind. Nor should we overlook rent-seeking producers who supply the resources employed by the industry. Whenever surplus food programs, school lunches, and the like are debated in the Congress, highly subsidized farmers and their lobbyists are among the conspicuous log rollers. Promoting the welfare of the farm sector is not incompatible with advancement of the urban poor. But under the current system, advancing the welfare of both is achieved by the least efficient means.

That altruism does not provide a fully satisfactory basis for explaining public welfare has been demonstrated, but even if altruism did provide an adequate explanation we would be left with thorny problems of explaining how much welfare should be offered, for whom, and by what means. Although private donors supply immense amounts of charity (more than $122 billion in 1990), much of it comes from relatively small numbers of wealthy people and their organizations. Of course, the mere existence of public welfare is an important cause of the low overall rates of charitable giving; why give voluntarily when you will in any case be forced to pay taxes? And this is so even though the tax laws are designed to encourage greater contributions. The fact remains that most people are otherwise unwilling to implement their public charitable impulses with more than, say, 3 percent of their income. This constricted sense of obligation is further supported by the unwillingness of Americans to adopt a negative income-tax law—a law that would reduce the inefficiencies of benefits-in-kind as well as reduce controls exercised over recipients. Generous Americans apparently approve of, if not insist upon, detailed controls over the use by recipients of official aid. In short, they are not at all convinced that beneficiaries will make the best use of discretionary income grants. Put crudely, many middle-class citizens believe that low-income persons will spend their money not on milk and bread but on liquor and drugs and less nutritious foods.

Distributive Justice in a Transfer Society

The volume of involuntary transfers in contemporary democracies is, as we have seen, overwhelming. That volume can and should be reduced and redirected in significant ways. State redistribution is not morally superior to that of markets or private charity. In fact, political distribution is at once both more impersonal and personally arbitrary than is the case with distribution by private institutions. Large-scale redistribution necessarily involves large-scale bureaucracies with all their inefficiencies and impersonal treatment of the individual. At the same time, discretionary choices on the part of legislator and bureaucrat make the citizen peculiarly dependent on what can only be viewed as arbitrary decisions. Those who choose to live by the state make a precarious choice. In short, while markets produce distributive outcomes that do not satisfy all, the polity can rarely satisfy anyone for long. Rent seekers, whether traditional producer groups or low-income claimants, must devote far too much of their time and resources to unproductive activity merely to protect what they have. Fervent pursuers of equality are apt to be bitterly disappointed because they are frequently outmaneuvered by wealthier rent-seekers. When the poor are taxed to support the middle and upper classes, it is not only galling but, perhaps, poetic justice for those who seek redress via the state. But the worst consequence is the sacrifice of individual liberty entailed by governmentally guaranteed income flows. To protect one citizen it becomes necessary not only to control others but also, to add insult to injury, to reduce their incomes arbitrarily. Coerced, collective altruism also fails to dignify the donor or recipient since coercion promotes mutual resentment. Finally, collective aid is not altruistic but coerced.

And who is to speak for the superior when greater equality prevails? Is it not an injustice to reward equally those offering superior skill, hard work, and greater contributions to society and those possessing less skill, less motivation, and making lesser contributions to society? Why should the free rider be paid the same as the dedicated, hard-working contributor? We doubt that, without recognition, contributors will continue to make the same efforts with the same beneficial effects. Some may even come to believe they are suckers. The high salaries paid to Michael Jordan, Pinchas Zukerman, Vladimir Horowitz, Paul Newman, and innumerable transitory rock stars are not only earned but constitute a measure of the esteem in which they are held by appreciative Americans and others. As individuals we do not hold them in the same esteem; still, we should not wish to deny their high incomes when countless others are more than willing to purchase expensive tickets to see and hear them in live performances. The willingness of American youth to pay top dollar to African-American entertainers has quite possibly done more to equalize race relationships than all governmental policies together (see Nozick 1974). In fact, imperfect markets have done more to advance the material well-being of the less fortunate than all that government could ever hope to achieve. Rewarding inequality whenever it serves to improve the lot of the least advantaged finds justification in common sense as well as in the philosophical arguments of John Rawls (1971).

We wonder, moreover, whether what Americans really mean by greater equality is purely an economic matter. What is wanted is greater equality of opportunity, a preference documented in countless public opinion polls. A freer private economy will not only reduce the role of government in pursuing that ideal but also generate more opportunities than are possible under any politically feasible or likely combination of governmental policies seeking income equality.

Americans not only value equality of opportunity; they value their privacy and their right to be different. Protagonists of equality never, it seems, make clear precisely what, other than wealth and income, should be equalized. Must everyone dress alike? Live in the same houses with the same furniture? Eat uniform meals? These are not rhetorical questions to be dismissed as the mouthings of an irritable, impatient, self-designated "aristocrat." De Tocqueville observed that the marginal importance of differences increases as equality is achieved. If this observation is correct, the egalitarian faces a serious dilemma. If everyone had the same income they would still trade possessions because their diverse preferences, or tastes in consumption, would require trades. Invidious comparisons cannot be avoided even in the equal society.

Most of all we appeal for a new approach to distributive questions. For too long the egalitarians have dominated the debate, set the issues, selected the premises, and put others on the defensive. Those who entertain any skepticism about political redistribution have been branded as uncaring, insensitive, and elitist. What is desperately needed is a reshaping of the agenda of debate. We must not concede that everything in life is a zero-sum game in which the powerful necessarily dominate choices. The fact that some possess more wealth than others does not imply a capacity to coerce others. Wealth is accumulated by activities that increase opportunities available to others. One need only consult the yellow pages of the telephone directory to see the enormous number of businesses that were created by the invention of the auto, assembly line, and more recently, the computer. Nearly all of these business are *small,* making small annual profits, but in the aggregate they employ millions of well-paid workers and serve the expanding needs of countless consumers.

These firms came into existence not by governmental dictate but by the entrepreneurial aspirations and skills of otherwise ordinary people. A complex, large economy such as ours offers an extraordinary array of opportunities, but mostly it offers the liberty to invent opportunities, to perceive and create "wants" where none exist. And for those entrepreneurs in need of investment funds, there are monies to be had. Banks and investment firms actively seek outlets, as do families in the pursuit of profit. The material well-being and self-regard of hundreds of millions of people have been advanced far more by the mundane daily workings of imperfect markets than by governments bent on redistribution and equality.

Bibliographical Notes

Much of politics in the twentieth century pertains to the efforts of some to have market distributions of wealth and income redistributed by political actors and processes. The term "welfare state" is frequently employed to describe what has taken place in democracies. For liberals, this development has been a welcome one. We believe it to be an unfortunate trend that we hope is peaking and possibly diminishing. In any case, the literature on what has occurred and whether it has been good or bad is voluminous. We do not pretend to have read more than a small fraction of what has been written.

Two of our favorites are not particularly well known but deserve to be: Yair Aharoni's *The No-Risk Society* (Chatham, N.J.: Chatham House, 1981) and Dan Usher's *The Economic Prerequisite to Democracy* (New York: University of Columbia Press, 1981). The first book catalogues and discusses a vast array of government programs that shift the risk from individuals and businesses to society, that is, to others. Dan Usher's book rather incisively argues that the market is a far better institution for distributive questions than are political processes. He also contends that democracy is unstable because of the incentives and opportunities presented to all citizens to plunder one another. Majority rule is one of the facilitating rules or institutions.

Another useful work that deals with a favorite liberal concern, that is, improving the lives of the poor but from a conservative perspective, is a book by Stuart Butler and Anna Kondratas, *Out of the Poverty Trap: A Conservative Strategy for Welfare Reform* (New York: The Free Press, 1987). The authors are noted members of the Heritage Foundation, a conservative think tank. They present challenging explanations of the existence of the poverty trap and devise imaginative policies for getting people out of it. They cite any number of successful efforts led by the poor themselves. Getting the government out of the poverty industry is the single most important policy axiom. Dependency is but one product of well-meaning welfare programs.

The two big books that must be confronted are, of course, John Rawls's *A Theory of Justice* (Cambridge: Harvard University Press, 1971) and Robert Nozick's *Anarchy, State, and Utopia* (New York: Basic Books, 1974). These two volumes by distinguished colleagues in Harvard's Philosophy Department set forth the foundations for judging fairness and for explaining the minimal state. The basic questions of each are different, but both authors manage nevertheless to define their concerns in such a way that the books are competitors in the field of justice and the modern state. Both books have stimulated much scholarly response and will endure.

References

Ando, Albert, Marshall E. Blume, and Irwin Friend. *The Structure and Reform of the U.S. Tax System* (Cambridge: MIT Press, 1985).

Hershey, Robert D. "US Study Finds Nearly 3 Out of 10 Get Benefits," *New York Times,* September 27, 1984, B10.

Murray, Charles. *Losing Ground: American Social Policy, 1950–1980* (New York: Basic Books, 1984).

Nozick, Robert. *Anarchy, State, and Utopia* (New York: Basic Books, 1974).

Okun, Arthur M. *Equality and Efficiency: The Big Tradeoff* (Washington, D.C.: Brookings Institution, 1975).

Rawls, John. *A Theory of Justice* (Cambridge: Harvard University Press, 1971).

U.S. Bureau of the Census. *Statistical Abstract of the United States: 1992,* 112th ed. (Washington, D.C.: U.S. Government Printing Office, 1992).

❀ 11 ❀

Micro-Politics
of Macro-Instability

ECONOMIC INSTABILITY PERSISTS despite the best efforts of political leaders, other public figures, and economists. Although pure and permanent stability may not be desirable, many people seem to place a very high value on reducing, if not eliminating, business cycles. In short, although stability is highly valued across a broad spectrum of society, it remains unrealized. In this chapter, we aim in part to explain the discrepancy.

As outlined in Part One, economic instability is thought by many to be an inherent tendency of the market economy. Many older Keynesians and most Marxists who share this pessimistic if not apocalyptic vision have defined the problem for decades; that they mislead makes little difference. Like Joseph Schumpeter, we believe that market economies are unstable but that the resultant instability is the by-product of some otherwise highly desirable properties of the economy. Schumpeter (1942) summed up this economic principle, aptly, as "creative destruction." Business cycles are not to be denied; they were, are, and always will be with us. Unfortunately, a once resilient market economy is now so buffeted by political forces that the most important cause of modern economic fluctuations is not the economy but the polity. Readers of the *Wall Street Journal* know all too well that their fortunes are often decided less by Wall Street than by Washington, D.C., less by the profit-and-loss column than by the vote calculus. Governmental failure, or politically generated instability, is a consequence of two basic factors characterizing politics: economic ignorance and the self-interests of political decisionmakers, including voters, interest groups, politicians, and bureaucrats.

Uninformed Governments

Let us begin with a generous recognition of the task confronted by government: The world is a highly uncertain place, and the theories and information provided by economists on macro-policies are woefully deficient. Economists do not know the workings of the economy in the sense that physicists know their universe; one reason for this deficiency, among others, is the lack of economic constants. Even when macro-economists agree on the relevant variables, they cannot agree on long-term forecasts or even short-run predictions. Data are rarely current, they are often incomplete, and they are seldom very reliable. Sizable ranges of uncertainty must be attached to all estimates, and one must expect that unexpected shocks—mostly political—can occur at any time to upset the most finely tuned and sophisticated monetary and fiscal advice. Knowing the current state of the economy is never likely to be very easy or reassuring. Since we cannot undo the past or know the future, large and frequent errors are to be expected.

But even if economists were able to capture an accurate picture at any one time, they would soon discover that it was outdated. Data are costly and time-consuming to collect, and the necessary collective action required to act on that information slow and uncertain. The time lags between adoption of, say, an expenditure program and its implementation are apt to number in months and even years. The multiplier effects of spending take time—usually too much time.

Scholars and politicians have assumed that they can know the effects of policy changes, that is, that if they alter a tax rate or spend a certain sum of public money on a particular type of activity, they can then accurately trace out the economic impact of those changes. The fact of the matter is that they have little reason to be confident. For example, the Reagan administration thought it knew what would happen to both demand and supply when reductions in the federal income tax were enacted during 1981 and 1986. It seems that the administration's optimistic estimates of dramatic improvements in both were seriously in error. Economic agents did not respond in ways predicted by Arthur Laffer. Then, too, economists really do not know the effects of major budgetary deficits, nor do they know what sequence they will follow. Some argue that all the effects are bad, including inflation and the crowding out of private investment, while others contend that at times they may be good and still others claim they are essentially neutral. Such confusion seems inexplicable to noneconomists. No wonder most presidents show little enthusiasm for their meetings with the Council of Economic Advisers.

To make things still worse, some theorists maintain that without major shocks governments are unable to "outsmart" people with changes in economic policy. Whatever countercyclical fiscal and monetary policies might be adopted are defeated because informed, rational citizens respond with counteractions to protect themselves in the market. Since policy is negated, it is wasteful. Unless a new policy is a complete surprise, it will fail to achieve the desired effects. If one accepts this rational-expectations analysis, one must conclude that macro-policy is largely futile.

With less threatening premises the economic adviser is still in difficulty because knowledge of the right variables does not easily translate into advice on how much spending and taxing is enough. How drastic must policies be to achieve the desired effects? And what if expectations change as a result of policy changes? In short, macro-policy advice is something economists should offer with humility rather than confidence. Ironically, leftist thinkers whose distaste for economics is well-known are the very persons demanding the most from economists. Their planned societies require economic knowledge that is unobtainable; governments are neither omniscient nor omnicompetent.

Self-Interest in Instability

Although students of international politics have long known that governments take advantage of and manipulate foreign events for their own purposes, economists and even political scientists have only lately begun to appreciate the role of political self-interests in economic instability. Ordinary citizens are well aware of the fact that campaigning politicians base their efforts on the presumed state of the economy, but few realize how politicians in office attempt to use governmental policy to influence elections. To some extent, politicians have created a political business cycle. Spending and taxing policies designed to improve their own electoral chances contribute to exaggerated economic fluctuations. And market fluctuations, in turn, provide rhetorical ammunition for politicians wanting to inject the government still more into economic life.

Actually, stability in politics benefits neither the politician nor the bureaucrat; neither would have the wealth, income, power, or status that accrue when there is more to do and nothing is done. Paradoxically, politicians become more important, have more money to spend, and derive more ego rewards if the economy is believed not to work right. Bureaucrats may be expected to demand larger budgets when contending with economic insecurity. We note, too, that Keynesian economists find more work and status when fighting unemployment or even inflation than they would if their only employment was in studying a steady-state economy, and even public choice analysts have a self-interest in complaining about large and active governments.

For politicians, fighting unemployment, if not inflation, is rewarding. Fighting unemployment brings out the compassion of liberal politicians and enables more money to be spent on helpful activities. Lowering taxes and spending more money creates not only economic but political good. Appearing to fight inflation and deficits is also politically astute. Actually fighting them may be political suicide. Since politicians recognize that most people view inflation as a negative force, most of the time they rail against it. But inflation also increases the revenues of government, usually at a rate faster than the rate of inflation. If prices rise by, say, 10 percent, revenues will increase by, say, 15 percent. The discrepancy comes about because of progressive rate structures. The more one earns the greater the rate of marginal taxation. Politicians appreciate this feature of the tax structure because it provides automatic revenue increases without having to publicly pass tax increases. So politicians, including the conservative ones, have somewhat ambivalent feelings about reducing taxes. Of course, in reducing the marginal rates, the 1986 Federal Income Tax Reform Act counters this automatic source of revenue.

Inflation also presents politicians with the opportunity to campaign for governmental controls (e.g., incomes policies) over the economy, a self-serving policy supported by some liberal and many new left economists. Wage and price controls have exerted a fatal fascination for centuries. The uninformed believe that if prices rise, controls will in fact stop further increases. From such myths controls are born and the bureaucracy needed to administer them.

Politically Manipulated Business Cycles

Sabotaging the economy is not deliberate. It is an inadvertent product of politically purposive actions inspired by the dominion of political incentives. Instead of alleviating cyclical difficulties, the sum total of economic policies often promotes disorder beneficial to a few citizens, mostly the political classes. These self-interests manifest themselves in a political business cycle.

Incumbent governments have shown a distinct propensity to adopt inflationary policies during the year or two prior to elections—not because they wish to increase inflation but because they want to decrease unemployment, a good in most voter minds. Spending to diminish unemployment, especially if accompanied by budgetary deficits, has the unfortunate effect of increasing pressure on the price level. Although preelection unemployment is artificially lowered, inflationary tendencies assert themselves after the election and in so doing anger increasing numbers of citizens. Anti-inflationary policies then seem in order, and a cycle of contrary or restrictive policies is superimposed over the electoral cycle. It might make considerable economic sense for a government to navigate a steady course between unemployment and inflation, but such a course most certainly would not constitute political success. Governments are not solely to blame, however, for voters actually prefer the succession of policies generating the instability they presumably do not want. Voters, it seems, act as though the immediate present is more important than vague memories of the past and a still more vague and uncertain future. Thus, voters are said to be myopic.

The political business cycle is illustrated in simple fashion in Figure 11.1, where the rates of inflation and unemployment are arrayed on the vertical dimension and the electoral periods on the horizontal line. The optimal political business cycle, or mix of two lines, indicates the course of unemployment and inflation rates. The rate of inflation rises over the electoral period and should reach its maximum just after an election, whereas the rate of unemployment should fall continuously between elections. Rational government will attempt to dampen inflation shortly after an election and will do so by implementing policies that necessarily increase the unemployment rate. Although this highly stylized model does not accurately portray the actual, messy course of events, it does serve to show typical intentions and policy choices. Although governments are indeed powerful, they cannot usually fine-tune the fiscal and monetary policies necessary to produce the model shown in Figure 11.1. The fact of the matter is that power is diffused and information limited; the citizenry soon learn that they can partially counter this obvious Machiavellian electoral strategy.

It should be noted, nevertheless, that several empirical studies have shown the existence of a political business cycle. For example, Bruno Frey and Friedrich Schneider (1981) found systematic evidence of such a cycle for the period of 1959 to 1974 in the United Kingdom. They discovered that a fall in the inflation rate of 1 percent increased the government's lead by 0.6 percent, whereas a fall in unemployment by 1 percent increased the

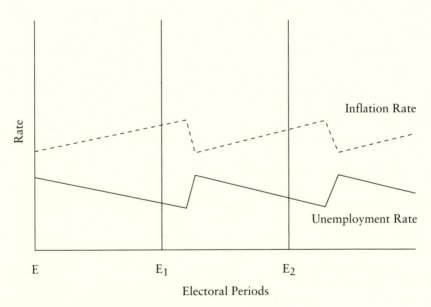

FIGURE 11.1 The Political Business Cycle

lead by a remarkable 6 percent. Fighting unemployment is definitely a superior political strategy, or at least it was during the period studied. All governments over this period in the UK were found to expand expenditures and reduce taxation when their leads in popularity were low. When their popularity was high, they were able to pursue more ideological policies without fear of retribution by voters. Evidence of the political business cycle is also strongly suggested by the monetary policies pursued by the presumably independent Federal Reserve Board from 1959 through 1981. Figure 11.2 shows that, of six presidential elections, four witnessed an expanded money supply prior to each election and a contraction soon after. Careful readers will also note that the scale on the vertical axis shows an increase over time from 3 percent in 1970 to 17 percent in 1986.

Some observers contend that the political business cycle was negated by the Reagan administration; we think not. The recession that plagued the first two or more years of Reagan's term began before he came into office; moreover, although Reagan reduced spending in some categories from what it might have been under Carter, he increased it in other areas, notably defense. In the end, the absolute size of the budget increased but at a lower rate than it might have under Carter, and deficits rose to their highest level in history. Despite income-tax cuts in 1981 and 1986, the total tax bill for most taxpayers increased. For these taxpayers, gains realized from the 1981 and 1986 reductions were more than equaled by greater Social Security payments, not to speak of other increases stemming from the 1984 and 1990 income-tax laws and various state and local tax increases. Handcrafted by political experts, Republican and Democrat alike, the 1984 measure did not become burdensome prior to the 1984 presidential and congressional elections. Enactment, in an election year, sounded "responsible" and seemed like a violation of the preelectoral business cycle, but the actual effects were all delayed. Worse, taxpayers were told that taxes were not increased; they were "reformed" so as to eliminate egregious loopholes and render the code simpler and somewhat fairer to all. Simplicity disappeared at the start of the reform process and fairness vanished when the politicians decided it was easier to get corporations to collect taxes in the form of higher prices. Again the rhetoric of revenue enhancement won out.

Although the rate of stagflation (what Arthur Okun aptly called the "Misery Index," that is, the sum of the rates of inflation and unemployment) was considerably reduced (from 18 percent to less than 10 percent) during Reagan's first term, the reduction was accomplished less by a repeal of the political business cycle than by the monetary policies of the Carter Federal Reserve Board. Slowing the growth of the money supply overcame the stimulative effects of administration fiscal policy and created a fairly deep recession. Owing to increased spending on unemployment insurance and other social welfare programs, the tax revenues of the federal govern-

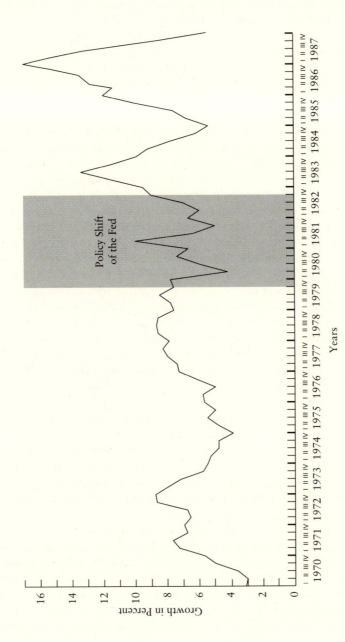

FIGURE 11.2   The Yearly Growth in the Money Supply (M1), 1970–1987

SOURCE: U.S. Bureau of the Census. *Statistical Abstract of the United States: 1990*, 110th ed. (Washington, D.C.: U.S. Government Printing Office, 1990), p. 506.

ment were insufficient; consequently, budgetary deficits and interest on the debt were increased by substantial amounts. These deficits are not necessarily worrisome during a recession but they do pose problems during recovery. A sustained recovery depends on the government adopting policies not likely to win much favor among congressional politicians. Reductions in spending and/or tax increases constitute the only credible strategies. President Reagan and his successor did not wish to reduce defense spending, and Democrats in Congress fought cuts in entitlement programs. Since these two forms of spending constitute most of the budget, there was little chance of success. Tax increases have little electoral appeal to politicians. Democrats may be more willing to pass increased tax measures than Republicans are, but they do not want to increase the taxes of the middle class or of lower income groups, nor do they wish to raise taxes during election years. That leaves the few upper-income taxpayers who, even if taxed at confiscatory rates, would not be able to finance the huge deficits. Despite a remarkable recovery (18 million new jobs) during the 1980s, the political business cycle has not been repealed by courageous and knowledgeable politicians facing up to their responsibilities. Although inflation was reduced by the 1990s to about 3 percent, unemployment in 1991–1992 grew to more than 7 percent. And, of course, deficits are at all-time highs.

A Note on Supply-Side Economics

Although much was written during the 1980s on "supply-side economics" and its notable role in Reagan policies, relatively little attention has been accorded its political relevance. A discussion of the political business cycle affords a convenient opportunity to do so. Although the economic virtues of this strategy of "pouring old wine into new bottles" are certainly debatable, there can be little debate about the political attractiveness of a program of policies based on the Laffer curve. A policy promising to increase government revenues by reducing tax rates is bound to win widespread favor. What liberals resist is the explanation and its implied approval of the private economy and the deregulation that accompanies much of supply-side analysis. Liberals have not been convinced that lowering taxes even by significant amounts has the predicted incentives effects. As is so often the case in economics, measuring the precise effects has proven devilishly difficult; as a result, everyone can maintain his or her own faith without much fear of falsification by empirical tests. In any case, supply-side economics may be viewed, for all practical purposes, as the extreme Right's ideological equivalent to the traditional Keynesian faith in macro-economics. Both provide the necessary rationale for combining "good" economics and "good" politics.

Just how supply-side economics is supposed to work is shown in the

form of the famous Laffer curve, which attempts to relate the rate of taxation with the size of governmental revenues. Figure 11.3 is a reproduction
of that relationship (see also Figure 7.1 and accompanying discussion).
This graph is of interest not only because of its substantive content but
because of its political implications. The figure shows that, except for that
point at which maximum revenues are obtained, all other quantities of revenue can be obtained by either of two rates of taxation, a higher and lower
rate. Thus, R_I can be achieved with either rates T_I or T_2. If our general
analysis is correct we should expect that a vote-maximizing government
ought to prefer the lower rate (T_I) since that would minimize collection
costs and taxpayer anger. As one reads the curve from left to right, the tax
rate increases as revenues increase to a maximum found at C, but there-
after tax rate increases lead to a fall in total revenues. The latter occurs
because taxpayers find less incentive to work and greater incentives to
avoid paying taxes. Presumably, at the lower rates they will continue to

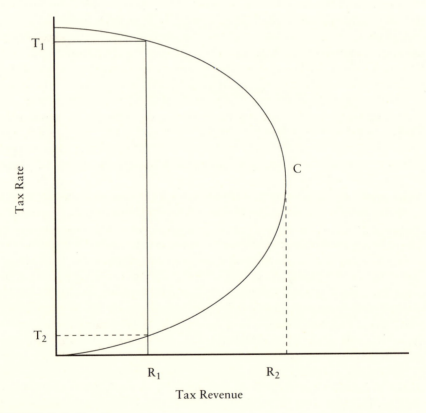

FIGURE 11.3   Tax Revenue

work hard as well as pay their taxes. Another way of saying this in more technical terms is that the activity being taxed will decline at a faster percentage rate than that at which the tax rate itself increases. Although it is in the government's interest to use the lower rate, given revenue "needs," it is also quite possible that the higher rates may prevail. Taxes are enacted for other reasons than revenue, and governments are, as we have seen, poorly informed and necessarily shortsighted. Governments may believe the curve is as depicted in the dashed lines. And lest we forget, taxes are sometimes supported as appropriate punitive measures, as is the case with some environmental and all sin taxes. Finally, of course, once a tax is enacted it is difficult to repeal.

One problem with the Laffer analysis is that careful analysts are just beginning to empirically establish the "exact" shape and position of the curve, and it appears there is not a single, determinate general curve. That fact, however, does not diminish the political uses of Laffer's theory.

Micro-Basis of Macro-Policies

Students of micro-economics or price theory have long bemoaned the tendency of Keynesian macro-economists to ignore well-established principles of individual choice and behavior when devising spending and taxing policies. The great aggregates of macro-analysis—saving, investment, consumption—are so defined that their composition appears neutral. All a government need do is construct a gigantic econometric model showing how government-induced changes in one or more of the aggregate variables will produce beneficial alterations in the others. The individuals and firms making up the real economy are really ignored because their choices are thought to be infinitely amenable to policy changes. The trouble is that macro-level changes must be consonant with the micro-foundations of individual choice. Since human nature cannot be ignored, incentives, prices, information, and expectations must be included, for they shape individual responses to changing environments. Fortunately, we need not create some new economics that will take account of individual choice; two hundred years of micro-economics have provided a solid basis on which to assess and base macro-policies. Conditioned by years of Keynesian supremacy, many economists and others ignore these verities. Elementary principles of the market are really quite universal, and as we have taken pains to point out, they are applicable far beyond the marketplace. Here we are concerned with the relevance of the market for macro-policy.

Taking the market seriously leads to quite different macro-policies than those to which we have been accustomed. But what is the micro-wisdom? In the first place, macro-policy should be based on the axiom that individuals are maximizers, mostly of their own income and wealth or welfare.

How they respond then depends on relative prices and taxes and not on the overall price level or aggregate averages and aggregate policies. In short, effective policies must take into account the detailed composition of the great aggregates. Nowhere is this principle more true than in the composition of the labor force. Unemployment policies not based on the changing nature of the population and of unemployment are doomed. Unfortunately, much earlier Keynesian analysis was fixated on the Great Depression, when the bulk of the unemployed were adult men. In contrast, today's unemployed tend to be youth and/or individuals in families containing employed workers. These individuals are not usually skilled, trained workers; rather, they lack skills and/or job experience or have the wrong skills. They remain unemployed because they are not employable in their present state. Then, too, many who find themselves unemployed have become so because of personal choice and are really between jobs. Fortunately for them, their unemployment is for a short time and cushioned by personal savings, family resources, and a variety of welfare programs and unemployment insurance. The new micro-economics suggest that these facts negate a great deal of Keynesian policy; unfortunately, one of the costs of these policies is that they may prolong unemployment and thereby further distort the allocation of resources. Since leisure is now made much less costly to both employee and employer, incentives are perversely affected; employment is discouraged. In the Netherlands and the United Kingdom, it hardly pays to look for work when for two or more years one can receive monthly incomes nearly equal to the earned wages. To deal with people between jobs and those without skills or with outmoded skills, government must surely devise policies that are different from those that were designed in the 1930s to deal with the massive involuntary unemployment of the Great Depression.

At the same time that economists are revitalizing the old explanations of unemployment they are also rethinking some other old lessons and their application to new circumstances, namely, decisions to save and invest. In short, much U.S. economic policy enacted since the depression has discouraged savings and investment. These policies are based on both a theoretical condemnation of savings and an obvious political strategy favoring borrowers. Consumption, savings, and investment are, according to Keynesian analysis, separate, uncoordinated decisions containing the seeds of their own destruction. In a depression, savings constitute an individually rational course of action leading to collective disaster. According to Keynes there can be too much saving, insufficient investment, and too little consumption. Since saving is now deficient, investment is also deficient. Far too many public policies have contributed to this bleak outlook.

Because the tax code has permitted borrowers to deduct interest costs from their taxable income, borrowers have been encouraged through tax subsidies to perpetuate their habit. We ourselves are among the millions whose borrowing via home mortgages and credit cards has been considerably eased by these tax subsidies. Those who choose to save find that they will be penalized because their earnings will be taxed not once but twice, first when income is earned and again when that invested income earns interest—even when the interest income was lower than the inflation rate. Naturally, the demand for borrowed money is increased, as personal private indebtedness clearly demonstrates.

That capital formation has become a major problem for Americans is no surprise. With the federal government competing for funds, private businesses find themselves "crowded out" of the capital market. A reduction in government borrowing would do much to ease the situation. But at the individual level potential savers and investors find that incentives to save and invest have been skewed to such an extent that they simply save and invest less than is desirable. The 1986 elimination of interest deductibility in the tax code will serve to redress the incentives of credit card users—but interest payments on homes are still tax deductible. Another beneficial provision would be to allow income earned from interest accounts to be exempt from taxation. Corporate tax rates should be reduced and government forced to rely more on consumption taxes. Such actions are consistent with the micro-foundations of price theory as well as the principles of social psychology. Reward those behaviors that are socially beneficial and tax the inefficient choices.

Although these reforms would help, so long as government engages in massive borrowing, saving and investing will be penalized. This must be because government has but three ways of financing deficits—raising taxes, borrowing, or printing money—and all tend to discourage work and productivity. If government raises taxes it reduces the incentive to work; if government borrows it competes with private borrowing and raises the interest rates; and finally, if government indulges in printing more money it creates inflation with all its attendant problems for more risky investment decisions.

Although laudable, these policy proposals confront persistent biases in American political institutions—biases stemming from powerful and perverse incentives. Since governmental decisions are rarely based on the economic criteria of marginal costs and benefits, policymakers have no definitive way of knowing whether the GNP is increased or decreased by more public and less private spending. In comparing alternative spending programs, they are left at a loss because they cannot scientifically decide whether, say, building public housing is more important than adding a new bomber to the Air Force.

Keynesian fiscal policy, at least as presented by writers of textbooks and popularizers, maintains that spending and taxing policies can be manipu-

lated in the interests of fighting both depressions and inflation. Such is not
the case; however objective the economist may be, fiscal policy lends itself
more to fighting depression than to stopping inflation. Reducing taxes
and increasing public expenditure is bound to be politically expedient
to a degree unattainable by increasing the tax burdens and reducing spending. Likewise, monetary policy finds itself inflation-oriented rather than
recession-oriented. Still, politicians are not happy about having to restrain
the supply of money. And whether fiscal and monetary policies make any
economic sense, or in whatever combination they may do so, the politician
must pay close attention to the distributive details of aggregate measures of
consumption and supply. Fiscal policies are translated into specific legislation having a vital impact on the composition of output and demand.
Whose investments are affected cannot be a matter of overall fiscal efficiency. *Whose* consumption is affected, and how, when, and to what extent, are all basic questions that politicians attempt to answer by their vote
calculus. Much the same considerations apply to monetary policies. The
proposal to eliminate credit-card interest subsidies in the spring of 1984
was met by a tremendous response from credit-card companies and
their card holders. Needless to say, this element of monetary policy was
settled in the predictable way: Millions of card holders, well aware of
their not inconsiderable potential losses, were readily mobilized by the self-
interested card issuers to defeat a much smaller coalition of merchants ex-
pecting substantial gains and a large number of cardless customers whose
gains would be minuscule.

Aside from these general considerations we must insist that government
not only has political self-interests in destabilization compounded by economic ignorance but that the very organization of the federal government
frustrates effective stabilization. Countless critics, including members of
Congress, have long maintained that the budget is *uncontrollable*. If the
budget is uncontrollable, who made it so? And if the budget is uncontrollable, how can Keynesian policies form the rationale of government stabilization? The realization of this dilemma, disheartening as it may be to fine-
tuners, has led Congress to follow not Paul Samuelson but political rules of
thumb derived from electoral necessities. Students of congressional budgeting have shown rather forcefully that Congress does not and cannot under
existing rules compare one spending program with another or one taxing
measure with another. And despite the Budgeting Act of 1974 and the
Gramm-Rudman-Hollings Act, and President Bush's pact, Congress does
not genuinely consider the total budget and its consequences. The task
is simply too great. Accordingly, they begin with the president's political
budget proposal and previous budgets and simply legislate sufficient
monies to placate various interests. Except for defense expenditures, spending proposals are rarely questioned by members of Congress. A new

member quickly learns that the best advice is that of former Speaker Sam Rayburn: "To get along, you must go along." Likewise, embattled presidents seeking reelection will use every available dollar to buy the votes of powerful interests.

These considerations lead us to conclude that although government may occasionally assist in stabilizing segments of the economy it does not and cannot stabilize the economy. Government is chiefly responsible for inflation, and it has contributed mightily to growing unemployment and the continuous misallocation of scarce resources. One agency encourages and provides for the improvement of tobacco growing while another warns smokers of the health hazards of smoking. Yet another agency works to increase the productivity of farmers while simultaneously limiting acreage and buying up surpluses to store at enormous cost. Then, at campaign time, some politicians exclaim that 20 million Americans are hungry and homeless. Another agency entrusted with public lands wastes timber and other resources when the price of those same resources is increasing. Such is the real political world of fiscal and monetary policy. Aggregate demand and supply remain intellectual and political problems.

The 1986 attempt to reduce the deficit provided a good example of these processes at work. The Congress reluctantly approved a measure that would reduce the fiscal 1987 deficit by $13.3 billion in a partial deficit-reduction measure induced by the stringent requirements of the Gramm-Rudman-Hollings law. Members of Congress wary of the forthcoming elections engaged, by their own admission, in cuts that were all "smoke and mirrors." Instead of reducing expenditures in both defense and domestic programs, the Senate enacted a series of perfectly Machiavellian measures such as selling some government assets, stepping up revenue collection, and applying assorted budgetary gimmicks. Approval of the package put off any further serious attempts to control the deficit until the next year when, of course, it was even worse. Even then, an increase in the cigarette tax was eliminated in an effort to affect the senatorial race in North Carolina. Then, too, a petty accounting maneuver moved the final payment of general revenue sharing forward a few days so it would count against the 1986 deficit rather than against that of 1987. One congressman was heard to say, "We're fine tuning the smoke and mirrors." Another called it a "package of golden gimmicks."

An Economic Bill of Rights

Given the current state of the macro-art and the nature of the political market, stabilization of the economy is a fanciful dream. Electing the right people is mostly irrelevant. Reforming human nature is as impossible as declaring an end to the scarcity of resources. Change in policy and intellec-

tual understanding is relevant and has some possibility of political enactment, but most important of all is a fairly radical yet realistic transforma-
tion of some basic political institutions. Although changing institutions is
more costly and uncertain than changing officials and policies, it is more
effective and less ephemeral. Fortunately, institutional reform is not only
possible but probable. The intellectual groundwork has been done, and reform even at the constitutional level is well under way. What was once
unthinkable is now almost fashionable. Politics does have limitations and
can be limited.

What is most needed is wider acceptance of the view that if government
were to follow the right micro-policies there would be little need for any
macro-stabilization. Accepting such views soon leads to an appreciation
of certain fundamental fiscal constitutional amendments designed to
overcome current spending biases. Along with James Buchanan, Martin
Anderson, Milton Friedman, and many other notable economists we support laws and constitutional amendments that would:

1. require a balanced budget;
2. require the federal government to keep increases in the money supply
   to a fixed low rate;
3. replace the present income tax with a flat-rate tax;
4. provide the president with a line-item veto;
5. set congressional term limits.

These proposed amendments individually and collectively would serve to
lessen the kind of fiscal irresponsibility we have described throughout these
pages. Each of these proposals has been carefully drafted and considered by
economists and others in a most thorough and thoughtful way (see Milton
and Rose Friedman 1984 and Anderson 1984). Two of them (2 and 4) have
been accepted by 32 of the required 34 states, and may soon obtain the
support of the remaining two states. The scare created by a possible constitutional convention may force Congress to adopt the amendments in order
to avoid a convention and maintain its own power of decision. In fact the
Senate has already passed the balanced-budget amendment; the House did
as well but not by the required two-thirds majority.

A balanced-budget requirement would have the salutary purpose and effect of forcing both Congress and petitioning interest groups to either eliminate or reduce existing programs or vote to raise the necessary taxes. Since
resistance to repeal of accustomed privileges is so powerful, we expect that
few old programs would be eliminated; at best some would perforce be
reduced. But new spending proposals would be effectively countered and,
in any event, deficit financing seriously curtailed.

Under the present system, tax receipts and public expenditures grow
much more rapidly than the GNP. That is why the federal government in-

curs ever-larger deficits (see Figure 11.4). Under the proposed amendment, a majority of Congress would have to vote to permit taxes to continue at their current pace. A limitation on taxation complements the balanced-budget requirement in that the latter could occur with ever larger budgets. We agree with Milton Friedman that an unbalanced small budget is preferable to a balanced large budget. Honesty is also promoted by this requirement because the amendment permits Congress to spend more rapidly than the economy grows, but only if Congress openly votes to increase taxes. Deficits are permitted but under specified conditions, the most important being the need to obtain a three-fifths majority vote. Budget growth then becomes a deliberate national policy rather than an unintended consequence of log rolling.

Since economists' knowledge about macro-policy is inadequate and incentives supporting expansionary budgets are overwhelming, wisdom suggests that some constraints be placed upon the monetary authorities. Discretionary monetary policy is destabilizing. Accordingly, we advocate that such discretion be eliminated and replaced by a rule enabling monetary

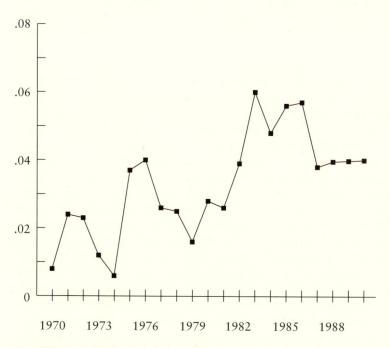

FIGURE 11.4   Ratio of Deficit to GNP
SOURCE: U.S. Bureau of the Census, *Statistical Abstract of the United States: 1992*, 112th ed. (Washington, D.C.: U.S. Government Printing Office, 1992).

growth to continue but at a constant, low, fixed rate approximating the long-run growth of the economy. Such a rule obviously injects more certainty into private planning. Under present arrangements traders spend far too much time anticipating the choices of the Fed and far too little in productive activity. Policy gyrations in which responses on the part of the Fed shift from too much money to too little, too soon, or too late should be effectively reduced.

Although the tax law of 1986 reduced the tax rates to two (15 percent and 28 percent), according to Milton Friedman a tax rate of no more than 15 to 16 percent would yield the same revenue as the current system. Because of its simplicity, a flat-rate tax should have enormous appeal to taxpayers. Of course, tax lawyers and accountants have a vested interest in complexity and may be expected to oppose the measure. Many politicians would oppose it because they can now have their cake and eat it too; in other words, they can express their support for high marginal rates on upper income groups but enact loopholes to lessen the real burden. Wiping the slate clean of tax privileges is also politically attractive; Congress can begin the new year selling new and still more valuable exemptions. We cannot ignore appearances, for when it comes to taxes, appearances are often more important than "reality" in politics. Although many middle-class voters fear they will actually pay more and some will, most will not. Still, their fears are real and must be countered. A flat-rate tax should reduce the number of people who engage in the underground economy and pursue tax havens freeing them to do more valuable things. A flat-rate income tax offers some greater sanity in financing the public sector (see Robert Hall and Alvin Rabushka 1983; 1985).

Furthermore, we believe it is time to provide the president with the same veto power possessed by most state governors, the power to veto line items in budget. Such a measure would counter the basic thrust of congressional budgeting, that is, it would enable officials and the president to consider each spending proposal independently of other spending proposals and revenue measures. Simply adding up the sum total of spending measures to produce an overall budget is unwise; such a process is inherently irrational. As it is, the president cannot veto a particularly odious expenditure because to do so would require him to veto the entire budget. Congress knows the strategic value of this all-or-nothing process and uses it to the hilt. A president with a line-item veto that could be overruled by a two-thirds vote by Congress would not allow abuse of the right but would confer the power to focus attention on at least the worst spending proposals. Proponents would have to present persuasive cost-benefit analyses to defend their redistributive plans.

With these constitutional revisions, we think that our fiscal Leviathan might be limited in much the same spirit by which government's power over civil rights is reduced by the Bill of Rights. It is very much within the American tradition to distrust government for it is the single most important monopoly in our lives. We want limitations placed on political exploitation. Individual and party competition, the chief constraints in liberal democratic theory, are in fact typically rather weak if not nonexistent. Entry costs into political competition are unduly high. Competition among governments offers some constraint but not much. Exit costs—the costs of migration to another locality, state, or country—are simply too high for most people. And even citizens who remove themselves from a monopoly must go to another only to face policy packages of a different mix that are still package deals. We are left then with constitutional constraints as the chief source of citizen protection.

Finally, we support the effort to impose term limits on Congress, an effort that has, as of November 1992, been enacted by fourteen states through referenda elections. We support term limits not simply to lessen the power of incumbents, but more pointedly because, as shown by the exhaustive research of James L. Payne (1991), the longer a representative's service in Congress, the more inclined is the member to vote for the growth of government and larger budgets.

Bibliographical Notes

Despite the importance of macro-economics, there is no single, readily accessible volume dealing with the political elements involved in policymaking. This being the case, we cite but four books containing various discussions—some technical— examining the micro-political foundations of macro-economic policies. The first is the wide-ranging and well-written *The Economic Consequences of Democracy* (New York: Holmes and Meier, 1977) by the brilliant English journalist Samuel Brittan. The book has some dated chapters on English politics but contains many fascinating discussions on economics and democracy, including the politics of spending and taxing. We have learned much from Brittan.

One of the very few books on macro-economics by a political scientist is the well-known *Political Control of the Economy* (Princeton: Princeton University Press, 1978) by Yale's Edward R. Tufte. The book is both scholarly and technical, so if the reader is an undergraduate the going may be a bit tough, but most of it is readable and in accordance with the ideas in the present book.

Perhaps the most important writing for the readers of this chapter to consult is the James M. Buchanan and Richard E. Wagner volume *Democracy in Deficit* (New York: Academic Press, 1977), a far-ranging analysis of the political legacy of John M. Keynes. The first third of the book deals with the history of Keynes's ideas and how they came to dominate academic and other circles, and the next third deals with the public choice aspects of Keynes's work, that is, how the ideas got translated into political strategies and policies. Finally, the authors consider and advocate constitutional reform to negate the baleful Keynesian doctrines and polices. The book was an eye-opener for us; it will be for others as well.

Finally, we cite a recent collection edited by Thomas D. Willett called *Political Business Cycles: The Political Economy of Money, Inflation and Unemployment* (Durham: Duke University Press, 1988). This well-reviewed book contains some twenty-one chapters dealing not only with political business cycles but many other interesting topics highly germane to our own discussion. Some of the chapters are not easy reading, but most can be grasped by non-economic specialists. We recommend especially Chapters 1 and 3, contributed by Willett and King Banaian, because they explain the various public choice models that have been advanced to understand macro-economic policies as products of a political process.

References

Anderson, Martin. *An Economic Bill of Rights* (Stanford: Hoover Institution, 1984).

Frey, Bruno, and Friedrich Schneider. "A Political-Economic Model of the UK: New Estimates and Predictions," *Economic Journal* 91 (1981), 737–740.

Friedman, Milton, and Rose Friedman. *The Tyranny of the Status Quo* (New York: Harcourt Brace Jovanovich, 1984).

Hall, Robert, and Alvin Rabushka. *Low Tax, Simple Tax, Flat Tax* (New York: McGraw-Hill, 1983).

———. *The Flat Tax* (Stanford: Hoover Institution Press, 1985).

Payne, James L. *The Culture of Spending: Why Congress Lives Beyond Our Means* (San Francisco: Institute for Contemporary Studies, 1991).

Schumpeter, Joseph A. *Capitalism, Socialism, and Democracy* (New York: Harper & Brothers, 1942).

U.S. Bureau of the Census. *Statistical Abstract of the United States: 1992*, 112th ed. (Washington, D.C.: U.S. Government Printing Office, 1992).

PART FOUR

In Praise of Private Property, Profits, and Markets

Studies by economic historians have concluded that those countries that respected, protected, and expanded property rights prospered and grew after the Middle Ages. In fact, the industrial revolution was only possible because of the expanded protection of property rights. Those countries not protecting property rights remained unindustrialized for a long time.

What do these historical facts have to do with modern democracy? We think a great deal. Overcoming the power of entrenched political interests and establishing rational policy today will require the same kind of commitment to property rights and markets. In addition, the power, reach, and size of government must be reduced.

Taking such steps requires some humility. Government cannot do all the things many wish it could. Just because our society sent people to the moon does not mean it can design political systems to solve all perceived problems. The American public and politicians alike must admit that prices contain more information than do government agencies and that free markets coordinate human activity far better than the best bureaucrat can.

If the American polity couples such a humility with the insights of public choice, it can design political institutions that will do far better than the ones it now has. Substantial, positive changes are possible. Our suggestions for change are presented in the next two chapters.

❦ 12 ❧

Rediscovery of Markets, Competition, and the Firm

THE U.S. MARKET ECONOMY came into prominence in the nineteenth century and remained relatively free until the 1930s when discovery of the redistributive potential of politics posed a potent threat to its continued workability. Of course, in some nations the market economy never developed much beyond local bazaars; in others, notably Italy and Germany, corporate fascism allowed capitalist institutions, but the state managed them for state purposes. In still others, Russia, for example, national markets never really got started under the czars and were for a brief time prohibited under state communism. Except for a capitalist underground economy, free markets remained illegal in the USSR until 1989–1990. So the reign of capitalism has not been universal or lengthy. Where it has taken root, capitalism has performed brilliantly but always under the threat of a redistributionist ethic and/or the power of ruthless rulers more interested in political power than in freedom and the GNP. Pervasive uncertainties intrinsic to capitalism, buttressed by the ambivalent moral status of capitalist institutions and ideals, also gave rise to passionate demands for reform and revolution, demands that went beyond simply gaining at the public trough.

The marketplace seemed to fail completely in the 1930s. As a consequence, socialism, public planning, and detailed regulation—that is, the substitution of political for economic processes—gathered a new momentum that has lasted more than fifty years. As wars and other governmental action seemed to rectify many economic ills, the case for the market was all too often left to embittered ideologues. Even Paretian welfare economics has been subverted and made the technical basis for an attack on market performance.

But over time, daily experience has acquainted ordinary people and scholars with the actual workings of political and bureaucratic processes; the virtues of the marketplace have been rediscovered and its principles cast in new and promising terms. These rediscoverers include such eminent European theorists as the late Frederich A. von Hayek and Ludwig von

Mises as well as the Americans Armen Alchian, James M. Buchanan, Milton Friedman, Douglas North, Richard Posner, and George Stigler, to list but the prominent. They have provided us with new meanings of competition, monopoly, the firm, property, goods, contracts and law, and the role of supply-side considerations in both micro- and macro-economics. Truly the past thirty years have witnessed a genuine renaissance in economics, yet very little of this quiet revolution has permeated other bastions of social science. The most auspicious result has been the rethinking of public policy by economists and advisers to conservative and liberal governments. Privatizing and allowing freer markets are no longer unthinkable here or abroad.

New Views of Market Processes

But a year after having published his startling *Road to Serfdom*, Frederich A. von Hayek, in a single essay, rewrote the meaning of competition for economists. Ironically, his technical understanding of the term was quite consonant with the more ambiguous understanding held by most laypeople. In "The Uses of Knowledge in Society" (1945), von Hayek argued that the standard neoclassical definition of competition emphasizing equilibrium had led economists astray from studying real world behavior in markets. His point remains true for many mainstream economists who still study final equilibrium states rather than the processes of unstable competition or, as von Hayek more appropriately termed it, "rivalry." Although von Hayek did not deny equilibrating forces, he wanted more attention devoted to disequilibrium, a process endogenous to free markets in which little can be controlled by any single seller or consumer. Capitalism produces a kind of partially ordered chaos, not quietly equilibrated firms and markets. Everything is in transition and doubt: knowledge, opportunities, and above all, expectations. Nothing is sacred. Wealthy one day and poor the next may be an exaggeration, but it does suggest the dynamism and uncertainty of market economies. For every competitor, there is a rival wishing to surpass him, and although some will be tempted to employ illegal and unethical means of advancement, most improve their fortunes by improving those of others—by inventing new and better goods and services, employing lower prices, and the like. The entrepreneur and his innovations occupy an analytical role in Austrian economics unknown to Anglo-Saxon neoclassical versions. The names of Schumpeter, von Mises, and von Hayek are central to this way of thinking.

The entrepreneur who constantly upsets routine through creative destruction is not content to make obvious decisions about the quantities to be produced but wants monopoly power, a power that is seductive because it cannot last long without the authority of the state. Businesspeople proceed to sell themselves and their products through advertising, product differentiation, brand names, collusion, price cutting, and trial and error—all perfectly natural forms of rivalry but known to conventional economists only as unmistakable signs of imperfect markets in need of remedial governmental intervention. The activities that make markets dynamic and competitive are, according to von Hayek, the very activities that liberal economists want suppressed or regulated.

Once the idea of rivalrous flux is accepted, a great many other new ideas and ideals flow forth to constitute a well-rounded paradigm of economic life. According to this view, market competition is considerably more robust than neoclassicists have thought to be the case. That political competition cannot perform the miracles of the market version is an important corollary; lacking a "hidden hand" of prices, the political process is often a zero-sum and sometimes a negative-sum game, whereas the market is a positive-sum or unanimous transaction.

In the new learning on markets both competition and monopoly have been redefined and refined in unexpected ways. For example, how much competition and/or monopoly exist depends on two factors: economies of scale and entry barriers. Both necessarily involve considerable governmental participation. In any case, how big a firm becomes and whether it is a price taker or price searcher depends on the size of the industry or market. When average costs for a firm are very low, the firm is apt to become dominant or be dominated by a small number of large firms producing most of the total product. Products that are easily produced at low cost lend themselves to mass production and few firms; complex, highly individualized products or services are apt to be offered by many firms, none of which has a large share of the market. Most academic critics of modern markets emphasize the overwhelming presence of monopoly; casual public opinion affirms the same misperception. Actually, while the large firms are extremely competitive, there has been a resurgence of small, specialized firms offering unique products and services. Indeed, we should think of every rock music group in this sense. If we do, we also learn that all monopolies are very short-lived. Furthermore, there are very few monopolies in the commonsense meaning of that term, that is, sellers without competition from close substitutes. Those who are inclined to question might ask the United States Steel Corporation about the mass production of aluminum, not to mention foreign steel competitors or the competition from other steel substitutes. Or one might ask the railroads about the trucking industry, the bus industry, and the airlines. Then, too, every monopolist's returns attract other potential monopolists and thereby bring about a dissipation of profits.

These strictures on the nature and significance of monopoly must be qualified by one very important factor, namely, the role of labor unions in a competitive economy. Labor unions have, in fact, been the most singular example of government-mandated monopoly. For decades, they have been awarded a special status in the law permitting them to benefit in ways not permitted other organizations, especially private firms. Unlike the private firm, which must worry about the elasticity of demand for its products, the union has been able to increase its members' wages by excluding those willing to work for less. Buttressed by closed shop privileges, the union has been able to exercise a degree of coercion unknown to other sellers. Still, many citizens seem to think that granting such power to unions benefits society. Nevertheless, we witness a pervasive weakening of these beliefs, not only in public opinion polls but in the decreasing membership of unions and their dramatically diminished power at the bargaining table. Even liberal academics now feel free to question the motives and power of unionized labor. Perhaps the knowledge that many industrial workers earn considerably more than many professors has something to do with the changing climate of opinion. In any case, although monopoly tendencies exist in the free market, the chief form of monopoly is found in government-mandated labor unions. If there is a role for antitrust laws, perhaps they ought to be applied to labor organizations.

Although the economies-of-scale explanation is important, probably the more significant aspect of monopolistic processes is a purely political phenomenon, namely, barriers to entry. Market advantages are available and are best obtained and most effective when granted by sovereign governments. Mercantile Europe provided a plenitude of examples, but for us the more relevant examples are found in the present-day United States. Not all industries seek the same forms of protection, partly because some are irrelevant to their situation and others are considered more or less politically infeasible. And in some instances, one form of protection actually maximizes privilege. For example, the auto industry prefers quotas to tariffs. Barbers, doctors, lawyers, and others prefer to restrict entry and restrain competition through licensing, thereby imposing professional standards and administering their own industries. Other occupations opt for patents and copyrights. In some cities, the taxi industry has managed to limit competition by requiring purchase of an expensive medallion (at an estimated cost of $150,000 in New York City). The shipping industry (high seas) has rules restricting the use of foreign vessels. Domestic content laws are highly popular among auto unions as well as domestic manufacturers of those parts. Peanut growers in the South must obtain a special "peanut allotment" to grow peanuts. Such allotments are exceedingly scarce, often inherited or sold at astronomical prices. Administering these various barriers are dozens of regulatory commissions in Washington, D.C., commissions that should be better known as cartel managers. By restricting competition, they attempt to stabilize if not increase the wealth and income of industries.

These official administrative agencies of political cartels must not be superficially thought of as mere captives of the industries they regulate. Consisting of self-interested members and staff, the commissions engage in exchanges with the regulated industries that are *mutually* profitable. As many analysts have noted, regulatory agencies place a high value on risk aversion, that is, not upsetting the congressional committee applecarts that provide budgets and overseeing their operations. Security becomes a major goal because jobs, salaries, status, and power are at stake and easily lost by unfavorable events and publicity. Predictability of decisions is another value jointly esteemed by client groups and bureaucrats. So, there is a powerful desire to codify and proliferate administrative practices and policies. Having comfortable relationships with clients as well as with the general public enables trouble-free days and enables the chief administrators to maintain more harmonious relationships with the president and Congress. A grateful industry will also discover the political talents and rent-seeking potential of retired administrators when it next considers hiring a Washington lobbyist. A cozy relationship may not be inevitable but it is certainly likely.

Unlike firms of the past, firms today are born in an already-functioning cartel arrangement closely regulated by political operatives. Entrepreneurs must not only have permission to enter business but must also meet diverse requirements ranging from having to pay innumerable and substantial fees and taxes to having their facilities approved, meeting zoning restrictions, and so on. Why, then, do new firms still organize? And how do they organize themselves?

The Business Firm:
New Understandings

In rethinking and explaining basic economic processes, attention has quite naturally focused on the role of the firm because it is the vehicle by which the profit-oriented entrepreneur combines and reallocates resources. Conventional textbook economics has always treated the firm as something of an "empty box," an artificial entity whose internal structure and decision-making are considered irrelevant in explaining market equilibrium. Because traditional price theory views the firm as but a mechanical response to market forces, purchasing inputs at fixed prices, transforming resources into products under certain technological constraints, and selling them in markets are all viewed as beyond its control. In short, the typical firm has very little to decide, and its decision processes are negligible. It is, indeed, an "empty box."

This view competes with Galbraith's view of powerful oligopolies; in addition, a newer conception has made considerable inroads. Consisting, in part, of behavioral approaches pioneered by Herbert Simon (1957), Austrian views of the market, and the rather special contributions of Ronald H. Coase (1937), Armen Alchian and Harold Demsetz (1972), and Oliver E. Williamson (1985), this new conception is distinctly different from traditional views and challenges the images that economists have typically employed. Once again, Ronald Coase led the way. He did so by raising two startlingly naive questions: Why do firms exist, and why are they organized as they are?

The firm exists, he claimed, because formal organization reduces the cost of doing things through multitudinous contracts, that is, the cost of production is reduced as hierarchies replace markets in which resource holders contract with one another afresh each day. Rejection of the contractual model by those who espouse market competitions is something of an anomaly. Nevertheless, entrepreneurs choose the very opposite practice for the sensible reason that individual contracting among the holders of resources would be extraordinarily complex, confusing, frustrating, and wasteful. So the typical firm is not a miniature market.

Instead, the firm is a "simple" hierarchy of owners, managers, and employees organized and coordinated by a formal division of labor. Combined, they are able to produce far more at a lower cost than might be possible without such organization. It is also important to note that each group of members is compensated in a different manner: Employees receive hourly wages; managers earn salaries and bonuses; and owners hope to receive residual payments called profits. Needless to say, such payments produce different interests among the team members, differences that must be resolved if the firm is to succeed.

Relationships among the firm members are governed by long-term rather than short-term daily contracts because such contracts enable reductions in contracting costs and increase stability of mutual expectations and performance. Such contracts also provide a more efficient means of controlling the behavior of members. In every team effort, there will be members tempted by the possibilities of free riding, shirking, or gaining at the expense of others. In large and complex impersonal organizations, the temptation is notably increased by both the greater probability of not being detected and the weakened ethical ties found among strangers. Since assessing contributions in a complex division of labor is difficult, the incentive to gain by shirking is further enhanced. Put another way, the lower the cost of shirking the more shirking will be "demanded" or practiced. Bosses or monitors are required to keep employees honest and make sure they share in the work. Communal organizations face this problem in a peculiarly wrenching way because their members assume that no one is tempted to shirk responsibilities; personal accounts of former commune members and social research, however, have shown that assumption to be a myth. And even when members of a commune do not shirk, they bring different skills, abilities, and motivation to the work. How shall they be paid? The shirker, of course, increases the social costs for colleagues, who must make up for the reduced contributions of shirkers.

As in large polities, monitors in the firm bear scrutiny. Managers of large and small corporations alike have interests of their own that may be satisfied at the expense of employees and/or owners—owners whose very absenteeism increases the possibilities of exploitation. The capitalist way of meeting this problem is to offer the bosses a bonus for doing a good job of monitoring. And this method works. Monitors who opt for possible gain at the risk of failing to increase production may end up being fired; again, dual incentives perform marvelous results, especially for consumers.

In earlier chapters we observed that private firms and public bureaucracies are financed in quite different ways; because the consequences are so critical the point is worth repetition and further examination. Government bureaus obtain annual budgets from a legislature to finance operations for set periods of time. Unlike the firm they do not depend on uncertain investments and market sales. Since the latter revenues are unpredictable, the firm must find investors willing to confront uncertainty. Some may invest because they enjoy risky situations, but most people will invest only because the expected future payment is sufficiently large to overcome their aversion to risk. As a reward for putting their wealth at risk, they are offered interest payments or the possibility of a profit and held responsible for only limited liability. The greater the risk, the greater the potential reward needs to be to encourage investors. Although there is also an unknown personality element involved in risk taking, economists generally prefer to assume that risk taking is dependent upon one's wealth while deciding among investment options. In other words, money may have diminishing marginal utility; those who have a great deal of it can easily afford to take the risk and will demand a smaller reward, whereas those with fewer dollars must be offered more to overcome their greater aversion to similar risk. So owners are the specialized carriers of risk who provide the investment capital needed to finance capitalist firms. Investments are assembled by spreading and reducing risks among the many investors, whose personal funds are limited. Not so ironically, U.S. trade unions have become substantial investors in the very companies for whom their members work.

This exegesis on the new theory of the firm helps to explain how the firm operates in actual market processes. Various firms have different degrees of autonomy in the market. Some are but "price takers"; others exercise some control over prices and are thus "price searchers" looking for optimal prices to charge buyers. In an older jargon, we are describing the competitiveness of markets. Everyone knows that some markets have more competitors than others and that the degree or intensity of competition varies greatly. Although both are important characteristics, numbers are more critical in price-taker markets and intensity is the critical factor in price-searching markets.

What is most significant in both markets, however, is the effort put forth by firms to produce products that persuade buyers to make purchases. Demand does not exist in noble isolation from the advertising efforts of businesses. Wants are created by firms inventing products and convincing customers of new needs. In that sense, supply precedes demand. Of course, once a demand has been created, firms must take account of it, but demand is neither universal nor permanent; improvements, refinements, and above all, new products constantly alter patterns of consumption. And price searchers must engage in a never-ending search for the "right" price. That they do can be observed by anyone who visits markets on a regular basis; the prices of everything are in constant flux, affording both unexpected gains and losses for all buyers and, of course, sellers. Unexpected gains and losses are far more commonplace for the harried businessperson than are the stable expectations depicted in the neat diagrams of a conventional economics textbook. Life on the supply side is never dull.

We are also suggesting that price searchers cannot set prices at will. The market power needed to do that simply does not exist; if it does, perhaps domestic auto companies lost billions during the last recession for diabolical reasons. As powerful as these corporations are, they must observe certain market realities; if they do not, competitors will, and will profit. Growth in firms stems from superior production and marketing strategies and not from some brutal tactic of size and monopoly power. The concentration in some industries is the result of superior performance as measured by satisfied consumers. It is because of this factor that the shares of the market held by large firms in the same industry tend to change over time. Ford was once the giant of the auto industry, then it was General Motors. And on a worldwide basis we cannot ignore Toyota and Nissan, firms that did not produce autos when Ford was king. And then there is Honda.

Perhaps the most visible activity of the modern large business is its advertising—an activity that draws especially moralistic condemnation from radicals and liberals with an aesthetic sensitivity. Even the mainstream economist is inclined to view advertising as a wasteful expenditure. This traditional view is based on the assumption that buyers are fully informed and therefore not in need of additional information. However, buyers are not and cannot be fully informed about more than a few products; instead, in a world where new products and services are constantly coming onto the scene, buyers remain ignorant until someone is willing and able to provide relevant information. That someone is the firm, especially, the new firm struggling to introduce whatever it has to offer. Because they are competing against literally millions of other goods, firms must catch the fleeting attention of the consumer. Their advertising efforts therefore become not wasteful but imperative. An average grocery store now stocks 17,000 different items. Since altering consumers' loyalties is a costly proposition, advertisers must be skillful, lucky, or both if they are to divert consumers from one product to another. Advertising is itself subject to diminishing returns. Many of the so-called excesses so disturbing to liberal thinkers are based on the false assumption that advertising is extremely effective; it may be, under highly restrictive conditions. Still, advertising is a perfectly understandable tactic on the part of firms. Attention is sought and gained through advertising; however, sales of the product hinge in the long run not on the advertising but on the ability of the product to satisfy the consumer. Advertising, in fact, conveys information—any information sellers think will be meaningful to buyers. If this information is not meaningful (that is, it does not result in increased sales), the advertiser searches for other themes. And buyers should be "grateful" for the information and the low cost at which it is, in fact, supplied. Just how socialists should and would provide consumers with information are issues they never seem to address. Perhaps the variety of goods and services would be so reduced and the homogeneity of products so increased in a socialist society that choice would become superfluous. Only superior goods fulfilling "real" needs would be offered. The alleged frivolousness of modern capitalist consumption would be a thing of the past. With spartan consumption the ideal, one wonders what might happen to newspaper want ads.

Virtues Reclaimed

Because of the incessant changes that take place in markets, trial and error provides a superb means for the achievement of individual and collective rationality in the production and distribution of private goods. The use of money and prices enables a highly decentralized decisionmaking system to react in responsive and responsible ways to changing demands and productive innovations. As a decentralized system, the market enables individuals possessing limited information to make more intelligent choices than could possibly be made by a board of dispassionate experts sitting miles away from the sites of action. Not only is much of the information provided by markets quantitative, and therefore easily understood and economically used by untrained individuals, but it is relevant to the immediate decision. As Adam Smith argued, the market also provides a powerful motivational system through the incentives of profit and loss—the carrot and stick, so to speak. Those who do not like what is provided in one market can usually give voice to their complaints and be heard by a responsive seller; those who prefer to vote with their feet may leave the store and try a competitor who is all too willing to have more business. The disaffected have options to a degree unheard of in history or in any contemporary society with a command economy and polity.

A number of themes emerge from this discussion. In the first place, markets, even the imperfectly competitive ones, achieve an extraordinary efficiency. Market economies have attained the highest GNPs in history because they not only provide incentives but also honor individual preferences accurately and quickly. The costly calculation of the welfare of others is minimized. Buyers, sellers, and entrepreneurs need only the information provided by price signals to make rational allocations. Operating within a decentralized authority system, they are able to coordinate their respective wishes rather than struggle with one another over fixed shares. As a result, economic dilemmas are handled with impersonality, efficiency, and a minimum of coercion. At the same time, the system penalizes incompetence, miscalculation, and dishonesty while rewarding effort, ability, foresight, and probity.

Moreover, these abstract arguments do not in any way capture the extraordinary capacity of the market to simplify allocative problems and thereby provide ready solutions that contribute to the welfare of the many. The rediscovery of the market has been enhanced by observation of the clumsy ways by which government regulators and socialist planners attempt to substitute themselves for the market. Although the airlines industry, for example, has been substantially deregulated, the federal government continues to attempt to impose its bureaucratic ways on an industry facing an overcrowding problem in major airports. Too many planes attempt to take off and land at peak hours on certain days of the week. This costly and annoying problem can be reduced by employing market principles to the problems. Increasing the cost of landing and taking off at busy hours will soon equate supply of slots and demand for flights at the appropriate quantity and price. Those who value certain flights most should be permitted the opportunity to put their money where their values reside. Those who value these flights less should be permitted the chance to purchase tickets for other, less convenient flights at lower prices. Were these opportunities not enacted by law they would soon achieve Paretian optimality, for no one for whom the value of remaining on the flight is greater than the value of the "bribe" has to give up a seat or flight. And anyone for whom the cost of the time lost waiting for a later flight is less than the value of the bribe will happily take the later flight.

But the uninformed public, professional regulators, and politicians will blame the airlines and argue that only the government can devise rules for the allocation of scarce time and runway space. But imagine the immensity of the problem if "solved" by rational discussion around the conference table. Whose time is more valuable? By how much? These questions are answered by the market without any discussion over eternal ethical principles. The existence of overbooked seats and overbooked runways is not evidence of market failure but of political failure. A market would solve the problem of underpricing by increasing the price of certain uses of the airport. Peak-hour use of privately held property elicits higher prices, while other less-valued times produce lower prices. Hotels offer weekend rates distinctly lower than those in force during the week. Telephone rates are set with these same considerations in mind. These sensible decisions come about because hotels and the phone companies are unregulated in these regards. But the spectacle of jammed flights and runways somehow seems to require collective solutions since it is assumed that markets created the problem in the first place. Such problems as those confronting airlines can be best understood and resolved through market principles. Agonizing ethical discussions and selfish politicking over transportation are not only unnecessary but wasteful.

A system of market choice seemingly encourages innovation beyond that known in any other type of economy. Discovery cannot be planned; it can only be facilitated by competitive markets. Although inventors may ruin the careers of others, they also create new careers and benefit the consumers.

To Adam Smith's great credit it was he who first understood how markets can produce a collective good from diverse self-interests. A price mechanism performs the task with efficiency unattainable by any board of planners equipped with the latest computers. Still, many concerned social scientists find it hard to believe that much general good can emerge from "base" self-interests, but that is because they fail to grasp the simple workings of the market. Nor can they grasp the operations of a political process that is unable, despite their fervent beliefs, to convert competitive self-interest into public good.

Finally, we agree with economists such as Milton Friedman who believe that the greatest achievement of the market economy is its success in maximizing individual wishes, or the freedom to choose. No one seriously contends that private choices are without constraints and public consequences; since consumers must face opportunity costs and prices on everything, they must recognize that freedom of choice and guaranteed outcomes are incompatible.

Bibliographical Notes

Although the rediscovery of markets, competition, and business firms has been under way for at least thirty years, the new learning has been developed and disseminated in a highly decentralized way. As a result, one confronts several different bodies of thought advanced by writers who often seem unaware of one another's existence. For example, the literature on firms has taken place within conventional economics and reflects that fact, that is, the material is often presented in technical terms. On the one hand, much of the reinterpretation of markets and competition is the work of "Austrian" economists (many of whom are Americans) and is written in a nonmathematical manner. On the other hand, Chicago economists have reinterpreted monopoly. Some of the new learning about the private-property, profit-seeking economy has been offered by legal thinkers and economic historians attempting to explain Western development. Although these literatures are highly complementary, they are diverse and expressed in a range of technical and nontechnical language.

Perhaps the best place to begin is with the extraordinary economics text *University Economics* (Belmont: Wadsworth, 1964) by Armen Alchian and William Allen, now in its fourth edition. This remarkable book is both an undergraduate text and a treatise—a highly original one. It does not just summarize and organize the new thinking but actually aided in developing that thought. Like Alfred Marshall's classic, this text will reward both undergraduate and advanced readers. The authors present a unique and original application of economics in both market and nonmarket settings. It is truly a great book.

One should also consult the work of a scholar already mentioned in previous chapters, namely Ronald H. Coase, whose major essays, including the one on the firm, are now available in paperback: *The Firm, the Market, and the Law* (Chicago: University of Chicago Press, 1990). This small volume clearly demonstrates why Coase has been one of the great economists of our time.

Oliver E. Williamson's *Markets, Hierarchies: Analysis and Antitrust Implications* (New York: Free Press, 1975) is another innovative study, although hardly the equal of Coase's works. A more recent attempt to pull together much of the new learning is found in Thrainn Eggertsson, *Economic Behavior and Institutions* (Cambridge: Cambridge University Press, 1990). This book is another in the distinguished Cambridge Surveys of Economic Literature series, and deservedly so. Parts of it may be difficult reading, but like many demanding books, it is well worth the additional effort.

We would be remiss if we did not cite at least one book by Israel M. Kirzner, the leading American "Austrian." We note but one of his writings: *Competition and Entrepreneurship* (Chicago: University of Chicago Press, 1973). This productive scholar has long promulgated Austrian ideas to an indifferent conventional audience in American economics. Only in recent years have his writings received their deserved recognition as important critiques of contemporary price theory and extensions of the work of von Mises and von Hayek. Their work, and the better-known works of Schumpeter, are finally being incorporated into the orthodox tradition and making it a far sounder body of analysis. We expect this healthy trend to continue.

References

Alchian, Armen, and Harold Demsetz. "Production, Information Costs, and Economic Organization," *American Economic Review* 62 (December 1972), 775–795.

Coase, Ronald H. "The Nature of the Firm," *Economics* 4 (November 1937), 346–405.

Marshall, Alfred. *Principles of Economics* (London: Macmillan, 1920).

Simon, Herbert. *Models of Man* (New York: John Wiley & Sons, 1957).

von Hayek, Frederich A. "The Uses of Knowledge in Society," *American Economic Review* 35 (September 1945), 519–530.

Williamson, Oliver E. *The Economic Institutions of Capitalism: Firms Markets, Relational Contracting* (New York: Free Press, 1985).

❦ 13 ❦

Privatization, Deregulation, and Constitutionalism

To act on the belief that we possess the knowledge and the power which enable us to shape the processes of society entirely to our liking, knowledge which in fact we do not possess, is likely to make us do much harm.

—Frederich A. von Hayek

FOR MUCH OF THE past century, government in the United States has been guided by the belief that the best form of government is one with wide-ranging discretion bolstered by good advice. As we related in Chapter 2, one of the earliest systematic statements of this belief was by Woodrow Wilson. In "The Study of Administration" ([1887] 1992), he asserted that the American Founders' arguments for limited government were based on "paper pictures" and "literary themes." He proposed a greatly expanded role for government—a government guided by technically expert civil servants "prepared by a special schooling and drilled, after appointment, into a perfected organization, with an appropriate hierarchy and characteristic discipline" (p. 21).

Although Wilson predated the rise of modern welfare economics by several decades, his vision of the appropriate role and form of government provided part of the intellectual backdrop for the standard economic approach to the study of markets and politics. As we described it in Chapter 12, a market system is based on the decentralized decisions of rational consumers and producers, each operating in his or her own self-interest. Consumers desire to attain the highest possible level of utility by consuming goods and services. They are, however, limited by the scarcity of their own resources and of the goods they seek. Producers are assumed to be profit maximizers who use real resources to create goods and services that can be sold at a profit. If they are to achieve their goals, they must use their real resources in the production of goods for which consumers are willing to pay the highest prices. This system automatically causes resources to flow to those uses where they make the greatest possible contribution to the maximization of consumers' utility.

Most proponents of governmental interventions in markets do not accept the above "invisible hand" description as a sufficiently accurate picture of market systems. They point out that markets suffer from imperfections that inhibit the free movement of the invisible hand and suggest these imperfections can be improved upon by government action. Accordingly, welfare economists see government as merely a means to achieving the normal ends of consumption and utility maximization. That is, it facilitates the allocation of resources desired by consumers. In his introductory textbook, Paul Samuelson (1980) states the argument as follows: "Whenever there are externalities, a strong case can be made for supplanting complete individualism by some kind of group action. . . . The reader can think of countless . . . externalities where sound economics would suggest some limitations on individual freedom in the interest of all" (p. 42). In addition to market failures, students of markets and politics raise other concerns and objections to markets. Markets are alleged to encourage "incorrect" values. Relying on markets to allocate income and wealth causes unacceptable inequities, which are compounded by the fact that disproportionate levels of income and wealth translate into disproportionate political power. Many claim that consumption and wants are manipulated by corporations that seek to promote private interests at the expense of the public interest. Market critics expect these outcomes because they believe that unfettered market activity conditions people to think of their self-interest rather than the common interest. The solution to these perceived ills, they contend, is the expansion of government.

In Parts Two and Three we constructed what we believe to be a serious challenge to these views of markets and politics. Government is not the frictionless plug welfare economists blindly propose as a means of stopping the losses caused by markets. The losses caused by extending the power of government into markets are real and the gains are illusory. Governmental choices are not based on a careful understanding and balancing of the complexities of macro- and micro-economics; rather, they are based on the imperatives of the ballot box. To paraphrase Adam Smith, it is not from the benevolence of the politician, the bureaucrat, or the voter that we expect our publicly supplied goods but from their regard to their own interest. Although the pursuit of self-interest can serve the interests of many, it does best when confined to the market. There is an invisible hand in politics but it operates in the opposite direction to Smith's invisible hand. Voters, politicians, and bureaucrats who believe themselves to be promoting the public interest are led by an invisible hand to promote interests other than those most widely shared.

Thus, politics is characterized by the oversupply and undersupply of public goods and excessive costs for both private and public goods. Although it reduces some negative externalities, it increases others. Indeed, government management of some resources causes their destruction.

Instead of being "government by the people," politics is often an intense competition for power to benefit particularized interests at the cost of wider society. Instead of politics ennobling participants, it promotes myth making, suppression and distortion of information, stimulation of hatred, and legitimation of envy. These claims should not be viewed as another refrain of the tired old song, "waste, fraud, and abuse." Although we agree with critics from the Left and Right who maintain that government is replete with waste, fraud, and abuse, we disagree with their analysis of the causes of the problems and thus with many of the solutions they propose.

Whether it is Jesse Helms, William Proxmire, Mike Wallace, or Chicago's Better Government Association making the revelations about wasteful government behavior, the problems are invariably presented as having been caused by incompetent, uncaring, or dishonest people. The solution from both the Left and the Right is straightforward—elect, appoint, or hire honest, well-trained people and government will function smoothly, efficiently, and fairly. Our analysis is entirely different. It exposes the problems of government as being far greater than those that might be caused by incompetent or grasping political actors. A government and polity composed entirely of saints would produce results approximating those we currently get from admittedly imperfect political participants. These problems will continue unless the rules of the game are changed.

In Chapters 3 and 4, we identified the incentives facing participants in political life and suggested these incentives matter a great deal since they structure choices and determine outcomes. In Chapters 6 through 11, we elaborated on those outcomes and demonstrated their perversity. Consider these, among the many we identified:

- Many welfare programs are traps, not safety nets.
- The costs of the Clean Air Act have been twice as large as the benefits.
- Political campaigns are characterized by discussions about which candidate is best at pork barrel (substitute "theft from nonconstituents" for "pork barrel") politics, not which candidate best serves the public interest.
- Taxpayer monies have been used to destroy important environmental amenities, including Yellowstone National Park.
- Regulations usually end up serving the regulatees, not the consumer.
- Fiscal policies exaggerate and exacerbate business cycles. Some cycles are caused by fiscal policies.
- Voters are rationally ignorant of the actions and often even the names of their politicians.
- Given voting cycles and the role of leadership, the results of many "democratic" decisions are arbitrary.

There are many lessons to be learned from these outcomes, but two important ones are: Good intentions do not guarantee good results and scientific management by government is impossible. Once naivete and good intentions are replaced by an understanding of the reality of politics, it becomes time to consider alternatives. Considering alternatives is the same sort of exercise undertaken by the American Founders 200 years ago. Their deliberations were based on the notions that incentives matter (or, as we might phrase it, "People respond to prices"), that processes are critical (institutions structure incentives), that good intentions are insufficient to counteract the abuse of power, and that government exists to protect rather than encroach upon liberty. Unfortunately, the problems we have identified have come about because American policymakers have lost sight of these basic precepts, especially during this century. Because government has grown, there has been an expansion of centralized command-and-control policies governing much of our economic, political, and private lives. These policies tend to cost more than they should and accomplish less than they could; they are often inequitable and inefficient—thus unnecessarily restricting freedom of choice.

Changing the consequences of government actions requires changing government's scope, tactics, and nature. It also requires that we as citizens change our expectations of what is possible while remembering that the ideal is often the enemy of the possible. We must begin by recognizing that government is not the benign instrument suggested by David Truman in *The Governmental Process* (1951) and taught by succeeding generations of political scientists. Nor is it the efficient manipulator of macro-policy that was envisioned by Keynes and his followers. We must also recognize that most of what is commonly viewed as market failure is misunderstood, caused by governmental policies, or the result of poorly defined property rights.

Those of us who would prefer to live in a world where people respected each others' rights, cooperated generously and voluntarily with each other, provided goods and services to satisfy the desires of the broad range of humanity, and expressed their true preferences must recognize government's comparative disadvantage at promoting these values. It is only after recognizing this basic fact that we can begin considering viable ways of promoting such values.

Recognizing the failures of government to promote widely shared values must be accompanied by a renewed acceptance of markets, property rights, and prices. We have provided the beginnings for rejecting the standard myths and misunderstandings about markets. The suggested readings at the end of each chapter will guide the interested reader to a fuller understanding of the subjects and topics we have introduced.

We set out to accomplish three tasks in writing this book. One was to explain the perversities of government; the second was to convey a new appreciation of markets. The third was to identify specific and general policy proposals. The proposals we outlined in the preceding chapters would reverse the policy trend of this century if adopted. They all call for a greater reliance on property rights, market processes, and private institutions and are wholly in keeping with the American political heritage of limited, decentralized government. We believe they would make for a more rational and peaceful polity. These proposals fall into four general categories—privatization, economic efficiency, deregulation, and constitutional reform.

Privatization

The term "privatization" was hardly used in the United States in 1980. Yet it gained buzzword status by 1986. Privatization is one of a number of techniques for providing public services through the private sector. Contracting government services out to private companies, establishing user fees, and "shedding" services, or selling them outright to the private sector, are a few common examples. Privatization can also mean increased reliance on voluntary, self-help associations and nonprofit organizations as well as on profit-seeking companies. The possibilities are almost limitless. Many forms of privatization can be used to reduce the size and scope of federal, state, and local government. Large portions of the federal estate would be managed more equitably and efficiently in the hands of private owners, including voluntary, nonprofit organizations such as environmental groups and hiking clubs. Many services, including social services, solid waste collection, electric power, fire protection, postal service, health care, accounting services, street maintenance and repair, park management, prelitigation arbitration, correctional services, education, police services, and other services commonly provided by government entities can be better provided by private-sector firms and organizations.

As we enter the third century under the U.S. Constitution, the privatization movement in the United States is reversing the trend of the past century. And most of the impetus for change is coming from the cities and counties, not from Congress, the federal bureaucracy, or the presidency. Because cities and counties do not have the federal government's luxury of concentrating benefits on their constituents by having nonconstituents pay the costs, they are beginning to experiment extensively with privatization. One outstanding example is La Mirada, California, a city of 40,000 people. More than 60 services are contracted out, and the city has just 55 employees. In Los Angeles, there are more than 200 city contracts for services such as trash removal and park maintenance. New Jersey has contracted out the function of issuing and renewing drivers' licenses to Sears Roebuck & Co.

The results of these privatization schemes and other reforms suggest that Thomas E. Borcherding's (1977) "Bureaucratic Rule of Two" can be reversed. According to Borcherding's rule, "Removal of an activity from the private to the public sector will double its unit cost of production." The experience of privatization suggests the opposite—that moving the provision of services from the public to the private sector can halve its cost. A particular privatization scheme will not automatically save a government 50 percent, but the potential for savings led *Fortune* to report in 1985 that "turning government over to business can cut costs 20% or more—often much more—without loss of quality" (Main 1985). Detroit provides a dramatic example. It cost the city $26 to collect each $15 parking ticket until a private collection agency was hired. The cost of collection dropped to $2 per ticket.

When a program or service is privatized properly, the costs are determined by competition, not by monopolist government agencies. The Urban Mass Transit Administration found that simply opening a service to competition among public and private operators reduced costs from 10 to 50 percent.

One of the most attractive qualities of privatization is that it allows for the continued supply of services rather than cutbacks in the face of fiscal downturns. Thus, it is possible to gain support from both the liberal and conservative ends of the political spectrum. Among the leading proponents of privatization during the 1980s, for example, were the Democratic mayor of Phoenix, Arizona, and analysts at the conservative Heritage Foundation. Because there exists a great deal of evidence that privatization works well, its implementation can be argued on pragmatic rather than ideological grounds. William A. Niskanen (1976), former member of the President's Council of Economic Advisors, described it best:

> [There is] the growing body of evidence that several forms of contracting out for government services can be far more efficient than the supply by bureaus. These methods promise both to reduce the total cost of government and to increase the level and quality of public services. Only the unthinking, uncreative, and inefficient have any cause to object. (p. 90)

Economic Efficiency

For services that are not privatized, more extensive implementation of user charges, fees, and permits would reduce inefficiencies and inequities. Users of services would express their demands by backing them with cash payments, and managers would obtain a more realistic measurement of the demand for the services. Parks, libraries, museums, wilderness areas, and city services are all candidates for a more extensive and cost-recovering set of user fees.

As part of promoting economic efficiency, we must recognize that relying on markets means accepting market verdicts. If timber cannot be cut economically, its extraction should not be subsidized. Water projects that cannot pay for themselves should not be built, and existing projects should, over time, move their water into the market, possibly by transferring rights to present users. Market forces should be allowed to establish farm prices and optimal farm numbers and sizes. Parks that produce too few visitors to cover at least operating costs should be sold or given away, possibly to environmental groups such as the Nature Conservancy or to local volunteer associations.

In many cases, a more rational use of fees, user charges, permits, and leases would lead to a decreased demand for many government-provided services. In the case of public lands, for example, a decrease in demand would promote long-run conservation of the resource and enhance the environmental quality of the land.

Governments should get out of the business of subsidizing development, especially on environmentally sensitive or important lands, such as prime farmlands, flood plains, estuaries, wetlands, and national parks. The principle behind the Coastal Barriers Resource Act of 1982, which ended subsidized development on 700 miles of undeveloped eastern coastal barrier structures, should be extended to other areas. Property owners should be free to use their land for productive purposes but should not be able to obtain crop support payments, subsidized construction loans, federal sewer grants, and other federal aids for use on their lands.

Attempts to mimic the market through establishing fees based on the "user pays" principle would provide substantial improvements over existing policies; however, it is important to understand the limitations of these policies. To say fees ought to be set and charged begs two critical questions—at what level should the charges be set and who gets to spend the money? The politics of setting the charges and allocating the income are still the politics of interest groups and politicians acting in their own interests. Irresponsible politicians could easily use the income from these fees for exploitative purposes. Still, fees would provide much better information about consumer demand than does the current system and could guide decisions about the appropriate supply of outputs. There would at least be real numbers to plug into cost-benefit and cost-effectiveness studies.

Regulatory Reform

Regulatory reform is necessary at all levels of government and at all points along the spectrum, from regulation of individuals to regulation of corporations. At the level of regulating individuals, governments need to stop attempting to protect people from their own choices and actions. The reasons are twofold—efficiency and freedom. When consumers' choices are reduced, citizens may have to spend more than necessary to purchase items that are less efficient than they could be. That is, they become poorer. The many safety regulations that exist are entirely paternalistic and reduce individual choice. They seldom accomplish the ends desired by their proponents. And once we recognize the pathology of public decision processes, it becomes clear that government regulators are not granted some special insight allowing them to balance others' lives for them. Individual citizens are far better suited to allocating their own incomes, time, and energies in ways that complement their values. We should remember Henry David Thoreau's concern: If he knew someone were coming to visit with the express intent of doing him "good," he would run in the opposite direction as quickly as possible.

Some regulation should be replaced by establishing property rights. We have already cited examples involving pollution rights, fishing rights, and hunting rights. Other regulations should be done away with altogether. For example, the minimum wage should be abolished or at least lowered for teenagers. Marketing orders, which essentially establish agriculture cartels, should also be abolished. Other areas ripe for deregulation include the surface transportation industry, communications, and banking. In addition, antitrust laws should be overhauled and the Consumer Product Safety Administration eliminated.

These proposals are meant to be suggestive of the broad range of economic activities that are currently controlled, regulated, and stifled by well-meaning but misguided regulation. There are many others that might be cited. We hope that our examples stimulate thought and possibly action toward a thorough rethinking of regulation and its effects.

Constitutional Reform

At a time when we are told that humanity consumes renewable and nonrenewable resources at a nonsustainable rate, market-oriented economists may be the world's only sane optimists—they understand how markets and prices ration scarce resources and produce superior substitutes. In that vein, we view ourselves as sanely optimistic political economists who place our faith in limited government, secure property, personal liberty, individual enterprise, and voluntary association. We have hopes for a humane society, but without constitutional reform, we must segregate our hopes from our expectations.

Many of the solutions to problems we have identified in this book will not be considered until politicians take a serious look at the long-run consequences of their decisions. But election cycles of two, four, or six years and institutional fiscal irresponsibility mean that politicians must respond to the short-run desires of constituents and special interests. Without real constraints imposed on politicians' abilities to respond to such demands, political decisionmaking will continue to be dominated by short-run considerations. Although we should not discount the abilities of political entrepreneurs or, indeed, the necessity of achieving constitutional reform, we can do little to solve the underlying problems if we simply rely on electing "good" or "better" politicians and do not fundamentally change the incentives these good people face.

A fundamentally different source of legitimacy for government action must be established. Currently, legitimacy for a program or expenditure is obtained by the approval it receives from politically powerful coalitions. But if politicians were constitutionally constrained, legitimacy would be based on constitutional principles, not on current wants. Consider what Dwight R. Lee and Richard B. McKenzie (1987) had to say about the potential of such constraints:

> When unrestrained political power makes politicians the lackeys for organized special interests and special interests become the victims of the productivity-destroying excesses of their own short-run demands, there is the potential for all to benefit by accepting some self-denying limits on government. If politicians could honestly say to politically organized groups, "My hands are tied; I cannot provide more benefits to special interest groups by imposing additional costs on the public at large," then the scope for short-sighted political exploitation of one group by another would be reduced. A government that can credibly tell people that there are *clear limits* on how much of their productive efforts will be taken from them will be in a better position to encourage productive investment than will a government that cannot commit itself to such limits. The best and maybe the only hope for motivating a move away from parasitic transfer activities and toward productive, wealth-creating activities that will, in the long run, make everyone better off, is having constitutional limits on the scope of government. (pp. 140–141)

But are changes at the constitutional level possible? Remember, we claim to be "sanely optimistic," that is, we hope for change but recognize that some of the major changes we believe to be absolutely essential have a low probability of being enacted. Our skepticism is based on two reasons, one practical and the other normative. The practical reason is that the constituency for constitutional reform may be large, but it is diffused, whereas the constituency for the status quo is concentrated and organized. The normative reason is that the balanced-budget norm that constrained government spending until the 1950s has been destroyed, in large part by the Keynesian legitimation of deficit spending.

Without the traditional constraints of antideficit norms and with the federal treasury being treated as a commons by 535 members of Congress, fundamental change will be difficult to achieve. But there is some hope in recent political events. For example, although the Gramm-Rudman-Hollings deficit reduction act failed to effectively restrain Congress and has had most of its teeth removed by court decisions, it is a move in the right direction. It demonstrated a willingness by members of Congress to look at fundamental rules that could redefine and shape the political order. The act also contained an important feature that may be necessary for fiscally restraining government—it automatically forced spending reductions if Congress did not make the cuts. It created a Dr. Strangelove kind of "doomsday machine" ticking away behind Congress that would automatically make spending cuts if Congress were unable to come to an agreement. Unless Congress is willing to implement other measures that provide similar incentives, it is doubtful Congress will make any meaningful cuts in spending; instead, it will continue relying on fiscal illusions and blame shifting.

Another ray of hope is provided by the fact that thirty-two state legislatures have officially called for a constitutional convention to propose a balanced-budget amendment. In addition, opinion polls conducted in the 1990s have consistently shown that a majority of the populace supports a balanced-budget amendment. Further, the tax reform movement of the past several years indicates a deep and powerful movement for constraining the tax powers of governments.

There are serious practical arguments against proposals to limit spending authority and taxing ability and to force a balanced budget. But the support and discussion generated by these proposals may indicate that the broad, unorganized coalition for constitutional reform can be organized *and* that a constitutional attitude is being generated and broadly accepted. It was a similar constitutional attitude that caused the American Founders to design a limited government. If this attitude spreads, it will become easier for political entrepreneurs to actually enact some of the proposals we believe are necessary.

Not Perfection, but Improvement

We propose privatization, economic efficiency, deregulation, and constitutional reform; at the same time, we fully recognize that markets are not perfect and people have motivations beyond obtaining material goods. We recognize also that transaction and information costs can be higher than we might prefer. Externalities exist, and public goods can be difficult to supply. In addition, we understand that goal-oriented, self-interested people are not perfect calculators—people acting in markets and in government make mistakes.

Yet all these aspects of markets do not mean government action is justified. Government failure is at least as pervasive as market failure. In fact, many market failures are caused by government, and few can be well addressed by government action. Because people turn to government when it appears that markets fail, there has been little or no incentive to solve perceived problems through contracts or other private solutions. Where it appears that public means exist for solving a perceived market failure (whether these means can actually accomplish the desired end is unimportant since illusion is more important in politics than reality), private means are ignored. We have no illusions that our proposals would result in a perfect polity, but we do believe that they can create a political economy of hope out of the current political economy of envy, distrust, and stagnation.

Bibliographical Notes

Scholarship on constitutions and constitutionalism has long been dominated by lawyers and political scientists, but that domination has weakened a bit since the advent of public choice theory. In brief, some economists interested in basic rules have seen fit to apply their powerful tools to constitutional questions and, of course, some legal minds, including Richard Posner and Richard Epstein, have pioneered in using economic concepts and ideas to reform the study and application of law. We are inclined to believe that this development has been one of the genuinely interesting and important intellectual changes of the twentieth century.

Anyone wishing to read in this area must begin with the work of Posner, now a federal judge. His textbook, *Economic Analysis of Law* (Boston: Little, Brown, 1986) is in its third edition. If one can read but one book in the area, this is it. The book deals with many matters besides constitutional ones. As such, it is a handbook on how to think about legal issues in economic terms.

To consider constitutional rules and their significance and choice, one must read James M. Buchanan and Gordon Tullock, *The Calculus of Consent* (Ann Arbor: University of Michigan Press, 1962), a foundation stone of public choice of such importance that Buchanan was awarded the Nobel Prize in economics in part because of this volume.

Two subsequent volumes involving Buchanan, as a sole author of one and as coauthor of the other, should also be cited. Buchanan's *The Limits of Liberty: Between Anarchy and Leviathan* (Chicago: University of Chicago Press, 1975) presents the economist as a political philosopher. Here, Buchanan explains how the state can be rationalized, something many others have done but in different ways from Buchanan. He treats law as a "capital good" in which all citizens have an investment. Accordingly, he advocates a limited government but one that can effectively maintain the value of the capital good. Thus, he resolves the paradox of individual rights and political enforcement. Ten years later, H. Geoffrey Brennan and Buchanan wrote *The Reason of Rules: Constitutional Political Economy* (Cambridge: Cambridge University Press, 1985), a book about rules—what they are, how they work, and how they can be properly analyzed. Somehow this book does not register with the impact of *The Calculus of Consent* or *The Limits of Liberty*, but that would be asking too much.

We will cite but two other writings: Richard B. McKenzie, ed., *Constitutional Economics: Containing the Economic Powers of Government* (Lexington: D.C. Heath, 1984), and Dwight R. Lee and Richard B. McKenzie, *Regulating Government: A Preface to Constitutional Economics* (Lexington: D.C. Heath, 1987). In the latter, two fine economists who also happen to be fine writers consider a number of constitutional issues, including how to think about constitutions, the economic consequences of the U.S. Constitution, constitutional bases of inflation, deficits, redistribution, and other equally important policies and issues. The approach and analysis is always refreshing and lucid. And the book provides an optimistic account of the possibilities for reform of a highly inefficient and often inequitable system.

References

Borcherding, Thomas E. "The Sources of Growth of Public Expenditures in the United States, 1902–1970," in Thomas E. Borcherding, ed., *Budgets and Bureaucrats: Sources of Government Growth* (Durham: Duke University Press, 1977).

Lee, Dwight R., and Richard B. McKenzie. *Regulating Government* (Lexington, Mass.: Lexington Books, 1987).

Main, Jeremy. "When Public Services Go Private," *Fortune,* May 27, 1985, p. 92.

Niskanen, William A., Jr. "Public Policy and the Political Process," in Svetozar Pejovich, ed., *Government Controls and the Free Market* (College Station: Texas A & M University Press, 1976).

Samuelson, Paul. *Economics,* 12th ed. (New York: McGraw-Hill, 1980).

Truman, David. *The Governmental Process* (New York: Alfred A. Knopf, 1951).

Wilson, Woodrow. "The Study of Administration," reprinted in Jay M. Shafritz and Albert C. Hyde, eds., *Classics of Public Administration,* 3rd ed. (Pacific Grove, Calif.: Brooks/Cole, 1992); originally published in *Political Science Quarterly* 2 (June 1887), 197–222.

About the Book and Authors

TRADITIONAL PUBLIC POLICY and welfare economics have held that "market failures" are common, requiring the intervention of government in order to serve and protect the public good. In *Beyond Politics,* William C. Mitchell and Randy T. Simmons carefully scrutinize this traditional view through the modern theory of public choice.

The authors enlighten the relationship of government and markets by emphasizing the actual rather than the ideal workings of governments and by reuniting the insights of economics with those of political science. *Beyond Politics* traces the anatomy of "government failure" and a pathology of contemporary political institutions as government has become a vehicle for private gain at public expense. In so doing, this brisk and vigorous book examines a host of public issues, including social welfare, consumer protection, and the environment. Offering a unified and powerful perspective on the market process, property rights, politics, contracts, and government bureaucracy, *Beyond Politics* is a lucid and comprehensive book on the foundations and institutions of a free and humane society.

William C. Mitchell is professor of political science at the University of Oregon and research fellow at The Independent Institute in Oakland, California. He received his Ph.D. in political economy and government from Harvard University, and he has taught at Cornell University, Northwestern University, UCLA, and the University of California at both Davis and Berkeley. Dr. Mitchell is book review editor for *Public Choice* and is a member of the editorial board for the journals *Western Political Science Review* and *Constitutional Political Economy.*

Dr. Mitchell was the first Distinguished Fellow elected by the Public Choice Society, and he has been a fellow of the Center for Study of Public Choice, George Mason University, and the Center for the Advanced Study in the Behavioral Sciences, Stanford University.

Dr. Mitchell is the author of *The American Polity, The Anatomy of Public Failure, Government as It Is, Political Analysis and Public Policy, Public Choice in America, The Popularity of Social Security, Sociological Analysis and Politics,* and *Why Vote?* A contributor to numerous scholarly volumes, his many articles and reviews have appeared in *American Behavioral Scientist, American Political Science Review, American Sociological Review, Contemporary Policy Issues, Ethics, International Journal of Comparative Sociology, Journal of Economic Behavior and Organization, Micropolitics, Policy Analysis, Public Choice, Public Productivity Review, Social Research, Western Political Quarterly,* and many other journals.

Randy T. Simmons is professor of political science and director of the Institute of Political Economy at Utah State University and research fellow at The

Independent Institute in Oakland, California. He received his Ph.D. in political economy from the University of Oregon, and he has been a policy analyst in the Office of Policy Analysis at the U.S. Department of the Interior and a fellow of the National Science Foundation.

Dr. Simmons is the author of the forthcoming book from The Independent Institute, *Endangered Species,* and he is a contributor to the books, *Rationality and Society, Framing Social Dilemmas* (D. Schroeder, ed.), *Controversies in Environmental Policy* (S. Kamieniecki, R. O'Brien, and M. Clark, eds.), and *Earth Day Reconsidered* (J. Baden, ed.). His many articles and reviews have appeared in *American Political Science Review, BYU Law Review, Contemporary Policy Issues, Forest Watch, Journal of Contemporary Studies, Policy Review, Public Choice,* and many other journals as well as in the *Baltimore Sun, Deseret News, Los Angeles Daily News, Salt Lake Tribune,* and *Washington Post.*

Index

Academia in Anarchy: An Economic Diagnosis (Buchanan and Devletoglou), 144

Academy in Crisis: The Political Economy of Higher Education (Sommer), 145

Acheson, James M., 20

Ackerman, Bruce A., 152

Administrative Behavior: A Study of Decision-Making Process in Administrative Organization (Simon), 36

Advertising, 29, 35, 127, 129, 199, 204
political, 79–80

AFDC. *See* Aid to Families with Dependent Children

Agenda control, 116–118

Aggregates, 93, 186

Agoraphobia, 127–128

Agriculture and the State (Pasour), 110

Agriculture industry and protectionism, 105–106, 110, 217

Aharoni, Yair, 174

Aid to Families with Dependent Children (AFDC), 17, 166

Akerlof, George, 144

Alchian, Armen, 198, 202, 208

Allen, William, 208

Altruism, and redistribution of wealth, 163, 168, 171, 172

American Public Choice Society, xiv

Anarchy, State, and Utopia (Nozick), 175

Anderson, Martin, 190

Anderson, Terry L., 161

Antitrust laws, 13, 19, 123, 133, 217

Aristotle, 43

Arrow, Kenneth J., 64, 77, 78

Audubon Society, 159

Auster, Richard, 125

Automatic deductions for taxes, 56

Automobile industry and protectionism, 104–105, 107

Automobile safety, 134–139

Baden, John, 158–159, 161

Balanced-budget
and government, 15–16, 218
requirement, 190–191, 219

Banaian, King, 194

Banking, 217
of discharge reductions, 9

Bargaining, political, 50–52, 68

Barter, 70

Bator, Francis M., xvii, 6–7

Baumol, William, xvii, 6, 8

Becker, Gary, 26, 109

Benefits
vs. costs, 9, 45, 67–70, 71, 74–76, 114, 148, 154, 170, 192, 216
marginal, 43, 88, 96, 114, 187
privatized, 8
public, 3, 166, 169, 171
socialized, 10
spillover, 58

Best of the New World of Economics, The (McKenzie and Tullock), 20

Black, Duncan, xiv, 77

Black Hole Tariffs and Endogenous Policy Theory (Magee and Brock), 109

Blood, Tom, 158–159

Bonner, John, 82

Borcherding, Thomas E., 215

Borrowing, 57, 186–187

Bovard, James, 110

Brennan, H. Geoffrey, 220

Brittan, Samuel, 193

Brock, William A., 109

Browning, Edgar K., 109

Buchanan, James M., xviii, 21, 64, 67, 100, 109, 119, 190, 193, 198, 220

Budget, 188, 203
deficits, 183
protection by bureaus, 61–62
See also Balanced-budget

Budgeting Act of 1974, 188
Bureau of Land Management, 161
Bureau of Reclamation, 154
Bureaucracy, 31, 115–116, 172
  vs. bureaucrats, 58–62
  exploitation by, 114–116
*Bureaucracy vs. Environment: The
  Environmental Costs of Bureaucratic
  Government* (Baden and Stroup, eds.),
  161
Bureaucrats, 75, 116, 118, 150, 164–165,
  178, 201
  vs. bureaucracy, 58–62
  relationship to politicians, 60
Bush, President George, 51, 53, 105, 108,
  153, 165, 188
Business cycles, 3, 14–15, 176
  political, 178, 179–183, 194
Butler, Stuart 174

*Cadillac Desert: The American West and Its
  Disappearing Water* (Reisner), 144, 154
Calculus of Consent, The (Buchanan and
  Tullock), 220
Capital, social, 164
Capitalism, 128, 163, 197, 198
Capitalism, Socialism, and Democracy
  (Schumpeter), 83
Capitalism and Freedom (Friedman), 64
Cartels, 102–104, 108, 123, 130–132, 217
  political, 200–201
Carter, President James, 33, 138, 181
Central Valley Project, 154
Chase, Alston, 144
Cheung, Steven N. S., 161
Chicago Board of Trade, 156
Choice, collective, 25, 39, 44, 48, 64, 93
  nature of, 44–46, 63
Choice, individual, 185–186, 207
Choice, public. *See* Public choice theory
Choice, social, xiv
Chrysler Corporation, 138
Civil service, 115–116
Clean Air Act, effects of, 151–153, 156, 212
Clean Coal/Dirty Air (Ackerman and
  Hassler), 152
Clinton, President William, 33
Coase, Ronald, 155, 156, 157, 160–161,
  202, 208
Coastal Barriers Resource Act of 1982, 216
Collective action, 20

Collective Action (Hardin), 101
Collective choice. *See* Choice, collective
Collusion, 19, 123, 130
  among industries, 108–109
Command and control regulation, 9, 148,
  149, 213
Common-pool goods. *See* Goods, common-
  pool
Communications, political, 72–73
Communism, 32, 82, 197
Community, 24–25
Competition, xvii, 5, 13, 25, 29, 60, 72, 98,
  102, 105, 114, 119, 127–128, 129–130,
  135–136, 141, 168, 187, 197–208, 215
  among bureaus, 115
  between elites, 28
  effect on interest groups, 63
  political, 50–52, 62, 133, 212
  protectionism and, 107–108
  restricted by regulation, 19
  viewed negatively, 3
Competition, imperfect, 131
  discussion, 12–13
Competition, perfect, xiv, 12, 26
Competition and Entrepreneurship (Kirzner),
  208
Compromise, political, 50–52, 63
Congress, 92, 170, 188, 191, 201, 214, 218–
  219
  term limits for, 193
Congressional Research Service, 167
Consensus, and veto power, 78
Constitution, U.S., 68, 221
  proposed amendments to, 190
  reform, 189–193, 217–219
*Constitutional Economics: Containing the
  Economic Powers of Government*
  (McKenzie, ed.), 221
Constitutions, 44, 49, 220, 221
Consumer
  compared to voter, xiii, 43, 46–47
  lack of information by, 14
  surplus, 102, 114
  welfare, 13
Consumer Product Safety Administration,
  217
Consumer protection, xix, 3, 127–144
  as rationale for regulation, 19, 138–139
Consumer sovereignty, 29, 31, 97, 139, 140,
  142, 144

Consumption, 43, 47, 96–97, 186–188, 205, 210

Contracts, xix, 5, 6, 44, 171, 198, 202

Controls, 1, 8–9, 105, 179
vs. market solutions, 150
pollution, 146–160

Corporations, taxing, 55

Costs, 51, 104–106, 109, 137
vs. benefits, 9, 45, 67–70, 71, 74–76, 114, 148, 154, 170, 192, 216
deadweight, 132, 139
entry, 193
exit, 115
external, 147
internal, 155
marginal, 43, 88, 114, 147–148, 187
opportunity, 44, 60, 69, 115, 122, 137, 207
political, 106–107
private, 7, 10, 94, 148
social, 3, 7, 102, 104–107, 131–132, 146, 148, 150, 155, 158, 203
socialized, 8, 135
spillover, 7–8, 9, 147
transaction, 18–19, 26, 72, 219
transfer, 102, 104

Crain, W. Mark, 139

Crandall, Robert W., 105, 138

Creative destruction, 176, 198

Crisis and Leviathan: Critical Episodes in the Growth of American Government (Higgs), 64

Cycles, business. *See* Business cycles

Cycles, voting. *See* Voting cycles

Cycling, 78

Dahl, Robert, 25, 35, 80

de Jasay, Anthony, 125

de Tocqueville, A., 173

Deadweight costs, 132, 139

Debs, Eugene, 48

Decentralization, 98–100, 214

Deductions, automatic, 56

Deficit financing, 57, 218

Deficits, 15, 183, 191, 221

Demand and Supply of Public Goods, The (Buchanan), 100

Demand creation, 204

Demand curve, 20, 68, 91, 92, 96, 125, 129

Demand revelation, 94, 98, 100

Demands, option, 12

Democracy, 22, 27, 35, 39, 48, 55, 67, 70, 77–79, 80, 163, 212
economic overview, 41–64
and redistribution, 169–172
value of, 82

Democracy and Welfare Economics (van den Doel), 83

Democracy in Deficit (Buchanan and Wagner), 193

Demsetz, Harold, 109, 202

Depressions and recessions, 53, 183, 188
Great Depression, 15, 186

Devletoglou, Nicos E., 119, 144

Distribution, of wealth and income, 3, 16, 35, 62, 112, 167, 172–174

Doel, Hans van den, 83

Downs, Anthony, xviii, 36, 72, 97, 116

Dupuit, Jules, 11

Dye, Thomas R., 36

Earth in the Balance (Gore), 34

Economic Analysis of Law (Posner), 220

Economic Behavior and Institutions (Eggertsson), 208

Economic Consequences of Democracy, The (Brittan), 193

Economic Prerequisite to Democracy, The (Usher), 174

Economic Way of Thinking, The (Heyne), 20

Economics, relationship to politics, xvii–xviii

Economics: Private and Public Choice (Gwartney and Stroup), 83

Economies of scale, 199, 200

Economists, welfare. *See* Welfare economists

Education
higher, state systems, 142–144
as public or private good, 98–99, 141–142

Efficiency, 7, 11, 13, 26, 30, 44, 59, 63, 66–68, 71, 76, 81, 114, 143, 155, 166, 215–216

Eggertsson, Thrainn, 208

Electoral rules. *See* Voting rules

Electoral system, 79

Elitism, 22, 25, 27–28, 35–36, 97, 148

Entitlements, 165, 183

Entrepreneurs, role of, 67, 77, 85, 100, 157, 159–160, 174, 198, 201–202, 206

Entry barriers, 19, 193, 199, 200

Environment, 20, 33, 212, 216
and government, 73, 146–160

Environmental markets, 158–160

Environmental Policy Center, 151
Environmental Protection Agency (EPA), 151
Environmental Protection Hustle, The
   (Frieden), 161
EPA. *See* Environmental Protection Agency
Epstein, Richard, 220
Equal opportunity laws, 76
Equality, democratic, 166–169, 172–173
Equality and Efficiency: The Big Tradeoff
   (Okun), 16–17, 64
Equilibrium states, 198, 201
Equity, 16–18, 19, 22, 80–81
Erlich, Paul, 34
European Public Choice Society, xiv
Exit costs, 115
Exploitation, 73, 104
   by government, 111–126
   by state universities, 118–123
Externalities, 7–9, 18–20, 26, 82, 146, 148,
   150, 153–155, 160–161, 211, 219
   negative, 7, 147, 211
   positive, 98

Favor-seeking, 59, 69–70
Federal Communications Commission, 32
Federal Income Tax Reform Act, 179
Federal Insurance Compensation Act (FICA),
   56
Federal Reserve Board, 181, 192
Federalist Papers, The, 41
Federalist 10, 25
FICA. *See* Federal Insurance Compensation
   Act (FICA)
Firm, business, xviii, 119, 161
   compared to government, 59, 61–62, 68,
   75, 125, 174, 185, 197–208
Firm, the Market, and the Law, The (Coase),
   208
Fiscal policy, 14–15, 180, 187–188, 212
Fiscal Theory and Political Economy
   (Buchanan), 64
Food and Drug Administration, 32
Food stamps, 10, 17, 166
Forced riding, 89–94
Fortune, 215
Free Market Environmentalism (Anderson
   and Leal), 161
Free riding, 8, 10–12, 20, 63, 70, 87, 89–94,
   96–98, 100, 102, 122–123, 130, 147,
   164, 173, 202
   by voters, 48

Free to Choose (Friedman), 64
Free trade, 108
Frey, Bruno, 180
Frieden, Bernard J., 161
Friedman, David, 70
Friedman, Milton, 64, 70, 75, 76–77, 128,
   159, 190–192, 198, 207
Friedman, Rose, 64, 75
Frolich, Norman, 100
Future, considerations for, 73–74, 75–77,
   152

Galbraith, John Kenneth, 29, 97, 201
*General Theory of Employment, Interest,
   and Money* (Keynes), 14–15
Global 2000 Report to the President, 33
GNP. *See* Gross National Product
Goods, common-pool, 96–97
Goods, private, 9–10, 29, 59, 63, 69, 88–89,
   98, 118, 147, 205, 211
Goods, public, xix, 3, 7, 18, 29, 45, 59, 63,
   69, 87–88, 97, 139–144, 147
   and altruism, 163–164
   and decentralization, 98–100
   discussion of, 9–12
   financing of, 95–96
   as outcome of self interest, 8, 22, 28, 67–
   68, 77, 164, 171, 207
   supplying, 88–94, 96, 98, 100, 123, 169,
   211, 219
Goods, toll, 96–97
Gordon, H. Scott, 20
Gore, Vice President Albert, 34
Government
   and balanced budget, 15–16
   compared to business firm, 59, 61–62, 68,
   75, 125, 203
   compared to market, xiii–xiv, 1, 34, 45,
   66, 82, 87
   expenditures. *See* Spending, governmental
   exploitation, 111–126
   failures, 41, 66–82, 219–220
   financing of, 57–59
   intervention in markets, xvii, 1, 4, 5, 6, 11,
   19, 23, 27, 30, 32–35, 39, 75, 127, 133,
   178, 211
   as a monopoly, 45, 123–125, 139, 140,
   193, 215
   planning, 33–35
   role of, xix, 6, 69, 85, 100, 103, 167, 189,
   210

Governmental Process, The (Truman), 35, 213
Graham, John, 138
Gramm-Rudman-Hollings Act, 188, 189, 219
Great Society, 165
Gross National Product (GNP), 42, 104, 132, 187, 197, 206
    ratio of deficit to, 190
Gwartney, James D., 83

Hall, Robert, 192
Hardin, Garrett, 20
Hardin, Russell, 101
Hassler, William T., 152
Haveman, Robert, 154
Hayek, Frederich A. von, 68, 197, 198, 208, 210
Head, John G., 21
Hershey, Robert, 166
Heyne, Paul, 20
Higgs, Robert, 64
Hirschman, Alfred O., 35
Hobbes, Thomas, 5
Human nature, politics and, 23–24, 185, 189
Hume, David, 11, 87–88
Huntington, Samuel, 69

Imperial Water District, 154
In Pursuit of Happiness and Good Government (Murray), 20
Incentives, 9, 49, 62, 67–68, 93, 108, 147, 149, 155–156, 158, 160, 179, 183–184, 185–187, 191, 206, 212–213
Income redistribution. *See* Redistribution of income
Inefficiency, technical, 92
Inflation, 15, 47, 74, 168, 178–179, 187–188, 221
    relationship to unemployment, 179–183
Information, 5, 7, 14, 16, 19, 26, 34, 43, 46, 71, 75, 127, 136, 150, 176, 185, 204–205, 219
Innovation, 76–77
Inside Bureaucracy (Downs), 36
Interest groups, 25, 27, 30, 47, 49, 62–63, 70, 75, 87, 92, 170, 190, 212, 216, 218
Interest-group liberalism, 26
Interests, xix, 211
Interests, public, xvii, 3, 25, 28, 30–31, 39, 52, 69, 75

Interests, self, 43, 49, 51–52, 108, 210
    conversion to public good, 8, 22, 28, 67–68, 77, 164, 171, 207
Interests, vested, 92, 128, 192
Internal costs, 155
Intervention. *See* Government, intervention in markets
Introduction to the Theory of Social Choice (Bonner), 82
Investment, 186–188
Invisible hand, 3, 4, 5, 25, 28, 35, 39, 42, 67, 166, 211
Iron triangle, 60, 92

Justice, 16, 22, 80–81, 172–174

Kelman, Steven, 64
Keynes, John Maynard, 14–15, 193
Keynesian economic policies, 15, 16, 31, 176, 178, 183, 185, 186, 188, 213, 218
Kirstol, Irving, 69
Kirzner, Israel M., 208
Kondratas, Anna, 175
Krueger, Anne O., 109

Labor, 127, 133, 186
Labor unions, 108, 129, 199–200
Laffer, Arthur, 177
Laffer curve, 112–113, 125, 183, 184–185
Lave, Charles A., 137–138
Law enforcement, 5, 59, 69, 123, 198
Leaky-bucket phenomenon, 167
Leal, Donald R., 161
Lee, Dwight R., 109, 218, 221
Legal system, 5–6, 44
Leone, Robert, 110
Levi, Margaret, 112, 125
Liberalism, 76
Liberalism Against Populism: A Confrontation Between the Theory of Democracy and the Theory of Social Choice (Riker), 82
Limits of Liberty: Between Anarchy and Leviathan, The (Buchanan), 220
Limits of Organization, The (Arrow), 64
Lincoln, Abraham, 78
Lindahl pricing, 96, 98
Lindblom, Charles E., 21, 25, 28–29, 35
Line-item veto, presidential, 72, 192
Liquor stores, state, 140–141

Log rolling, 52, 63, 69, 71–72, 80, 104, 108,
    112, 115, 171, 191
Logic of Collective Action, The (Olson), 20,
    100
Lovejoy, Dr. Thomas, 34
Lowi, Theodore, 26

McKay, Bonnie J., 20
McKean, Roland N., 67
McKenzie, Richard, 10, 20, 218, 221
Macpherson, C. B., 24
Macro-economics, 198, 211, 213
    micro-economics as basis for, 183, 193
    uncertainties of, 176–178
Madison, President James, 25
Magee, Stephen P., 109
Majority, 44–45, 68, 75, 77, 80, 93, 108
Majority rule, 125, 174
    problems of, xviii, 78, 79, 104, 112
Making Public Policy (Kelman), 64
Management of public agencies, scientific,
    30–32, 34, 35
Marginal benefits, 43, 88, 96, 114, 187
Marginal costs, 43, 88, 114, 147–148, 187
Marginal utility, 43, 203
Market, compared to government, xiii–xiv, 1,
    34, 45, 66, 77, 82, 87
Market failures, xvii–xviii, 41, 219–222
    as justification for government
        intervention, 1, 4, 6, 27, 30, 97, 178
    theories of, 6–19
Markets, xviii, xix, 4–6, 80, 108, 128–129,
    195–208, 211, 213–214
    environmental, 158–160
    imperfect, 13, 82, 173–174
    limitations on, 157–158
    nature of, 3–6, 128
    perfect, 17, 26
    problems with public goods, 10–12
    producer-rigged, 102–104
*Markets, Hierarchies: Analysis and Antitrust
    Implications* (Williamson), 208
*Markets or Governments: Choosing Between
    Imperfect Alternatives* (Wolfe), 64
Marshall, Alfred, 208
Marxism, 112, 125, 158, 164, 176
Median voter. *See* Voters, median
Merit wants, 97
Metzenbaum, Senator Howard, 152
Michels, Robert, 36

Micro-economics, 198, 211
    as basis for macro-economics, 185–189,
        193
Mills, C. Wright, 36
Mind and Society, The (Pareto), 36
Misery Index, 181
Mises, Ludwig von, 68, 197, 198, 208
Mitchell, William C., xv
Monetary policy, 57–58, 177, 180, 181–188,
    191
Money, 70
Money creation, 57
Monopoly, 12–13, 16, 29–30, 60, 108, 123,
    127, 129–133, 139, 193, 198–200, 215
    cost of, 13, 132
    of school districts, 98, 141–142, 144
    state liquor, 140–141
    of tenure, 122–123
Mosca, Gaetano, 35
Munger, Michael, 104
Murray, Charles, 20, 167
Musgrave, Richard, 97
Mutual gains, 67, 128, 130
Myopia
    of institutions, 73–74
    of politicians, 113
    of voters, 179, 212

Nader, Ralph, 133, 135
National Clean Air Coalition, 151
National defense, 6, 10, 69, 90, 92, 93–94,
    123, 183
National Park Service, 159
Natural Resources Defense Council
    (NRDC), 151, 152
Nature Conservancy, 159
Negative-sum game, 199
New Deal, 164–165
New Politics of the Budgetary Process
    (Wildavsky), 36
*1984 Annual Report of the President's
    Council on Environmental Quality*,
    161–162
Niskanen, William A., Jr., xviii, 60, 114,
    115, 215
Nixon, President Richard, 16, 51
Nominal income, 57
Nominal tax rate, 56
No-Risk Society, The (Aharoni), 174
North, Douglas, 112, 198

Nozick, Robert, 175

Oates, Wallace, 8
Occupational Safety and Health
    Administration (OSHA), 133
Okun, Arthur, 16–17, 64, 181
Olson, Mancur, xviii, 20, 100, 109
Oppenheimer, Joe, 100
Opportunities, 5, 16, 173, 174
Opportunity costs, 44, 60, 69, 115, 122, 137, 207
Optimality, 26, 88, 91–92, 93–94, 148, 150, 206
Oregon Liquor Control Commission
    (OLCC), 140
Orr, Daniel, 109
OSHA. *See* Occupational Safety and Health
    Administration
*Out of the Poverty Trap: A Conservative
    Strategy for Welfare Reform* (Butler and
    Kondratas), 175

PAC. *See* Political action committees
Page, Benjamin I., 110
Paretian welfare economics, 197
Pareto, Vilfredo, 36
Pareto efficiency, 26, 66–67, 206
Parks, privatization of, 159–160
Pasour, E. C., Jr., 110
Passions and the Interests, The (Hirschman), 35
Payment-in-kind (PIK), 106
Payne, James L., 193
Perot, Ross, 33
PIK. *See* Payment-in-kind
*Playing God in Yellowstone: The Destruction
    of America's First National Park*
    (Chase), 144
Plott, Charles, 77
Plural elites, 28
Pluralism, 25–27
Plurality, 44, 78
Policies, 168
    efficiency of, 149–153
Political action committees (PACs), 106–107
*Political Business Cycles: The Political
    Economy of Money, Inflation and
    Unemployment* (Willett and Banaian), 194
Political Control of the Economy (Tufte), 193

Political Economy of Rent Seeking, The
    (Rowley, Tollison and Tullock, eds.), 109
Political Leadership and Collective Goods
    (Frolich, Oppenheimer and Young), 100
*Political Parties: A Sociological Study of the
    Oligarchic Tendency of Modern
    Democracy* (Michels), 36
Political profit, 52
Political scientists, as allies with welfare
    economists, 22–23
Political system, 41–42, 44–48, 63
Politicians, relationship to bureaucrats, 60
Politics
    fiscal aspects of, 49–50
    and human nature, 23–24
    participation in, 24–25, 46, 48
    relationship to economics, xvii-xviii, 42
Politics and Markets (Lindblom), 21, 35
Politics-administration dichotomy, 30–31
Polity, as an economy, 41–44
Pollution, 9, 217
    by government agencies, 153–155
    controls over, 146–160
    market, 155–158
Polyarchy, 25, 28–29
Portney, Paul, 152, 153, 156
Posner, Richard, 109, 198, 220
*Power and Market: Government and the
    Economy* (Rothbard), 125
Power Elite, The (Mills), 36
Preface to Democratic Theory, A (Dahl), 35
Preferential Policies (Sowell), 110
Price fixing by state universities, 118–123
Price-searching, 129, 199, 203–204
Price-taking, 199, 203–204
Pricing, 5, 9, 11–12, 14, 15, 45, 61, 70, 88,
    105, 143, 158, 185, 199, 201, 207, 213, 217
    Lindahl, 96, 98
    public, 94–95
Pricing, market, in provision of public goods,
    95–96
Privatization, of goods and services, 94–95,
    98, 141, 159–160, 198, 214–215
Profit
    middle class, 81
    political, 52
Profit maximizers, 73, 102, 210
Profit seeking, 102, 148
Profscam, 118–123

PROFSCAM: Professors and the Demise of Higher Education (Sykes), 145

Progress and Privilege: America in the Age of Environmentalism (Tucker), 161

Progressives and "good government," 32–33

Property rights, xviii, xix, 5, 42, 44, 74, 119, 148–149, 154–162, 195, 213–214, 217

Protectionism, 104–106, 107, 138–139

Public Choice, xiv

Public Choice Studies, xiv

Public choice theory, xiii-xv, xviii-xix, 39, 41, 67, 80, 100, 114, 119, 164, 170–171

Public goods. *See* Goods, public

Public Goods and Public Welfare (Head), 21

Public interest. *See* Interests, public

Public Use of Private Interests, The (Schultze), 8, 64

Publicness, 11, 88, 92, 96–98

Question of the Commons: The Culture and Ecology of Communal Resources, The (McKay and Acheson), 20

Rabushka, Alvin, 192

Rawls, John, 175

Rayburn, Speaker Sam, 189

Reagan, President Ronald, 53, 69, 105, 108, 138, 153, 165, 177, 181, 183

Real tax rate, 56

Reason of Rules: Constitutional Political Economy, The (Brennan and Buchanan), 220

Redistribution
coercive, 163–175
and democracy, 169–172
of income and wealth, 16–18, 59, 63, 67–68, 80–81, 106, 138, 192, 197, 221
voluntary vs. coercive, 172

Regulating Government: A Preface to Constitutional Economics (Lee and McKenzie), 221

Regulation, 1, 8–9, 18–19, 30, 32, 75, 129–130, 132, 136–139, 149, 157, 197, 201, 212, 216–217

Regulations, safety, 133, 217

Reisner, Marc, 144, 154

Rent control, 76

Rent game, 103, 107

Rent-seeking, 26, 102–103, 107–109, 111, 119, 121, 123, 131–133, 139, 163, 169–172, 201

Republicans and the welfare state, 76

Resources, 33–34, 149
allocation of, 44, 74, 75, 91, 96, 104, 112, 155, 186, 201, 206–207, 210–211, 217
exploitation of, 73

Resources for the Future, 152

Riker, William H., 77, 82

Rise and Decline of Nations, The (Olson), 109

Risk, 67, 134, 136, 201, 203

Road to Serfdom (von Hayek), 198

Romer, Thomas, 116, 118

Roosevelt, President Franklin D., 164

Rose, Richard, 69

Rosenthal, Howard, 116, 118

Rothbard, Murray N., 125

Rowley, Charles K., 109

Rule and Revenue, Of (Levi), 125

Ruling Class, The (Mosca), 36

Safety
automobile, 134–139
consumer, 133–134
worker, 133

Samuelson, Paul, xvii 5–6, 10, 11, 147, 188, 211

Savings, 186–188

Scelte Pubbliche, xiv

Schneider, Friedrich, 180

Schultze, Charles L., 8, 64

Schumpeter, Joseph, 83, 176, 198, 208

Scientific management of public agencies, 30–32, 34, 35

Self interest. *See* Interests, self

Services, public, 6, 45, 59, 214–216

Sherman Anti-Trust Act, 123

Sierra Club, 151, 159

Sikorski, Jerry, 153

Silver, Morris, 125

Simmons, Randy T., xv, 152

Simon, Herbert, 32, 36, 201

Sinclair, Upton, 31

Smith, Adam, 3, 4, 25, 42, 67, 166, 205, 207, 211

Social choice, xiv

Social costs. *See* Costs, social

Social Security, 17–18, 53, 56, 76, 114, 139, 166, 181

Social welfare, 11, 75, 92, 102, 104–107, 112, 131–132, 148

Socialism, 1, 70, 74, 197

Sommer, John W., 145
Sowell, Thomas, 110
Spending, governmental, 8, 47, 49, 52–54, 90–91, 92–93
Spending and taxing, 178, 185, 193
Spitz, Elaine, 24
SSI. *See* Supplemental Security Income
Stability, economic, 14–16, 176, 188
  political interests and, 178–179
State, The (de Jasay), 125
State as a Firm, The (Auster and Silver), 125
State liquor stores, 140–141
Steffens, Lincoln, 31
Stigler, George, 22–23, 26, 81, 198
Stockman, David, 69
Stroup, Richard L., 83, 159, 161
Studds, Representative Gerry, 34
Subsidies, 19, 72, 76, 104, 147, 149, 157, 188
  agricultural, 106, 154, 171
  cross-subsidies, 123, 130, 170
  educational, 119
  for environmental protection, 151
Summed Marginal Benefit (SMB) curve, 91
Supplemental Security Income (SSI), 17
Supply, 45, 93
Supply and demand, 88, 95, 100, 120, 129–130, 134, 204
Supply-side economics, political relevance of, 183–185, 198
Surplus, 102, 105, 114
Sykes, Charles J., 118, 145

TANSTAAFL, 70
Tarbell, Ida, 31
Tariffs, 104
Tax rates
  flat, 192
  real and nominal, 56
Taxation, 9, 11–12, 15, 45, 47, 52, 81, 87–88, 94, 114–115, 118, 157, 167, 178–179, 181, 191–192, 219, 186–188
  discussion of, 54–58
  as government exploitation, 112–114
  and redistribution, 17–18, 29
  as regulation, 130, 148, 149
  relationship to government revenues, 184–185
Taxes
  property, 139
  vs. vote loss, 55, 58, 183

Taylor, Frederick, 31
Tenure, 119, 121, 122–123
Theory of Justice, A (Rawls), 175
Theory of Public Choice: Political Applications of Economics (Buchanan and Tollison, eds.), 64
Thoreau, Henry David, 217
Toll goods. *See* Goods, toll
Tollison, Robert D., 57, 109
Tolls, 95
Toward a Theory of the Rent Seeking Society (Buchanan, Tollison and Tullock, eds.), 109
Transaction costs. *See* Costs, transaction
Transfer costs. *See* Costs, transfer
Transfers, 59, 102, 104, 132, 166–168, 172–174, 218
Transition rules, 170
Treatise of Human Nature (Hume), 87
Truman, David, 25, 26, 35, 213
Tucker, William, 161
Tufte, Edward R., 193
Tullock, Gordon, xii-xv, xviii, 10, 20, 67, 79, 81, 109, 220

Unemployment, 15, 74, 164, 171, 178–179, 186
  relationship to inflation, 179–183
United Mine Workers, 151
United States Army Corps of Engineers, 153–154
United States Supreme Court, 13
Universities, state, 142
  as exploiters, 118–123
University Economics (Alchian and Allen), 208
User fees, 9, 94, 159, 214–216
Usher, Dan, 174

Veto, line-item. *See* Line-item veto, presidential
Veto power and consensus, 78
Vote loss vs. taxes, 55, 58, 183
Voters
  compared to consumer, xiii, 46
  geographical distribution of, 79
  median, 79, 81, 90–91, 93, 98, 116–118
Votes
  equality of, 68
  public money spent on, 52–54, 60
  trading, 69, 70–72

Voting, 23, 24–25, 28–29, 64, 70–73, 77–80, 212
  fiscal aspects of, 46–48
  with one's feet, 115, 123, 125, 205
Voting cycles, 77–78, 212, 217
Voting rules, 90
Vouchers for schools, 99, 141, 143

Wage
  minimum, 76, 217
  private vs. public, 116
Wagner, Richard E., 57, 193
Wall Street Journal, 176
Wallich, Henry, 70
Water marketing, 154–155, 216
Waxman, Henry, 153
Weber, Max, 59
Welfare, 90–91, 98, 104, 166–167, 171–172, 186, 212
  motivations for, 164
  social, 11, 75, 92, 102, 104–107, 112, 131–132, 148
Welfare Economics and the Theory of the State (Baumol), xvii, 6

Welfare economists, xvii, xviii, 4, 6, 9, 11–14, 18, 19, 33, 148, 197, 211
  as allies with political scientists, 22–23
  arguments of, 3
Welfare state, 76
Western Governor's Association, 154
Who Gets What from Government (Page), 110
Who Profits: Winners, Losers, and Government Regulation (Leone), 110
Who's Running America: Institutional Leadership in the United States (Dye), 36
Wildavsky, Aaron, 36, 69
Wildlife markets, 158–159
Willett, Thomas D., 194
Williamson, Oliver E., 202, 208
Wilson, James Q., 69
Wilson, President Woodrow, 30–31, 210
Wolfe, Charles Jr., 64

Young, Oran, 100

Zero-sum, transfer, 131
Zero-sum game, 58, 127, 174, 199